OUR ROVING BIBLE

Our Roving Bible

TRACKING ITS INFLUENCE THROUGH ENGLISH AND AMERICAN LIFE

By

LAWRENCE E. NELSON

Director of the Division of Languages and Literature
Director of Graduate Studies, University of
Redlands, California

The Bible is a book-making book. It is a literature which provokes literature.

—C. B. MCAFEE

ABINGDON-COKESBURY PRESS

New York • Nashville

K

Printed in the United States of America

FOREWORD

THIS book begged to be written. It presents evidence, objective and abundant, that for centuries the Bible has shaped English and American thinking in more ways and to a greater extent than has hitherto been generally realized. It shows that for a generation the Bible has been entering English and American literature at a rapidly accelerating rate.

These facts, of prime importance for any accurate evaluation of current trends of thought, are not elsewhere available in panoramic form. Therefore—this volume.

Nearly a century and a half ago, in the *Edinburgh Review,* Sydney Smith said, "The author . . . should gaze at Noah, and be brief. . . . He should learn, as they did in the ark, to crowd a great deal of matter into a very small compass." This has been done herein.

CONTENTS

THE BIBLE ENTERS ENGLISH

1. Angels and Earthly Creatures

The Bible has been a greater influence on the course of English literature than all other forces put together.

—WILLIAM LYON PHELPS[1]

THE Bible is the most gadabout book since time began. It has roved the face of the earth, often appearing in the most unexpected places. It has been the world's most exciting best seller for every year since Western printing was born. It now speaks—in print—more than 1,068 languages. One of these languages is English, into which it was catapulted A.D. 597.

Long ago Bede told the tale of its arrival. There had been a bargain day in Rome. Merchants had brought blond slaves for sale. Monk Gregory paused before the price-tagged lads.

"Who are these?" he asked.

"Angles."

"Not Angles but Angels," he quickly quipped, and hurried off to the pope to insist that the fair-haired English be evangelized at once. Might he be one of those sent? [2]

The pope agreed. Not so the populace, who insisted that he continue to grace Rome. Gregory remained, and soon was made pope. When the gloss of his new glory had somewhat worn off, he remembered his angelic islanders and ordered priests to England, with Augustine as leader.

Of England, a dot perched precariously upon the western edge of the world, people knew little but imagined much. Historian Procopius, hair acreep from certain eerie ghost stories, had labeled it "The Island of Silence and the Dead." These things had their effect. As Rome receded and England loomed, the missionaries grew scared. They hustled Augustine back to beg the pope to let them return home. Gregory ordered them on.

They arrived and found—ironic answer to their panic fears—a bishop snugly ensconced as queen's chaplain. The king had married a Christian Frankish princess and given her freedom of worship. Two other faint traces of Christianity they found in

England. Irish missionaries were seeping in. Vestiges of the faith remained among the natives whose Christian ancestors had been dispossessed by invading Anglo-Saxons a century and a half before. With these exceptions England was so very pagan that the king met Augustine only in the open air, where witchcraft was reputedly weakest. Yet he proved gratifyingly tolerant. The newcomers' words were new, and one should not lightly change religions, he said. But they might remain, preach freely, and convert as many as they could. He would pay their living expenses.

Under such favoring conditions Christianity spread rapidly. This ushered into England a new era, marked by a civilization so potent that when, two centuries later, Charlemagne sought an outstanding educator to head the palace school, his choice fell on English Alcuin.

Augustine's band had brought into England a force far more powerful than witchcraft—a handful of Latin books, sometimes called England's first library, reputedly nine in number: a two-volume Bible, two copies of the Psalms, two of the Four Gospels, an apocryphal *Lives of the Apostles,* a *Lives of the Saints,* and an *Exposition of the Gospels and Epistles.*[3]

So complete was the domination of the culture represented by this Bible-centered library that even the alphabet of England changed. The Latin alphabet routed the old magic Teutonic runes of early English so thoroughly that today only one pallid ghost remains—the supposed *y* (actually a runic *th*) with which the proprietor of "Ye Old Hotte Dogge Stande" proudly lays ignorant claim to a pseudo culture.

Englishmen everywhere began to place the sign of the holy cross beside their signatures as an oath of good faith, the wreckage of which custom yet survives in the present pathetic scratch of the illiterate—"John Smith, his (X) mark."

Under the impact of new ideas and new emotions the language expanded.

> With the Bible came words redolent of the East, like *camel, lion, palm, cedar,* and terms of drugs and spices, like *cassia,* and *hyssop,* and *myrrh. . . . Gem,* too, is a Bible word, and *crystal,* which our ancestors used . . . for ice as well, as they believed rock-crystal to be a form of petrified ice.[4]

With the Bible the missionaries had brought also their own Roman culture; and soon the English language blossomed, not only with such ecclesiastical terms as "mass," "creed," and "shrine," but also with such homely secular words as "box," "cup," "mat," and "pillow." Familiar native words changed their meanings. "Church"—a word picked up in the freebooting days—ceased to signify to the English a place to be looted and burned. "Bless" lost its heathen meaning of "to consecrate with blood." "God," "love," and "sin"—words familiar from pagan days—acquired Christian significance. Developments in literature paralleled these far-reaching changes in language. As monkish scholars wrote down the people's pagan poems, they piously inserted Christian elements, often with ludicrous results.

The epic *Beowulf,* for example, deals with events in northern Europe before the Anglo-Saxons met Christianity, as it plainly states. The people, eager for relief from the marauding raids of the monster Grendel, "vowed in their heathen fanes altar-offerings," for "Almighty they knew not." Yet so Christianized did the text become that the songs attributed to these pagans are based upon Genesis, and Grendel and all other monsters are presented as lineal descendants of Cain, exiled for Abel's murder. Even more startling is the "Charm to Heal Bewitched Land," wherein worship of the ancient earth goddess—"Hail be thou Earth, Mother of men"—hobnobs with church masses; twig crosses inscribed with the magic names of Matthew, Mark, Luke, and John; prayers to Mary; the Lord's Prayer; pleas to "grow and multiply and replenish the earth"; benedictions; and amens "in the name of the Father, Son, and Holy Spirit."

Soon pagan old and Christian new became so inextricably intertwined that English literature has never yet been able to disentangle them. These twin strands appear in the still popular old Cornish charm,

> From Ghoulies and Ghoosties,
> Lang-Leggety Beasties,
> And things that go Bump in the Night,
> Good Lord, deliver us! [5]

Composed of these same twin strands is nineteenth-century Dante Gabriel Rossetti's poignant "Sister Helen," with its pagan melting of waxen image to cause the death of a recreant lover and its agonized refrain to the Virgin Mary. So also, in Thomas Hardy's *The Return of the Native,* is Susan Nunsuch's dark reversing of the Lord's Prayer thrice as she grimly burns the pin-stuck image of Eustacia Yeobright. So too, in Robert Louis Stevenson's *Treasure Island,* is the fear engendered by Silver's discovery that, in giving him the black spot of deposing, his comrades have rashly mutilated a page of a Bible. So is Julia Peterkin's Scarlet Sister Mary, who gets religion but resolutely refuses to discard her love charm.

But the coming of the Bible to England did much more than merely give a Christian tinge to pagan literature. It soon initiated a glowing new literature of its own, of which the reputed beginnings are quaintly told by Bede in his classic tale of Caedmon. Humiliated by his embarrassing inability to sing when the after-dinner harp came his way, Caedmon one day slipped away and fell asleep in the stable. Roused by a celestial being who bade him chant the beginning of created things, he hesitatingly composed, "Now must we hymn the Master of heaven . . . ," the surviving nine lines of which "probably form the first piece of extant literature composed on English soil." [6]

His new gift known and tested, Caedmon was told each day a portion of Scripture, which next morning he brought back versified. Thus, "keeping in mind all he had heard, and as it were chewing the cud," he extracted from the Bible the beginnings of a new English literature.

Others followed the path thus happily opened, and poetic paraphrases of stirring portions of Scripture became a literary fashion, bringing in such poems as "Genesis," "Exodus," "Daniel," "Judith and Holofernes," and "Christ and Satan."

These were biblical poems with a difference. Into them the authors poured the exultant love of icy seas, of raging storm and mighty battle, which long had raced in their northern blood. Shields rang and spears splintered with thrilling zest.

When Pharaoh overtook the fleeing Israelities at the Red Sea,

> then the hearts of men lost hope when they saw Pharaoh's host come sweeping on from the south, bearing their shields, the troops gleaming —spears were strong, battle drew nigh, shields shone, trumpets sang—banners reaching aloft, the host treading the road. Birds of prey, greedy for battle, dewy-feathered, dark lovers of carrion, screamed in

wheeling flight over the corpses. The wolves sang their dread evensong in hope of the feasting; savage beasts behind the foemen awaited, unsorrowing, the fall of the host; the watchers of the ways cried out at midnight. The fated soul took flight; the people were hemmed in.[7]

The poet is merely describing a battle which might have occurred —and did not!

In the "Andreas," when a storm arose,

then the whale-mere was troubled and stirred; the swordfish sported, darted through the deep, and the grey gull wheeled about, greedy for slaughter; the candle of the sky grew dark, the winds rose, the waves dashed, the floods were fierce, the cordage creaked, the sails were soaked.[8]

Good St. Andrew notes with professional eye the skill with which God and his angels (traveling incognito) handle the craft, and revels in its speed.

As the Bible won its way, a change of climate occurred in English literature. The fundamental joyousness of its message and its warm Oriental imagery conquered the cold cast of Anglo-Saxon thought and softened its savagery. Wintry seas and gloomy fens ceased to have a monopoly. "Guthlac" and "The Phoenix" present landscapes dowered with delight: "Peaceful was the scene of victory and new the abode, pleasant the jargoning of birds, blossoming the land; cuckoos proclaimed the spring." [9] A subjectivity new to English literature appeared, and lyric joy arose.

But the flowering time was brief. As, in the fifth century, Angles, Saxons, and Jutes swept down upon the hapless Britons, so in the ninth century the Danes descended upon the Anglo-Saxons. So terrible was the devastation that Alfred, coming to the throne, could find not a single person south of the Thames, and few north of it, who "could understand their rituals in English, or translate a letter from Latin into English." [10]

Ill as he was, and beset by the cares of a postwar administration, Alfred began rebuilding the shattered culture. Learning Latin at thirty-nine and gathering about him a pitifully few scholars, he began translating famous books into English. The books he Englished for his people were all Bible-marked. His Orosius contains 26 biblical references; his Bede, 40; his Gregory's *Pastoral Care,* 541. Sixty per cent of these allusions are to the Old Testament. To his own code of laws he prefixed the Ten Commandments and parts of the three following chapters of Exodus.[11]

Alfred died. A century later arose Aelfric, greatest English prose writer and most distinguished theologian of his time, and unrivaled for five centuries thereafter. Of the 1,422 allusions to Scriptures in his writings, 70 per cent are from the New Testament, 304 being drawn from Matthew alone.[12]

Five hundred years in the future the Puritans were to turn back sternly to the spirit of Alfred and his sources, leaning heavily upon the Old Testament for their allusions. Yet another four hundred years and our twentieth-century writers were to find themselves the spiritual children of Aelfric, turning naturally and increasingly to the New Testament for quotation and allusion.

Forty-one years after Aelfric's death William the Conqueror, twanging out a mighty and mouth-filling oath—"By the Splendour of God!"—won the battle of Hastings and became the master of England. The Anglo-Saxon period, which the Bible had reached, captured, and made great, was over.

What part would the Book now play, as English life, literature, and language passed reluctantly beneath the conquering yoke of Norman French culture?

THE BIBLE DOMINATES THE MIDDLE ENGLISH PERIOD

2. Men with Growing Wings

Pretzels were originally given by priests to good children who learned all their prayers. The design represents folded arms in the attitude of prayer.[1]

For long it seemed that the Bible might play no further part in English, that the language itself might perish. England's population was tiny, some four per cent of its present size. The land was ruled by French-speaking courtiers, gentry, churchmen, and king. English speech almost disappeared from cultured use. As late as the fourteenth century English schools still taught Latin through French. For three centuries French remained the official language of the law courts.

But the first requisite for a successful funeral is a willing corpse, and the English language was not yet grave-ripe. Battered and with inflectional corners knocked off, it survived and finally absorbed its conqueror to the extent that modern English has been jestingly defined as "French, badly spoken."

The French changed many things in England, among others the naming habits of the English. Although the Bible had been in England for five hundred years, the people still gave their babies the accustomed Teutonic names—Aelfric, Alfred, Caedmon, Cynewulf. Except for a few ecclesiastical titles adopted at ordination, there were no scriptural names in England when the French came.

The adoption of French personal names had two results: it greatly reduced the range of possible choice, and it greatly increased the proportion of biblical and saints' names. Whereas in the *Domesday Book* there was no "Philip," no "Thomas," and but a sprinkling of "Johns," by 1300 one Englishman of every five was named "John."

It was of course impossible for Englishmen and Englishwomen to maintain their individuality on these terms. Various methods to secure a personality arose. The surname was adopted. . . . Among the middle and lower classes these did not become *hereditary* till so late as 1450 or 1500.[2]

Because of the Norman devotion to the church the largest class of other French words taken over by the English was ecclesiastical: witness such terms as "cell," "chaplain," "passion," "paradise," "sacrament," and "saint." Many of these—such as "blame," "lesson," "nature," "order," "rule," "save," and "tempt"—have since so accumulated secular meanings that their earlier religious use has been obscured. "Parlor," for example, once meant the room where monks were permitted to talk.

But English did not limit its new diet to French. Back from the Crusades, those spectacular manifestations of the Bible's influence, came crusaders laden with rich spoil of new culture and new words. Souvenir bottles filled at the river Jordan, wherein John the Baptist, the second Elias, had baptized, popularized the names "Ellis" and "Baptist," increased the vogue of "John," and gave us a once-popular new term for a chamberpot—a "jordan." Names of colors—"azure," "saffron," and "scarlet" (originally a kind of cloth)—arrived. From Damascus came "damask," as later came "poplin" from the "papal" city Avignon, and "gauze" from that Gaza from which Samson once carried the gates. Far wandering, "cotton" and "sugar" entered the language. Oranges followed in the wake of returning warriors, as did Eastern cosmetics. "Lute" added its romantic and "mattress" its prosaic touch, while "Bedouin" and "caravan" stirred imaginations. That they might abuse "misbelieving" Mohammedans more roundly, French crusaders concocted "miscreant." Inactive besiegers of Palestinian castle Hasart originated a dice game which gave us "hazard."[3]

While the language was widening horizons, English literature was modestly launching what was destined to become its most prolific and enduring secular theme—the Arthurian legend.

Presumably living in the early sixth century, Arthur was originally neither English nor king. In Nennius' Latin *History of the Britons* he was a victorious general of the Britons against encroaching Anglo-Saxons. In the eighth battle he "carried on his shoulders an image of the Blessed Virgin: on that day the heathen were put to flight." In the twelfth battle he slew 960 in one day, no man helping.

Two other marvels Nennius notes: a stone bearing a footprint of Arthur's dog, Cabal, was always in place next morning, however often moved; the size of Arthur's son's tomb varied however often measured. "I myself have tested this," vouched Nennius.

A Welshman proverbially "has imagination enough for fifty poets without judgment enough for one." By the fourteenth century Celtic tales made Arthur a fairy king surrounded by a freakish array of courtiers. One could run more swiftly than any beast; two others could outspeed their own thoughts; a fourth could span three hundred acres at a single bound; a fifth walked upon trees and mountain tops so lightly that no leaf or grass blade bent; a sixth guided men as well in a land unknown as in one known. A seventh could drink as much sea as would float three hundred ships. An eighth could hold his breath under water for nine days and nights. A ninth draped his red beard across forty-eight rafters in Arthur's hall. A tenth could slice the corner off a fly's eye without harming it. An eleventh, "though he were buried seven cubits in the earth, fifty miles off would he hear the ant in the morning when it started from its nest." [4] It was high time for some literary artist to take these tales in hand.

The ground work had long been laid. About 1137 Geoffrey of Monmouth, using a probably mythical "very ancient book in the English tongue," had written in Latin his *History of the Britons*, in which Arthur blossomed forth as a brilliant king and world conqueror. He was, however, sadly lacking in supporting cast. There was as yet no Lancelot, no Tristram, no Round Table, no Holy Grail. A Norman poet, Wace, had turned Geoffrey's history into lively French verse. Finally, seven centuries after Arthur supposedly lived and four centuries after Nennius had put him into a book, English Layamon, about A.D. 1200, translated and enlarged Wace's poem. At last Arthur was in an English book.

In his wanderings he had acquired an outward polish of culture. One of his Christmas dinners was a social event. Celebrities thronged to it from many lands—seven kings' sons and seven hundred knights, to say nothing of the elite from his own realm. Dinner was served with a flourish:

> Then men blew the trumpets, and spread the tables; water men brought on floor, with golden bowls; next soft clothes, all of white silk. [5]

But the veneer of culture was still pitifully thin. Arthur quelled a dinner quarrel among his guests with savage brutality:

> Sit ye, sit ye quickly, each man on his life! And whoso will not that do, he shall be put to death. Take ye me the same man, that this fight first began, and put withy on his neck, and draw him to a moor, and put him in a low fen; there he shall lie. And take ye all his dearest kin, that ye may find, and strike off the heads of them with your broad swords; the women that ye may find of his nearest kindred, carve ye off their noses.[6]

Anyone renewing the strife might have his choice of being "dead, or with horses drawn in pieces."

This grisly doom pronounced and the corpses removed, Arthur became again the suave and gracious host. Afterward, however, he had the Round Table built, that its pacifying equality of seating might lessen the dinner dangers of his court—a scheme so successful that Thomas Jefferson borrowed it for his presidential dinners when he entered the recently completed White House in 1801.[7]

By the fifteenth century Arthurian material had become so voluminous that Thomas Malory discarded nine tenths of it when he wove the remainder into his monumental *Le Morte d'Arthur,* which England's first printer, Caxton, rather grumblingly published in 1485, never dreaming that of the seventy-one books from his press this would be the one to carry his name most resoundingly down the centuries.

Gradually the Arthurian tale found itself being drawn ever more irresistibly into the orbit of the biblical. One author identified Arthur's spear, Ron, as that with which the Roman soldier had pierced the side of Jesus. Another considered Arthur's sword, Excalibur, to have been the one used to behead John. The Round Table became identified in some quarters with the table of the Last Supper. Joseph of Arimathea's staff, planted at Glastonbury, burst into bloom each Christmas and thus became the famous Glastonbury thorn.

> The staff it budded and it grew,
> And at Christmas bloomed the wholdaroo;
> And still it blooms at Christmas bright,
> But best they say at dark midnight.[8]

Joseph had brought with him to England the cup of the Last Supper, which was devotedly guarded at Glastonbury. In course of time, however, according to legend, sin arose among its guardians, whereupon the cup promptly disappeared, to be seen thereafter only by the pure in heart. Sought eagerly by the best of Arthur's knights, it became the Holy Grail, symbol of all man's highest and most enduring quests.

So thoroughly in the course of time did the once brutal, immoral, and pagan Arthur become Christianized that had Shakespeare's blundering clowns in *Love's Labour's Lost* completed their proposed presentation of the Nine Worthies of the World, they must have included Arthur, who had become chief of the three Christian Worthies.

Shakespeare's portly Sir John Falstaff lightly hummed a ballad of King Arthur as he strolled into the Boar's Head Tavern in Eastcheap; and when Falstaff died, the untheologically trained Mistress Quickly was sure he went, not to Abraham's bosom, but to Arthur's: "Nay, sure, he's not in hell. He's in Arthur's bosom, if ever man went to Arthur's bosom." [9]

Milton played long with the idea of putting Arthur and his knights into an epic, but abandoned them for *Paradise Lost* and *Paradise Regained,* in each of which he mentioned them appreciatively.

Arthur had by now so grown into English thought that not even the classicists and the satirists of the late seventeenth and the eighteenth centuries could ignore him, though they manhandled him grotesquely. Blackmore, in his *Prince Arthur,* aped Vergil's *Aeneid* throughout—"Arms and the man I sing," becoming, "I sing the Briton and his worthy arms." The fall of Troy became the fall and redemption of man; the counterplotting pagan deities were metamorphosed into good and bad angels.

Fielding, burlesquing heroic plays in his *The Tragedy of Tragedies,* turned Lancelot into Tom Thumb, who became lunch for a cow, and Guinevere into Queen Dollallolla, "a woman entirely faultless, saving that she is a little given to drink, a little too much of a virago toward her husband, and in love with Tom Thumb." [10] Arthur's knights became courtiers, Noodle, Doodle, and Foodle.

Nineteenth-century romanticism rescued them from these maltreatments. Scott read the tales absorbedly, and used them occasionally. Southey edited them. Wordsworth, Peacock, Bulwer-

Lytton, Arnold, Morris, and, in America, Lowell, tried their hands at them. But the magic popularizer was Tennyson. For half a century he found the theme "the greatest of all poetic subjects." *The Holy Grail* came to him "suddenly, as if by . . . inspiration." To him Arthur became the human soul seeking perfection, his castle the symbol of man's slow climb from savagery to angelage.

> And four great zones of sculpture, set betwixt
> With many a mystic symbol, gird the hall;
> And in the lowest beasts are slaying men,
> And in the second men are slaying beasts,
> And on the third are warriors, perfect men,
> And on the fourth are men with growing wings.[11]

Two years after these lines appeared, Walt Whitman in America pontifically announced that romance, and particularly Arthurian romance, was quite permanently dead:

> Ended the quest of the holy Graal,
>
> . . . .
>
> Arthur vanish'd with all his knights, Merlin and Lancelot and Galahad, all gone, dissolv'd utterly like an exhalation;
> Pass'd! Pass'd! for us, forever pass'd, that once so mighty world, now void, inanimate, phantom world,
> Embroider'd, dazzling foreign world, with all its gorgeous legends, myths,
> Its kings and castles proud, its priests and warlike lords and courtly dames,
> Pass'd to its charnel vault, coffin'd, with crown and armor on,
> Blazon'd with Shakespeare's purple page,
> And dirg'd by Tennyson's sweet sad rhyme.[12]

But the Arthurian theme, not noting this public report of its demise and interment, proceeded to a vigorous new growth. A. C. Swinburne used it. With it Mark Twain flamed invective against social injustice. Richard Hovey died with his five volumes unfinished. Thomas Hardy levied on the theme, as did Laurence Binyon. In *Galahad* John Erskine fathered a literary problem child. From Edwin Arlington Robinson's restless, probing mind came *Merlin, Lancelot, Modred;* and with *Tristram* he won the Pulitzer prize. John Masefield added the voice of England's poet laureate. In 1939 came T. H. White's *Sword in the Stone* and *Witch in the Wood.*

Whitman was clearly wrong concerning the Arthurian death. Many medieval themes have grown mossy and been quietly entombed. Yet the tales of Arthur, nobly enriched by the Bible and made by it a symbol of the soul's quest for the best, have survived with vigor undiminished and with brightness undimmed.

But we must return to the Norman period and find what more it brought to English life and thought.

3. God's Playtime

God created man in his own image—and man returned the compliment. —ANONYMOUS[13]

"How CAN Hebrew still be a known language, since it was in existence before the annihilation of tongues at the tower of Babel?" inquired a puzzled medieval critic.

"Shem and his sons were absent on that day," was the ingenious response.[14]

Had they lived in medieval England, Shem and his sons would likely have been somewhere rehearsing a play. Probably never again will audiences find heroes and villains so real as the mystery and miracle plays made the personages of the Bible to people of the Middle Ages. Originating in the solemnity of the Mass, these plays were, at first, shot through with all the irresistible ardors and fervors of Christmas and Easter, and were restricted to episodes suitable for those seasons. Their popularity, however, soon extended them to the more dramatic portions of the entire Bible and to the lives of saints. They thus became "a sort of living picture book" of religion, all the more effective because the common people did not possess the Bible in their own tongue.

Becoming too elaborate—and possibly a bit too loose-tongued—for presentation in the churches and by clerics, they passed to the out-of-doors and the laity. English climate making Christmas and Easter unsuitable times for out-of-door plays, Corpus Christi Day was commandeered. Coming in early summer, it was already a day of elaborate paradings, in which walked living likenesses of holy personages, bearing identifying symbols.

Here Adam and Eve would pass, lifting between them the Tree of Knowledge; and here John the Baptist leading a lamb; there Saint

George on his warhorse, trailing after him the green-scaled, gilt-hoofed body of the slain dragon; or red-bearded Judas, bending beneath the weight of his moneybag, and closely followed by the horned and blackened devil, considerately bringing along the gallows.[15]

Biblical plays fell quite naturally into the festivities of such a day. The trade guilds, in whose hands they now were, mindful of the monetary as well as the social and religious possibilities, evolved one- to three-day fairs at which plays were presented from early morning until late afternoon for the edification and amusement of the crowds which streamed in from the surrounding countryside. Performed in 125 English towns, many of these plays have been lost; but 161 have survived, of which four cycles, of from 25 to 48 plays each, are complete.

Sometimes plays were assigned according to the occupations of the guilds which gave them. In York, plasterers presented the Creation, armorers the expulsion from Eden, shipwrights the building of the ark, fishers and mariners the Flood, shoers and curers of horses the flight into Egypt, while bakers provided the Last Supper and sledmen took the journey to Emmaus.

Naïve realism marked their production. Under the "pageant"—the wagon on which they were acted—was Hellmouth, spouting sparks and smoke. Into it demons, abristle with horsehair and adorned with fearsome animal faces, gleefully hurled lost souls wearing red, black, and yellow coats. Good souls glistened in white, while the angels, duly plumed, gleamed in gold. Gilt-and-silver-helmeted Herod, flashing a Mohammedan's curving scimitar, was gay in blue satin, while Pilate in green bore a leather club stuffed with wool. Christ's tormentors were recognized by black jackets painted with nails and dice. He himself, in gilt wig and beard, wore white sheepskin, as the Lamb of the World, and red sandals, symbol of one who has trodden the winepress alone. The devil—black, horned, clawed, shaggy, with cloven foot and forked tail and sometimes pipes of burning gunpowder in his ears—sufficed to give even good children nightmares.[16]

Spectacular effects were sought. One Hellmouth, a triumph of ghastliness, was "the head of a whale with jaws worked by two men, out of which devil boys ran." In the Norwich Grocers' play, "Father" took a bloody rib from man's side and turned it into a woman; "beholde here she ys." The Towneley "Creation" was vivid with lanterns, hawthorn branches, and wooden images of bird and beast. One York play showed "Zacchaeus climbing into a sycamore tree," and another presented at the Crucifixion that "Longeus with a lance" whose loafing fame gave name to the modern "lounge." Elsewhere we find "the barrel for the earthquake," pulpits for angels, and "starch to make a storm."

Comparative costs sometimes startle. One versatile actor received two and a half times as much for cockcrowing as for hanging Judas; a pair of God's gloves cost half as much as the ale drunk while the players dressed themselves, and two thirds of the amount spent for the "making of three worlds." The Holy Ghost's coat cost two shillings onepence; and four pairs of angel wings, two shillings eightpence. A modest fourpence purchased a pound of hemp with which to mend the angels' heads. The Coventry Smiths stingily paid "God" but two shillings, while "Caiaphas" and "Herod" starred at three shillings fourpence each.

Into such plays by amateur actors in holiday mood many "indecorous impromptus" were inevitably introduced, lightening the solemn fare with homely wit and bringing forth forerunners of the comedians and villains who played so large a part in later English drama. Of such stuff was wrought the comedy in the Coventry *Second Shepherds'* play. The rascality of thievish, loafing Mak, the unconcealed suspicions of his fellow shepherds, his successful filching of the sheep despite their aggressive precautions, his inability to gain admittance at home until he has convinced his peevish wife that he comes not empty-handed, the wily couple's bold hoodwinking of the searching shepherds by wrapping the sheep in baby clothes and putting it into the cradle, the tricked herders' unexpected return with gifts for the new baby and the resulting discovery of the outrageous hoax—all these give rough-and-ready humor. The defrauded shepherds toss Mak in a canvas and, worn with their labor, return to the fields for a nap, from which they are roused by an angel singing the birth of Christ. Trying their own voices on the new tune, they set out for Bethlehem, where they give the Infant their presents: a bob of cherries, a bird, and—gift of the youngest shepherd—a tennis ball!

Take and play with it withal
And go to tennis.[17]

English slapstick comedy also was cradled in biblical drama. In the various Noah plays the rheumatic old countryman's grumbling unwillingness to start building the ark, his glaringly henpecked home life, his obstinate wife's refusals to budge from her spinning and her gossips, the stinging ear boxings and sound drubbings so enthusiastically exchanged as she belatedly arrives aboard (sometimes propelled boisterously by her broad-shouldered sons), her tempestuously expressed wish that her own husband and those of all wives in the audience were dead, must have evoked chuckles and howls of delight.

Cain's grudging selection of his worst sheaves for the altar; his fire's stubborn refusal to blaze even under prodigious puffings and blowings; his coughings, chokings, and swearing when smoke gets into his eyes and lungs; his bickerings and fist fights with his temper-trying plowboy, raised many laughs.

In Chaucer's *Canterbury Tales* the quarrelsome drunken miller cried out in the high-pitched voice traditionally used by Pilate in the miracle plays. From this same squeaky Pontius Pilate, from Judas, with a change of sex, and from Tobias' dog, in the Apocrypha, were developed the Punch (Pontius), Judy (Judas), and dog Toby (Tobias) of the modern Punch-and-Judy shows. Mary Magdalene's riotous drinking scene in the plays so pleased the populace that it left the word "maudlin" (Magdalene) in the language.

Audiences might laugh uproariously at the antics of common people and lesser devils, but tyrants and principal devils were on a different plane. They were expected to roar and rant, to "outbellow and outbuffet" such spectators as dared to heckle their villainies. Of these roarers and ranters were Caesar Augustus, threatening to behead anyone in the audience who uttered a word during the performance; Herod, whose famous rantings made Hamlet warn the players against tearing a passion to tatters and trying to out-Herod Herod; Lucifer, vaingloriously trying to fly off the stage and tumbling ignominiously into Hellmouth; and the devil, suddenly appearing in the midst of the audience "in the most orryble wyse." These made the English stage noisy and were the material out of which melodramatic villains might well be fashioned.

Then there were the Jews. Though members of this "most durable people in human history" were barred from England from 1290 until the mid-seventeenth century, medieval legends were filled with their machinations. They lied, they cut little boys' throats, they stole the consecrated wafers of the Mass, they used Christian blood for the Passover, and they did many other reprehensible things. These legends, and constant presentation of the Jews as enemies and persecutors of the Christ,[18] doomed them to be dramatic scapegoats.

> Barabas and Shylock and a host of others coming down well towards the end of the nineteenth century are, in their viciousness and comicality, their more than ludicrous dress and execrable dialect, but the direct heirs of the Jews as portrayed in the early miracle plays.[19]

Even so seemingly harmless a thing as our "Hip! Hip! Hurrah!" bears the bloody stain, "hip" supposedly being the initials of "*Hierosolyma est perdita*" (Jerusalem has fallen), the soldiers' mob cry in savage, medieval Jew-hunts.[20]

Beginning in 1378, a new type of play, the morality, developed and for a time became the most prominent form of drama.

> A morality may be defined as a dramatized allegory; it sets forth some moral, theological, political, or educational doctrine by means of one-dimensioned characters, who represent good or evil councillors of the hero—Man. In the earliest moralities . . . the grand theme is Christian life and death. . . . In later moralities . . . one of the grand themes is Knowledge. . . . Another theme is Protestantism. . . . In the sixteenth century morality as in the twentieth century sensational movie, there were nine reels of wickedness and but one final reel of repentance.[21]

Dealing poignantly with that most momentous of all human problems, how to prepare for death, the early morality *Everyman* is still good theater. Sir Ben Greet's company loved to present it simply, along with Shakespeare's plays. Later it was elaborately presented, with tremendous fanfare of publicity, in Hollywood's gigantic Bowl, to the acclaim of crowded thousands. Most other moralities, dealing with lesser themes, are so superlatively dead that "the very word is like a yawn." [22] They committed the unpardonable literary sin of forsaking concreteness to follow after the strange gods of abstractness.

Buffeted by the new spirit of Renaissance, by rising religious and political controversies, and by the sudden tidal wave of Elizabethan secular drama, medieval religious plays came to a somewhat abrupt end, departing this life about the close of the sixteenth century. They left a noble memory and bequeathed to an unsuspecting world a hidden linguistic legacy, which it was somewhat slow in discovering.

Certain residues were of course easily recognized. Scholars smiled over the unconscious wrong done womankind in "termagant." Because this supposed Saracen idol, a ranting character in the moralities, wore a long robe to show his Eastern origin, the audiences ignorantly supposed him to be feminine, and a termagant became and still is a scolding woman.

But a new class of surnames, which long puzzled philologists, had arisen, Why were so many people named "King," "Prince," "Duke," "Earl," "Abbot," and "Pope"? And why should people be named "Godde" (God), and its derivatives "Good," "Goodman" (Godman), and the like? At last an answer was ferreted out—they were nicknames from the medieval plays. The Hugh who played the part of Deity became, to his jesting neighbors, Hugh Godde. This was the easier since nicknames were but a recent development. Kings, princes, abbots, and popes being stock characters in those plays, opportunities for such nicknamings were numerous.

The mystery and miracle plays, which boldly allowed God himself to dangle his feet from jolting pageant wagons, and the morality plays, served an age well and went their way into the limbo of lost fashions, only to revive hesitatingly in the nineteenth century and to flourish again in the twentieth.

What else did religion give to the middle English period?

4. O Mighty Lady

"The design of God in creating woman was to complete man." True, just as much as God's design in creating man was to make a clay model for woman! —MARY DODGE[23]

ARTHUR, so the record runs, plunged into battle wearing an image of the Virgin Mary upon his shoulder or, as a later chronicler notes, drawn in red gold upon the inner side of his shield. In this exaltation of the Mother of Christ he was prophetic, for one of the notable phases of the later Middle Ages was the cult of the Virgin which swept over Europe, leaving indelible marks upon languages and literatures. Boundless adoration of her became the unavoidable duty of poets.

Christ's dear mother, Mary mild,
Light of life, Maid undefiled,
Low I bow and bend the knee,
Mine heart's blood I offer thee.[24]

Hauntingly beautiful lyrics lauded her loveliness.

All of a Rose, a lovely Rose,
All of a Rose I sing thee a song.

That Rose is Mary, Heaven's Queen—
From her breast a flower sprung! [25]

This powerful laudation of the Mother and Babe was one of the flowerings of that secular literature which developed increased tenderness toward women and children.

To mispraise women it were a shame,
For a woman was thy dame;
Our blessed Lady beareth the name
Of all women wherever they go.

A woman is a worthy thing
They do the wash and do the wring,
"Lullay! Lullay!" she doth to thee sing,
And yet she has but care and woe.[26]

While women were for centuries still to "do the wash and do the wring," yet this surging tenderness made it easier to acknowledge all members of the sex as "worthy wights." Dyspeptic priests, seeing them in their yellow robes, were less prone to liken them to yellow toads, or devil's mousetraps, baited with yellow cheese.[27] Priests might still warn men that in hell exist heat, cold, thirst, and darkness, but less frequently would come the smashing climax that "with the worm, Woman, Man is caught as the fisher catches the fish with his bait." [28]

The literary manifestations of the growing interest in Mary were many and varied. One tireless admirer wrote in her honor the nearly thirty thousand lines of *Cursor Mundi* (*Runner O'er the World*), so called because in the proud—or possibly rueful—words of the author, "almost it over-runs all." This literary marathon starts with the Creation and runs to the day of doom and the world thereafter. John Lydgate wove into the *Lyf of Our Lady* in English verse not only her story as related in the Gospels but also many of the apocryphal accounts of her life and death.

Mary in medieval story was ever grateful—sometimes almost pathetically so—for any attention paid to her. The pious tumbler doing gymnastics for her before her shrine won her praise, for he was bringing her his best. She made burning coals seem to be sweet flowers and spices under the little Jewish lad who had been cast into an oven by his father for accompanying Christian playmates to Easter Mass and for praying there to the Virgin and her Son. Through her grace a Christian boy, slain for singing a hymn to her as he passed through the Jewish quarter, warbled sweetly after death, though his throat was slit. The bishop discovered in the mutilated throat a lily, golden-lettered with the name of the hymn, upon removal of which the corpse fell silent. At the Requiem Mass, however, it suddenly burst forth in another hymn to Mary.

One Saturday, visiting a monk who devoutly recited a hundred Hail Marys, she increased his daily stint to a hundred and fifty—fifty for joy at the Annunciation, fifty for joy that she should bear Christ, and fifty that she should go to him for bliss. The monk, grieved that Mary possessed no petticoat, since the cloth supplied by his previous devotions had proved too scanty, dutifully recited the added *Aves*. A week later she returned with a new petticoat, declaring that the monk should be made an abbot.

When the citizens of a besieged city bore in procession her kirtle, the enemy, blinded by the sight, was captured. From the knee of a man whose leg had been amputated she pulled a new leg. A monk who had learned and recited all the matins, hours, and special prayers that he could unearth was so ill with quinsy that he was thought dead. She cured him by stroking the swelling and by sprinkling milk from her breast into his mouth.

A merchant of Constantinople borrowed from a Jew, pledging the Virgin as security. Suddenly at Alexandria he remembered the payment due next day. Putting the money into a chest, he cast it into the sea, praying the Virgin that it might reach the creditor safely and on time. The Jew received it, knew its purpose, but hid it and, when the merchant returned, denied payment. At the church where the pledge had been made the Virgin's image revealed the cheat, to the chagrin of all the other Jews.

When a harlot tempted a hermit he prayed for her. She abusively declared that she needed no prayers, whereat he asked her to pray for him, which she did in a chapel of Our Lady. Christ was incensed that such a one should dare pray for his friend, the saintly hermit; but Mary's intercession won his forgiveness. She then exhorted the harlot to repent and be shriven, for in forty days she should die and pass to bliss everlasting.

A lecherous sacristan who always greeted her image as he passed was drowned while abroad on an evil errand. Devils wrested his soul from the angels, but Mary, defending him on the ground that he had ever greeted her in kindly fashion, persuaded God to let it return to the body long enough to repent and reform.

A clerk, lusting to see Mary's body, was told by an angel that the penalty must be either death or blindness. Choosing loss of sight, he shrewdly planned to look with but one eye. Next day, remorseful for his trickery, he confessed and begged for complete blindness. Mary appeared and warned him of the ills of total blindness. But he was content—he had seen her; his only request was that he might be admitted to heaven. She granted his prayer and next morning restored his sight.

She banned forever from an abbey on Mount Sinai all such "filths" as flies, toads, lizards, lice, and fleas.

For there were wont to be so many such manner of filths, that the monks were in will to leave the place and the abbey, and were gone from thence upon the mountain above to eschew that place; and Our Lady came to them and bade them turn again, and a from thence forwards never entered such filth in that place amongst them, ne never shall enter hereafter.[29]

This curious blending of the devotional and the mundane is well illustrated by the activities of the Guild of St. Mary, organized in 1355 to provide doles for the sick and needy, funeral expenses and prayers for the dead. On each February second "all the brethren and sisteren"—under penalty of half a pound of wax for unexcused absence—met at a fit and appointed place away from the church, "and there, one of the gild shall be clad in comely fashion as a queen, like to the glorious Virgin Mary, having what may seem a son in her arms." With much music and gladness, and many blazing candles, the group escorted her, accompanied by Joseph and Simeon and two angels, to the church, where they all offered their wax lights, together with "a penny each." This done, they went home joyously. But their duties were not yet ended. "On the same day, after dinner, the brethren and sisteren shall meet together, and shall eat bread and cheese and drink ale, rejoicing in the Lord, in the praise of the glorious Virgin Mary." [30]

With the rise of Protestantism and the passing of time, many of the pious tales concerning Mary have languished. Her effect upon language, however, has been more durable. She has given name to such plants as herb Mary, Mary's bath, Mary's flower, Mary lily, Mary's seal, marigold, St.-Mary's-thistle, and even (God save the mark!) St.-Mary's-garlic!

But it is as *Our Lady* that she sponsors many other plants of unusual beauty or delicacy: lady's-bedstraw, lady's-bower, lady's-comb, Our-Lady's-cushion, lady's-delight, lady's-finger, lady's-foxglove, lady's-glass, lady's-glove, Our-Lady's-hair, lady's-laces, lady's-lint, lady's-looking-glass, lady's-mantle, Our-Lady's-mint, lady's-thimble, lady's-thistle, lady's-tresses, and Our-Lady's-tree, a birch so green in winter that to pious minds it seems a miracle.

Dolls became "Little Maries," and those manipulated by strings are still "marionettes."

The Priory of St. Mary of Bethlehem, founded at London in 1247, cared for the sick and by 1402 had become famed for its work with the insane. Harmless patients released from the Bethlehem or Bedlem House were known as "bedlams," and our present designation of a confused, unintelligible din as a bedlam is high tribute to the work done long ago at the Priory of St. Mary of Bethlehem.

London streets likewise still bear eloquent testimony. In Maiden Lane once stood an image of the Virgin. Lad Lane was, for like reason, Lady's Lane. Covent Garden was Convent Garden, and in Mincing Lane the mynecen (nuns) owned tenements. Traditionally,

> Amen Corner, at the west end of Paternoster Row, London, is where the monks used to finish the *Pater Noster* as they went in procession to St. Paul's Cathedral on Corpus Christi Day. They began in Paternoster Row with the Lord's Prayer in Latin, which was continued to

the end of the street; then said *Amen* at the corner or bottom of the Row; then turning down *Ave Maria Lane,* commenced chanting the "Hail Mary," then crossing Ludgate, they entered *Creed Lane* chanting the Credo.[31]

Whether or not this is the actual origin, the naming still stands, it having been the site of a noted bookshop burned by the 1940–41 bombings of London. Books of a famous publishing house located there were long advertised in magazines under the caption "The Amen Corner."

"By Mary" became the now discarded oath "Marry!" "By Our Lady" resulted in "B'rlady" and possibly that most naughty British adjective, "bloody." Most important of all were the changes wrought upon the naming habits of the nation—changes that started with the Norman Conquest, but intensified later. "Mary," hitherto in somewhat bad repute, became the most popular of all feminine names, so popular that in America at present it is borne by six million women. From it have developed sixty-five other names, as well as the generic term "gangster's *moll.*"

Paralleling "Mary" comes "John," with one American man in twelve now so named, and ninety-three additional given names developed from it.[32] As for surnames, America now has more than a million Johnsons, two thirds of a million Joneses, and thronging Jacksons, Jenningses, Jenkses, Evanses, Micklejohns, Hankinses, Hansons, and Hancocks, the last three being from the Hans in Johannes.

"Mary" and "John" are but two of many biblical names—"Ruth," "Elizabeth," "Lois," "Paul," "James," "Thomas," "Peter"—which have come into common use.[33]

That "John" in particular has saturated English thought is eloquently witnessed by such familiar phrases as "John Bull" and "John Doe," "Johnny Reb" and "John Chinaman," "Jack Sprat" and "Jack Horner," "Jack and the Beanstalk," "Jack Frost" and "Jack Robinson," "Jack and Jill," "every man Jack" and "Jack-in-the-box," "Jack Tar," and the now vanishing "Jack of all trades," as well as the notoriously long-suffering "John Q. Public." In addition there are cheap-jacks, jackanapes, jackscrews, jackknives, bootjacks, jack pots, jackstraws, jack-o'-lanterns, jackasses, and jack rabbits, not to mention jacksnipes, applejack, flapjacks, demijohns, and the unpleasant gentry known as highjackers.

This Scripture-rooted naming forms but one phase of that wider and more varied utilization of the Bible which arose during the Middle Ages, the thoroughgoing extent of which we nowadays find it extremely difficult to realize.

5. Toy of the Laity

When Adam delved and Eve span
Who was then the gentleman?
—ANONYMOUS[34]

MUCH of the rich religious color which once glowed in men's minds has faded and become half forgotten. A gossamer afloat during "goose summer" days is now but a fine-spun spider web, not a raveling from Virgin Mary's winding sheet, fallen to earth as she ascended to heaven. Ancient pagan wassail bowls, long ago transformed into monkish "loving cups," are now but mantel-gracing contest trophies. The once noble Salisbury rubric's "kiss of peace" has shrunk to a perfunctory kissing of the bride. Awe-some relatives in canon law have dwindled into prosaic "in-laws."

The man in the moon is now the man in the moon only, no longer that biblical sinner (Numbers 15:32-36) who gathered sticks on a Sunday, nor yet that Cain with his dog, symbol of Satan, and his thorn bush, emblem of the Fall, announced in the Prologue of Shakespeare's *Midsummer Night's Dream.*

Hot cross buns baked on Good Friday are no longer kept all year, so that a few crumbs in water may cure whatever ailment arises—especially diarrhea. Pancakes are but pancakes, though once they gave their name to the bell which summons to shriving. The latticed lids of mince pies at Christmas no longer symbol forth the holy manger, nor do most people now feel that

A man had better ne'er be born
As have his nails on a Sunday shorn.[35]

The inn sign the Pig Washael, or Virgin's Greeting, has now become chain restaurant and candy shop, flaunting a pig joyously dancing on its hind legs and playing a flute—The Pig and Whistle. The "God encompasseth us" has become the Goat and Compasses. The saints have been well camouflaged. St. Audrey's Fair has left us but a sneering adjective, "tawdry." St. Olave's Street is now

Tooley Street; St. Osyth's Lane, Sise Lane; St. Peter's Ey, Battersea; St. Maidulf's Borough, Marlborough; St. Ebbe's Row, Tibb's Row. Among personal names St. Aubyn has become Tobin; St. Osith, Toosey; St. Maur, Seymour; St. Clair, Sinclair; and St. Pierre, Simper. Tiffany no longer suggests that the proud bearer was born on the Epiphany, nor Pankhurst that one's birthday was Pentecost. Biblical Adam, Bartholomew, David, Goliath, Jacob, Job, Judah, Matthew, Noah, Peter, and Philip would have extreme difficulty recognizing as their respective namesakes the present Atkinson, Babcocks, Dawsons, Gullys, Cobbs, Chubbs, Judsons, Mayos, Noyeses, Perkinses, and Phelpses. Towns named Kirby no longer shout forth what a high honor it once was for a village to have a church within its borders. Dwellers in Halifax have probably never heard of the virgin slain and beheaded while defending her honor, whose "holy hair" gave their town its name.[36]

Medieval minds ran normally in churchly channels. Was there a special Mass on the eve of Christ's birthday? A new word, "Christmas," was born. Did the time of a church service change? Noon (Latin *nona hora,* "ninth hour," 3:00 P.M.) calmly followed the service to its new time, twelve o'clock. Did a plant bear blossoms shaped like the bells jingling on the bridles used by pilgrims to the tomb of Thomas à Becket at Canterbury? Then the plant was a Canterbury Bell. Since Judas was traditionally red-haired, all redheaded and, especially, red-bearded people were treacherous scoundrels, whose blood was a potent ingredient of poisons.

> In never a house where a red man be
> Nor woman of the same colour certainly
> Take never thine inn for no manner need
> For these be folk to hold in dread.[37]

Why should not the Stone of Scone, coronation seat of English kings, be treasured? It was the rock upon which Jacob pillowed his head at Bethel as he dreamed of a ladder to heaven and heard God's promise of wide dominion. Did a medieval poet arise? His works dripped with scriptural allusions. Of 6,074 lines in the poems "Patience," "Pearl," and "Purity," 2,400 are biblical.[38]

A mere listing of surviving biblical quotations in English literature written between 1066 and 1350—the lean years when the language was struggling for survival—crams nearly three hundred closely printed pages.[39] Even light literature—satire, parody, burlesque—took churchly mold.

> The complete service of the Mass was applied to the worship of Bacchus and Venus, and of gaming. We have an excommunication pronounced by order of Venus, and the hymns to the Virgin are turned into mock hymns in honor of wine. The mock *Regula Libertini* appears more than once. The church Catechism and Paternoster . . . were regularly parodied. . . . Erotic stories were told in the language of the Bible. Saints' lives were parodied.[40]

A child's primer would contain the alphabet, the Exorcism, the Lord's Prayer, and such things as the Hail Mary, the Creed, the Ten Commandments, the Seven Deadly Sins, the Seven Principal Virtues, the Seven Works of Mercy Bodily (from Matthew 25), the Seven Works of Mercy Ghostly, the Five Wits Bodily, the Five Wits Ghostly, the Four Cardinal Virtues, the Seven Gifts of the Holy Spirit, and perhaps a quotation from the thirteenth chapter of First Corinthians, or the Beatitudes, with selected sayings of St. Augustine.[41]

A cross before the first line in the primer reminded the child to pray, "Christ's cross me speed," before starting to study, and left us the word "crisscross" and the game tick-tack-toe, just as the priest's black winter hood gave a name to dominoes, and the red-inked dates in the church calendar gave us the popular phrase "red-letter days."

Anyone learning Latin was presumably "clergy." Let him but read correctly his "neck verse," usually the beginning of the Fifty-first Psalm, and he was largely exempt from penalties visited upon lesser men.

> If a clerk had been taken
> For stealing bacon,
>   For burglary, murder, or rape,
> If he could but rehearse
> (Well prompt) his neck-verse
>   He never could fail to escape.[42]

Not until 1841 did the last vestige of this law disappear.

One of the striking things about the medieval age was its mathematical certainty about things religious. God took just three days to manufacture the "timber" for his universe, ending March 24.

Lucifer—the "light bearer" whose sulphurous doom named, in due course of time, the first vile-smelling matches—was created on Sunday and fell on Monday, falling forty miles a day for 7,700 years. God made 153 kinds of fishes. Birds he made of water—sea birds of sea water, river and lake birds of fresh water, field birds of grasses' dew, woods birds of trees' dew, and marsh birds from fens' moisture. Goliath's eyes were three feet apart. There were seven skies. Even as late as 1509, St. Paul's School was limited to 153 charity students, because that was the number of fishes in the miraculous draught recorded by John.

Even in such a system of surenesses, questions were arising. Were Abraham's angelic visitors really riding horses? Did the star of Bethlehem actually speak with human voice? "Some find this hard to believe." [43] The age of cocksureness was nearing its end.

Urbane Geoffrey Chaucer, with his "private renaissance," possessed few characteristics of a reformer. Several of his jolly Canterbury crew liked miracle plays—among them Absalom, and the miller, and the wife of Bath. Treacherous Nicholas, too, inquired of his intended dupe, "Haven't you heard what trouble Noah had in getting his wife aboard the ark?"

Chaucer's characters quoted Scripture with appalling intimacy. The oversexed Wife of Bath knew all that the Bible said "of bigamye or of octogamye." The rascally pardoner could twang off a sermon with the best of men, while the honest, prosy parson droned texts interminably. In two prose tales alone Chaucer Englished 160 Bible passages. He quoted from 40 books of the Bible and Apocrypha, and mentioned by name, from one to 20 times each, 69 biblical persons and 47 saints and theologians.[44]

If the retraction at the end of the Parson's Tale is genuine Chaucer became more pious as he grew older, for he begs "meekly for the mercy of God that you pray for me that Christ have mercy on me and forgive me my guilts; and namely for my translations and inditings of worldly vanities," among which he classes most of his best known works, including such Canterbury tales as tend to sin. But for his Boethius and other books of saints' legends, homilies, morality, and devotion, "thank I our Lord Jesus Christ and his blissful mother, and all the saints of heaven. . . ." Even while writing *The Canterbury Tales* he lauded Christian sincerity in the poor parson.

But Cristes lore, and his apostles twelve,
He taughte, but first he folwed it himselve.

As for the parson's plowman brother,

God loved he best with al his hole herte
At alle tymes.

But Chaucer saw, mocking these high sincerities, a host of shams, and would not keep silent. "I pleynly speke in this mateere," he quietly said, and proceeded to draw relentlessly the amorous, pilgrimage-traipsing woman, the unhealthily cloistered monks, the ruthless begging friar, the pimply summoner, the shameless pardoner with his pillowcase pieces of Our Lady's veil and his bulging wallet, "bret-ful of pardoun, come from Rome al hoot."

Far less tolerant was William Langland. A loyal churchman, he saw his church owning one third of the wealth of all England, and asked hotly what it was doing to help the common man. "A puritan two hundred years before Puritanism existed under that name," [45] he hammered out "that splendid, violent, cantankerous, and mystic vision of social evils and heavenly remedies," [46] *The Vision of Piers Plowman,* clinching his points with 514 Latin quotations from the Bible.[47] Here is no Chaucer, smiling at the pardoner. "If the bishop were holy and worth both his ears," he blurts out, "his seals would never be sent to deceive people so." "He that graspeth at her gold," he shouts of bribery, "so God help me, shall pay for it bitterly, or the book lieth." Of crafty men he charges bluntly, "They care not one goose wing for God."

Langland was not alone in rebelling.

Of this imagination was a foolish priest in the county of Kent called John Ball, who . . . used oftentimes . . . to go into the cloister and preach . . . "Ah, ye good people, the matter goeth not well to pass in England, nor shall not do so till everything be common. . . . Let us go to the king . . . and shew him how we will have it otherwise, or else . . ." [48]

John Ball and fifteen hundred of his comrades died, but their challenging rhyme, "When Adam delved and Eve span, who was then the gentleman?" still lives.

Meanwhile scholarly John Wycliffe was persistently asking, Why keep the Bible from the people?

In Anglo-Saxon times Bede had translated John; Aldhelm, the Psalms; and Alfred, the four Gospels. Ælfric had translated the first seven books of the Old Testament but, pressed to continue, had balked. He trembled lest, reading the Bible for themselves, foolish men might try to live as the patriarchs had, or might question established rules. "The itch of disputing is the scab of the church," [49] and the Bible in English might well cause an epidemic of intellectual itchiness.

Wycliffe, nearly eight hundred years after its arrival in England, Englished the Bible, to the consternation of his contemporaries.

> This Master John Wycliffe translated from the Latin into the tongue of the Angles (though not of the Angels) the gospel which Christ intrusted to the clergy and learned men. . . . Thus to the laity and even such women as can read this was made more open than formerly it had been even to such of the clergy as were well educated and of great understanding. Thus the evangelical pearls have been scattered abroad and trampled by the swine, and that which used to be dear to clergy and laity is now a common jest in the mouth of both. The gem of the clergy has become the toy of the laity.[50]

Men fought Wycliffe most venomously. He was to them

> the Devells Instrument, Churches Enemy, Peoples Confusion, Hereticks Idoll, Hypocrites Mirrour, Schismes Broacher, Hatreds Sower, Lyes Forger, Flatteries Sinke: who at his death despaired like Cain, and stricken by the horrible judgment of God, breathed forth his wicked soule to the dark mansion of the black devell. [51]

But no amount of execration could stop the forces loosed by him and his followers, and after a century a notable reinforcement arrived, when in 1481 there appeared:

> Pyes . . . of Salisbury . . . good and chepe . . . if it pleases any man spirituel or temporel to bye.[52]

This, one of the first printed advertisements ever read by Englishmen, was not some baker's method of selling pastry, but notice that England's first printer had just issued, "good and chepe," the Salisbury rules for finding the dates of Easter. It was now mechanically possible to produce Bibles cheaply. Whereas a hand-written Bible had cost perhaps two hundred dollars, the time was to come when one, well bound in limp leather, could be sold profitably at twenty-five cents.

But printing did not solve all problems. In 1491—one year before Columbus found a new world, and two years before the pope divided it, giving us the word "demarcation" thereby—the boy was born who as "the most habitual bridegroom in English history" was to precipitate with his matrimonial ventures such religious turmoil as England had never hitherto known.

THE BIBLE HELPS THE MODERN AGE BE BORN

6. Defender of the Faith

Little Miss Muffet sat on a prophet—
And quite right, too!

—OGDEN NASH[1]

By one of history's ironic jests it was upon Henry VIII that a grateful pope, as payment for the king's pamphlet against Luther, conferred the resounding title "Defender of the Faith." When, a few years later, this same five-Masses-a-day Henry rudely wrenched England from the papal hold, he conveniently forgot to return the ego-tickling title. His successors liked it and kept it.

The rupture with Rome arrived somewhat unpremeditatedly. A time came when Henry desired a loosening of his matrimonial bonds. He anticipated no particular trouble; his sister Margaret had recently encountered little difficulty in a similar quest. But his marriage had required a special license; the pope disliked setting aside a predecessor's ruling. Besides, the wife Henry wished to discard had a nephew who may not, as has been charged, have been so politically powerful that he "owned Rome and everybody in it," [2] but who had influence enough to cause Henry's urgent demands to meet persistent side-steppings and chafing delays.

Rome's grip on England and deference to Spain galled, England's monasteries bulged with tempting wealth, and events in Germany, thanks to Luther, suggested an easy and profitable way out. In Anglo-Saxon times invading Danes had destroyed 53 English monasteries. Thirty-seven had disappeared at the Norman Conquest. Under the Defender of the Faith 613 were suppressed. With them went 90 "colleges" under the care of the religious, 110 hospitals, and 2,374 chantries.[3] Men who objected to this program too strenuously were executed. The rich properties thus thrown into the hands of Henry were sold at scandalously low prices to his friends or to those he wished to make his friends. This automatically built up a potent defense against possible restoration; too many people in high places would have lost money.

Englishmen, seeing what was happening in the name of religion, and not daring to express their feelings too openly, fell back upon an ancient weapon—satiric rhymes. It was a dangerous weapon. Only a few years earlier, in the reign of Richard III, the poet Colingbourne had been hanged for writing

> The Cat, the Rat, and Lovel our Dog,
> Do rule al England, under a Hog.

His meaning had been too clear. As *The Mirror for Magistrates* puts it:

> The Chyefe was Catisby whom I called a Cat,
> A crafty lawyer catching all he could.
> The second Ratclife, whom I named a Rat,
> A cruel beast to gnawe on whom he should.
> Lord Lovell barkt & byt whom Richard would.
> Whom therefore ryghtly I dyd terme our Dog,
> Wherewyth to ryme I cleped the Kyng a Hog.[4]

When open criticism becomes too hazardous, subterranean criticism thrives. Under Henry and succeeding rulers there rose what in later years came to be known as the Mother Goose rhymes, in which, under seemingly innocent exteriors, were hidden wryly pointed jibes. "Robin the bobbin, the big-bellied Ben," was corpulent Henry himself, who, gobbling up religious establishments, "Ate more meat than three-score men," and devoured church, steeple, priests, and people.[5] "And yet he complained his belly wasn't full" because Parliament, though finally forced to fall in line with Henry's plans, proceeded too slowly to suit the king's imperious will. "Robin the bobbin, the big-bellied Ben," already current as a metaphor for a greedy priest, was a slap at Henry as Defender of the Faith and titular head of the Church of England.

For generations monks had placidly fished their well-stocked ponds on Thursdays to catch their Friday's food. Henry was busily adding to his already vast holdings these properties, so

> Little Tommy Tittlemouse lived in a little house;
> He caught fishes in other men's ditches.[6]

Since the great Cardinal Wolsey, sensitive to such barbs, tried to buy up all copies of lampoons against himself, he drew an inordinate share of attention. The fun is greater when the victim writhes.

Little Boy Blue, come blow your horn,
The sheep's in the meadow, the cow's in the corn

would remind this famous "Boy Bachelor" of his reputedly humble origin as son of an Ipswich butcher and cattle grazer, and pointedly suggest that he wake up to what was going on about him instead of remaining wrapped in his pleasant dreams of power.[7]

Jack and Jill
Went up the hill
To fetch a pail of water

taunted Wolsey and Bishop Tarbes for going to France to try for a marriage between Mary Tudor and the French king, and with intriguing for the holy water of the popeship which the cardinal so eagerly desired.[8]

How shall he marry
Without e'er a wife?

boldly charged Wolsey with love dalliance and the siring of illegitimate children.[9] When the proud cardinal fell from his pinnacle of power there was much scurrying about; the full-robed pope, disguised as

Old Mother Hubbard,
Went to the cupboard

in various vain attempts to get the poor dog, Wolsey, a bone of renewed preferment, but "The poor dog had none," and Wolsey died impoverished.[10]

Far more elaborate in its symbolism was the jingling "Sing a song of sixpence," the sixpence being the church dole; the pocket full of rye, the confiscated lands, the wealth of which the king so gleefully computed in his counting house; the four and twenty blackbirds, the two dozen deeds to church properties which the Abbot of Newstead sent in a pie as a present to Henry that they might sing melodiously to his greed. The Queen was Catherine of Aragon, eating England's bread and Spain's honeyed promises of support in her troubles. In the garden was the pretty maid, Anne Boleyn, hanging out the dainty frocks brought from France, her nose to be snipped off first by the priestly "blackbird," Wolsey, who at the king's secret command wrecked her engagement to marry Lord Percy, and later by that grimmer blackbird, the headsman.[11]

When Cranmer, after Wolsey's fall, astutely suggested that the proposed divorce be referred to the universities for a ruling, the king rapped out that he had the right sow by the ear, but the people impishly rhymed:

To market, to market,
To buy a fat pig.

Then home again, home again,
Jiggety jig.[12]

The pie-probing exploit of Little Jack Horner arose when Abbot Whiting sent him to Henry with a pie containing deeds to twelve churchly estates, by means of which he hoped to save the remaining holdings. In transit, by accident or otherwise, a hole was made in the crust, through which Jack "put in his thumb" and extracted the deed to Mell's Park, asserting upon his return that the king had graciously given him this considerable plum. Jack's defenders claim that the plum was not extracted, but bought.[13] Be that as it may, "The house that Jack built" still stands, a comfortable residence for his descendants.

Bishop Still was the man all shaven and shorn, who married the maiden all forlorn, lovely Joan Horner, great-niece to Little Jack Horner. This famous jingle has been traced to an old Jewish hymn following the Passover liturgy, wherein "my father" bought a kid for two pieces of money. Cat ate kid, dog bit cat, staff beat dog, fire burned staff, and so on to the triumphal climax:

Then came the *Holy One,* blessed be He!
And killed the angel of death,
That killed the butcher,
That slew the ox,
That drank the water,
That quenched the fire,
That burned the staff,

That beat the dog,
That bit the cat,
That ate the kid,
That my father bought
For two pieces of money.[14]

The kid is interpreted as the Hebrews; the father, Jehovah; the two pieces of money, Moses and Aaron, who led the Hebrews from Egypt; the cat, the Assyrians; the dog, the Babylonians; the staff, the Persians; the fire, the Greeks under Alexander; the water, the Romans; the ox, the Saracens, who subdued Palestine; the butcher, crusaders who wrested the Holy Land from the Saracens; the angel of death, Turks who took the land from the Christians. God will overthrow the Turks and restore the Jews.

Incidentally, the children's number game (One, two; buckle my shoe) finds close kin in both a Passover liturgy and a Christian chant of the Creed, in each of which, after every new line, all that preceded was repeated. The Jewish chant begins:

One: who knows? One: I know: One is our God in heaven and earth.
Two? . . . There are two tables of the Covenant.
Three? . . . There are three Patriarchs.

In the Christian chant one was God; two, the tables of Moses; three, the three patriarchs; four, the four Evangelists; five, the five wise virgins; six, the six waterpots at Cana; seven, the seven sacraments; eight, the eight Beatitudes; nine, the nine choirs of angels; ten, the Ten Commandments; eleven, the eleven thousand virgins; twelve, the Twelve Apostles.[15]

This credal chant has given rise to chants, folk songs, and children's verses in many lands, with many variants. In one "the charmed waters" which were turned into wine at Cana appear rather startlingly as "the charming waiters," and in the southern Appalachian Mountains as "the cheerful waiters." [16]

In England it took on a new guise as the anecdote of the soldier arrested for carrying a deck of playing cards to church. "The ace," he claimed in his defense, "reminds me that there is but one God; the deuce of the Father and Son; the trey of the Holy Trinity; the four of Matthew, Mark, Luke and John; the five of the wise and foolish virgins; the six of the days in which the world was made; the seven of the day on which the Lord rested; the eight of the good people saved from the flood; the nine of the lepers whom the Lord cleansed; the ten of the Commandments."

Laying aside the knave, he went on: "The queen puts me in mind of the Queen of Sheba, and thus of the wisdom of Solomon; the king calls to mind the King of all, and likewise His Majesty, King George, to pray for him."

"What is the knave for?"

"The sergeant who brought me here is the greatest knave I know. The three hundred sixty-five days in the year are shown by the number of spots in the pack, the fifty-two weeks by the number of cards. So you see this pack is my Bible, my prayer-book, and my almanac." [17]

Returning to the time of Henry VIII,

Jack be nimble,
Jack be quick,
Jack jump over
The candle-stick

is a vivid reminder of that stern necessity which lay upon churchmen to get upon the right side of things quickly if they would avoid the unpleasant consequences of opposing the king's will.

Even after Henry's death the making of such rhymes served as an escape valve for pent feelings. The three blind mice were Messrs. Cranmer, Latimer, and Ridley, who greatly annoyed the farmer's wife, landowning Queen Mary, by opposing her determination to restore England to Rome, and got their life tales quite appreciably shortened thereby.

Another Mary, Queen of Scots, as little Miss Muffet, sat on a mysterious something called a tuffet, dining in truly Scottish simplicity, until a very ogreish spider, John Knox, intruded. Her privacy was often thus rudely broken.

Goosey, goosey gander,
Whither shall I wander?
Upstairs and downstairs
And in my lady's chamber.

There I met an old man
Who wouldn't say his prayers,
I took him by the right leg
And threw him down the stairs.[18]

Intruders not only threw Cardinal Beaton downstairs: they hanged his stabbed and bleeding body from the castle walls.

Peter Piper, gay Earl of Leicester, picked a peck of very pickled peppers when, with one wife killed, he assertedly tried to murder the second that he might marry a third. When, with the second still alive, he married the third, the courtiers labeled them, though both were cousins to the queen, Leicester's Old and New Testaments.

When the very learned Reverend Doctor Henry Sacheverell preached, as late as 1709, two exceedingly bold sermons on the relations between church and state, he "scratched out both his eyes," so thoroughly that he was condemned of seditious libel, his sermons were burned, and he was forbidden to preach for three years.

And when he found his eyes were out,
With all his might and main,
He jumped into another bush,
And scratched them in again

so cleverly that he quickly regained favor and became Rector of St. Andrews.[19]

Like foam upon troubled waters, these light rhymes were once surface indications of a subterranean turmoil, a turmoil out of which emerged three important cultural changes.

7. Geneva Jigs

You that loyal Britons be,
Hallelujah sing with me.

Cho. *Hallelujah sing with me,*
You that loyal Britons be.

—GEORGE WITHER[20]

ENGLAND revolutionized its singing habits, its reading habits, and its writing habits.

The first great change in English song in the time of Henry VIII was the sudden loss of its rich treasury of Latin hymns. Augustine and his comrades had marched to their first meeting with an English king singing a hymn. Cædmon had initiated native English poetry by writing a hymn. Aldhelm, haunting English highways and byways, had used hymns to attract hearers, thus becoming "a sort of early Saxon Sankey," or possibly a predecessor of the Salvation Army street corner meeting. King Alfred had carried a hymnbook with him on his hunting trips. Both in England and elsewhere "that most social type of poem, the hymn," had deeply penetrated the common life. So greatly had hymns multiplied in various countries that one modern collection of medieval hymns, restricted to those omitted from other recent collections, fills fifty-four large volumes.

> No literary work of the dark ages can be compared for the extent and far reaching results of its influence with the development of popular Latin poetry. The hymn went further and affected a larger number of people's minds than anything else in literature.[21]

For centuries these hymns of the church, a part of that tremendous flood of vocal worship which inundated all Christian lands, rolled out over the English countryside. Then they stopped abruptly. With the founding of the English church, the issuance of an English prayer book, and the turning of the liturgy into English, this vast reservoir of song was discarded as popish.

To make matters worse, England, impoverished by loss of the Latin hymns, for long failed to develop a native hymnody, despite the fact that secular music flourished and almost every Elizabethan and Stuart poet tried his hand at sacred verse. Two tenaciously held ideas blocked the native hymns from the churches. The Puritans rejected them as "human composures"; and as for Anglicans, the new songs necessarily lacked the sanction of ancient ecclesiastical usage.

In desperation the people turned to the Bible and began "to dyngen upon David"—that is, to sing psalms. In 1560 Bishop Jewel noted that a remarkable change had come over London. Psalm singing had started in one church and then quickly spread. Sometimes six thousand people would sing together at St. Paul's cross. Between 1600 and 1653 there were 206 metrical versions of the complete Psalter published, together with 19 versions of prose and verse mixed, and 27 versions of selected psalms.[22]

This sudden preoccupation with psalmody would have delighted fourteenth-century Richard Rolle, who had prefaced his own translation of the Psalms with lyrical vigor:

> Psalm singing chases fiends, excites angels to our help, removes sin, pleases God. It shapes perfection, removes and destroys annoyance and anguish of soul. . . . As a lamp lighting our life, healing of a sick heart, honey to a bitter soul . . . this book is called a garden enclosed, well sealed, a paradise full of apples.[23]

Sir Thomas More also had greatly loved the Psalms; every morning he recited seven of them (the 6th, 32nd, 38th, 51st, 102nd, 130th, and 148th). While he was in the boat on his way to the Tower (and to his death) he sang psalms, by which recreation, as he told his son-in-law, he "gave the devil a foul fall indeed."

Queen Elizabeth, as usual, hedged. She contemptuously dubbed the current psalm roarings "Geneva Jigs," yet she encouraged the people in them and even tried her own hand at paraphrasing.

If psalm singing contained but half the virtues claimed by Rolle, then during the latter part of the sixteenth century and all of the seventeenth, England's greatest benefactors were Sternhold and Hopkins, whose compilation of the Psalms in meter swept the nation. No book in English has been more harshly attacked, and none, save only the Bible and the Prayer Book, more universally used. The British Museum possesses more than 650 editions of it, published at dates ranging from 1564 to 1841.

With no sense of ludicrousness pious audiences gravely sang:

> Ye monsters of the bubbling deep,
> Your Maker's praises spout:
> Up from the sands, ye codlings peep,
> And wag your tails about.[24]

Of the Scottish Psalter, largely from Sternhold and Hopkins, Thomas Fuller said that two hammers on a blacksmith's anvil would make better music. Edward Phillips jeered:

> Like a cracked saint's bell jarring in the steeple
> Tom Sternhold's wretched prick-song for the people.[25]

The Earl of Rochester, hearing the sounds issuing from a church, sneered:

> Sternhold and Hopkins had great qualms,
> When they translated David's Psalms,
> To make the heart right glad:
> But had it been King David's fate
> To hear thee sing and them translate
> By God! 'twould have set him mad! [26]

Wesley in his day dubbed them "miserable, scandalous" doggerel, while Ruskin in turn damned them as "half paralytic, half profane." But the people liked them.

In 1623 George Wither issued the first real approach to an English hymnal, *Hymns and Songs of the Church.* In addition to biblical translations it contained original hymns which so won royal favor that Wither gained a fifty-one years' patent and an order for them to be inserted into every English metrical psalm-book issued.

This brought down upon Wither the wrath of the Company of Stationers since it endangered that company's monopolies; they taunted him with making money out of the praises of God. His hymns, the Stationers raged, were popish, superstitious, obscene, and totally unfit to keep company with David's Psalms. Besides, the disgruntled attackers added piously, such writings should be left to the clergy—who, it was assumed, would publish through the Stationers. Young people bought Wither; older ones clung to Sternhold and Hopkins.

Eighteen years later Wither issued *Hallelujah, or Britain's Second Remembrancer,* addressing to the High Courts of Parliament "the sweet perfume of pious praises compounded according to the art of the spiritual apothecary." He prescribed when or by whom each hymn should be taken: "When we put on our Apparel"; "A Hymn whilst we are Washing"; "When we ride for Pleasure"; "A Rocking Hymn"; "For one that is promoted"; " For a Widower, or a Widow delivered from a troublesome Yokefellow"; "For Them who intend to settle in Virginia, New England, or the like Places." Still Sternhold and Hopkins remained the favorite.

At the end of the seventeenth century Tate and Brady's new version stirred up yet more heated discussion. Was it, after all, lawful for the people, especially women, to sing in church? Was it a fit thing for human compositions to be sung in public?

Shortly before this new melee arose, little Isaac Watts had tittered during family prayers. Explaining this scandalous breach of decorum, he confessed that, seeing a mouse run up the bell rope by the fireplace, he had made a rhyme:

> A mouse for want of better stairs
> Ran up a rope to say his prayers.[27]

At twenty-two, objecting to the songs heard at church, he was challenged by his father to write a better one. The answer was:

> Behold the glories of the Lamb,
> Amidst his Father's throne:
> Prepare new honors for His name,
> And songs, before unknown.

In 1707 he issued his epoch-making *Hymns and Spiritual Songs in Imitation of the Psalms.*

"Does Dr. Watts indeed presume to instruct the Holy Ghost in writing Psalms?" sneered the conservatives. Watts's answer was six hundred new hymns. A whole vista of Christian experience and emotion was opened as fit theme for song. No longer must church singing be restricted to the ancient hymnbook of the Jews. "Why must we, under the gospel, sing nothing else but the joys and hopes and fears of Asaph and David? As well have compelled David to sing the words of Moses and nothing else all through his rejoicing days!" [28]

The year that Watts published his first hymnal, Charles Wesley was born. A hymn writer of a hymn-writing family, Wesley shattered all precedents, publishing four thousand hymns and leaving two thousand or more in manuscript. This prodigious output, and the use made of it in the Wesleyan revival, changed markedly the temper of life in England and America. Religious experience was exalted and enthusiasm, long out of fashion, encouraged.

The mass of hymnody which has arisen since the Wesleys' time is enormous. One famous collection contains more than six thousand volumes. These hymns went everywhere. Cowboys

sang "Dan Tucker" until a horse would kick up his heels, and they sang "My Lulu Gal" with additions not to be printed, but they sang also "Nearer My God to Thee," " The Old Time Religion," "Jesus, Lover of My Soul," and "In the Sweet By and By." " 'Old Hundred' had a more soothing effect on wild cattle on the run than any other tune I knew," one veteran recalled. Reed Anthony, Andy Adams' cowman, tells how he and other Confederate soldiers guarding a herd of Texas steers saved the life of one because he would always walk out and stand attentive to the notes of "Rock of Ages" sung by his herders. Half the tunes of genuine cowboy songs sound as if they had been derived from camp-meeting hymns. The tune of "Jesse James" will make a sinner want to go to the mourners' bench. And those old, slow, mournful tunes made Christians out of many a herd of devil-hardened steers.[29]

These hymns have ranged from the most exalted literary standards to the most debased trashiness. What could be worse than Joanna Southcott's hymnal?

> The blades that I have call'd be wheat,
> Are those that judge the calling great,
> That they from Satan shall be free,
> And Pharaoh was a type of he.[30]

On the other hand, the better modern hymnals contain much of the best work of our ablest modern poets.

Hymns have now sunk so very deeply into our national thought that they have become poetic folk patterns. They are the only poems which many people know. No other poetry is so widely known or read by so many people weekly. From no other source except the Bible are so many familiar passages indelibly lodged in the public mind. Because of this, hymns are now being frequently used in secular literature—plays, novels, and short stories —sometimes in their purity, and sometimes debased to

> On the level
> 'S not the devil,
> Jesus is my Saviour now,

which was sung to the tune of "Yes, Sir, That's My Baby," in Steinbeck's *The Grapes of Wrath*.[31] An even more raucous parody was

> At the cross, at the cross,
> Where I lost my shirt and drawers,

And the but—tons they all
Rolled away, rolled away——[32]

which was screeched by an irritated bum in a twenty-cents-a-night flophouse in a recent short story.

Dramatic tribute to the power of hymn singing came in World War II, when selected hymns were stowed, along with first-aid kits, rations, and New Testaments, on every lifeboat and raft in the merchant marine.[33]

The religious upheavals which began in Henry VIII's time had also their effect upon the singing of Christmas carols. Caroling had originally possessed no flavor of religion or of song, being but a popular May dancing for women. Music and men were soon added. Godly people frowned upon it.

. . . carols, wrestling, or summer games,
Who-so ever haunteth any such shames
In church, or in churchyard,
Of sacrilege he may be a-feared.[34]

As the singing element became dominant, "those masterpieces of tantalizing simplicity," carols, were born. Many were secular.

As I came by a green forest side,
I met with a forester that bade me abide,
Whey go bet, hey go bet, hey go how,
We shall have sport and game enow.[35]

Since, however, the frequent church festivities—especially those of Christmastime—and the mystery and miracle plays encouraged carols which were of a religious nature, the Bible from Genesis to Revelation was soon ransacked for themes. Christmas was then a long-drawn-out affair.

On the fortieth day came Mary mild
Unto the temple with her child,
To show her clean that never was defiled,
  And therewith endeth Christmas.[36]

Its dominance in the year's merrymakings led carols finally to be called Christmas carols. But rising puritanism became a foe to reveling, and though Robert Herrick might yet melodiously pen,

What sweeter musick can we bring
Than a caroll, for to sing
The birth of this, our heavenly king?[37]

caroling soon felt the nipping frost.

In 1643 England's Roundhead Parliament banned all observance of saints' days and sternly forbade observance of Christmas, Easter, and Whitsuntide, standing ready to enforce the ban with troops. In America, Massachusetts enacted in 1659 that

> anybody who is found observing, by abstinence from labor, feasting, or any other way, any such day as Christmas Day, shall pay for every such offense five shillings.[38]

Though the Restoration legalized Christmas, the sophisticated turn of the times was not conducive to caroling. Indeed, it was not until late in the nineteenth century—long after Scrooge, in Dickens' *A Christmas Carol,* hearing

God bless you, merry gentleman,
May nothing you dismay!

had grasped a ruler and chased the shivering caroler from his door—that carols largely regained their lost favor, to become in the twentieth century the Christmas staples of church and radio.

While these changes in the singing habits of the people were taking place, a significant development in the nation's reading was occurring.

8. Best Seller

Adam was the first man and Eve she was his spouse;
They lost their job for stealing fruit and went to keeping house.
All was very peaceful and quiet on the main
Until a little baby came and they started raising Cain.

—ANONYMOUS[39]

WHILE sixteenth-century England was deliberately losing the Latin hymns, it was unwillingly gaining the printed English Bible. This was not easy, nor was it accomplished without martyrdoms.

"It is not good to disturb a hornet's nest," Henry had warned those inclined to cavil about his marriage annulment; those who insisted on giving England a printed English Bible stirred up several most lively hornets' nests.

In the first place, there was a distinct cultural odium attached to Englishing the Scriptures. Modern languages, especially English, lacked prestige; they were, for dignified prose literature, not quite respectable. Sir Thomas More issued *Utopia* in Latin. It was translated into German, French, and Italian; then after thirty-five years had passed, and the author had been dead sixteen, it reached beggarly English. Roger Ascham apologized for putting one of his own books into English. Even at the end of the sixteenth century, Francis Bacon carefully translated one edition of his essays into Latin, that they might survive this ephemeral English language.

Even if the Bible were to be turned into English, another complication arose—into what sort of English should it be turned? Bishop Gardiner vigorously objected to the style of Tyndale's New Testament because it was too clear! Among the hundred and two Latin words which he urged retaining in any English version "for the dignity of the matter in them contained" are such monstrosities as *"holocausta," "panis," "peccator,"* and *"zizania."* [40] On the other hand, scholarly but storm-centerish Sir John Cheke, tutor to Prince Edward, felt that the fad for classical terminology had gone to nonsensical extremes, and he began a New Testament which should contain nothing but native words. Lunatic became "moon'd"; captivity, "outpeopling"; and publicans, "tollers." Parables were "biwordes," and a proselyte a "freschman."

But far bitterer than these scholarly sparrings were ecclesiastical anathemas. Twenty-four years after John Wycliffe's death the reading of any of his writings or translations had become a penal offense in the jurisdiction of Canterbury; six years later a sterner enactment provided that any who read the Bible in English should "forfeit land, catel, lif, and goods from their heyers for ever." Finally, his moldering bones were dug up, burned, and dumped into the river which flowed past his church.

In spite of this fierce opposition, his hand-written Bibles were so popular that even now a hundred and seventy known copies survive. In the sixteenth century, printing had made hand-written books unnecessary, and the Renaissance had made a much better text possible; yet even after fifty years of printing in England, there existed no printed English Bible, and in official quarters none was desired.

"We had better," shouted one of William Tyndale's debate opponents, "be without God's laws than the Pope's."

"If God spare me," vowed Tyndale in return, "I will one day make the boy that drives the plough in England to know more of Scripture than the Pope does."

This reply drove him from England forever. "I perceived that not only in my lord of London's palace, but in all England, there was no room for attempting a translation of the Scriptures," [41] he sadly confessed, after bitter experiences. Having translated his New Testament at Hamburg, he was busily seeing it through the press at Cologne when a priest, suspicious from a chance remark of the printers, plying them with wine, discovered the damning secret. Saving such printed sheets as he could seize, Tyndale hurriedly fled and finally, probably at Worms, about 1526, issued the first complete printed New Testament in English. In bales, barrels, and boxes of merchandise copies were smuggled into England. Many were seized and burned. After ten years, Tyndale was betrayed, captured, strangled, and burned. But since an estimated fifty thousand copies of his Testament had been distributed, "It passeth my power," wrote Bishop Nikke, "or that of any spiritual man, to hinder it now."

Events were moving at a dizzying pace. One year before Tyndale's death, Miles Coverdale, using Tyndale's work, had issued, probably at Zurich, the first complete printed Bible in English. Two years later this was reprinted in London, "set forth with the kynges most gracious licence." England finally had a Bible in English, and printed in England.

Coverdale, having powerful friends at home and abroad, managed to die a natural death, but John Rogers, who issued a Bible under the name of Thomas Matthew, was burned. This melancholy event added measurably to the vividness of ensuing American education, for the admonitory rhymes which Rogers supposedly wrote to his brood of ten children in honor of the occasion, and sundry smudgy pictures depicting the event itself, with his wife and moon-faced progeny placidly observing the paternal incineration, long formed a part of the famous *New England Primer*. That these highly publicized rhymes were actually written by a man named Smith in preparation for his own martyrdom, and that records indicate that Mrs. Rogers did not take the children to see their father burned, is quite beside the point. Millions of American children gazed upon the pictured faces of the Rogers children as they glimmered eerily through their sire's billowing smoke, read his good advice, and were presumably edified thereby.

Meanwhile, affairs had so reversed themselves in England that three years after Tyndale's death the Great Bible was issued, officially ordered set up in the churches, and members of the clergy were urged expressly to "provoke, stir and exhort every person to read the same, as that which is the very lively word of God."

Four years more and all translations bearing Tyndale's name were again banned, all notes in other texts ordered obliterated or removed, and the reading of the Bible, either privately or publicly, was forbidden to all women (except noble ladies or gentlewomen, who might peruse it "in their garden or orchard" or other retired place) and also to apprentices, artificers, husbandmen, journeymen, laborers, and serving men, under penalty of a month's imprisonment. Three years later Coverdale's New Testament was added to the banned list. The Bible was restricted because it had proved too popular. So many people had crowded about the six copies set up in St. Paul's that Bishop Bonner had been forced to forbid their use at the time of service, because of the disturbing noise. One John Porter, "a fresh young man, and of a big stature," had been especially well liked, as "he could read well and had an audible voice."

"I am very sorry," fumed the king in his message to Parliament at the end of 1545, "to know and hear how unreverendly that precious jewel, the Word of God, is disputed, rhymed, sung, and jangled in every ale-house and tavern. This kind of man is depraved and that kind of man, this ceremony and that ceremony."[12]

At Henry's death his son, aged ten, succeeded. The official attitude changed. During the six and a half years' reign of Edward VI, English prayer books, "to be understanded of the people," were prepared; and thirteen editions of the whole Bible, with thirty-five separate ones of Testaments, poured from the presses. Apparently they were needed. In 1551 the Bishop of Gloucester, testing the biblical knowledge of his clergymen, had found that of 311, 171 could not repeat the Ten Commandments, 10 were unable to give the Lord's Prayer, 27 could not name its author, and 30 could not tell where it was to be found. One had no idea of the scriptural authority for the Apostles' Creed, unless it was the first chapter of Genesis, but added complacently that it didn't matter, since the king had guaranteed it to be correct.[43]

At Edward's death Mary, his half-sister, came to the throne. In the five years of her bloody effort to restore England to Rome, all printings of the English Bible in England ceased abruptly, and three hundred of her subjects died as martyrs. These are the days of which Benjamin Franklin in his *Autobiography* says of his ancestors:

> They had got an English Bible, and to conceal and secure it, it was fastened open with tapes under and within the cover of a joint-stool. When my great-great-grandfather read it to his family, he turned up the joint-stool upon his knees, turning over the leaves then under the tapes. One of the children stood at the door to give notice if he saw the apparitor coming, who was an officer of the spiritual court.[44]

Mary died brokenhearted, and her half-sister Elizabeth followed her to the queenship. As the Roman Church considered Elizabeth's birth illegitimate, she necessarily tended toward Protestantism, but she astutely realized that her safety lay in pursuing a middle course, balancing one faction against another, and building up her own personal supremacy. This she accomplished with consummate skill.

Elizabeth, an energetic student, was ostensibly much interested in the Bible. At sixteen she had almost completed Cicero and had read much in Livy. It is reported that she started the day with the New Testament in Greek and went thence to Greek orations and tragedies; that when she received news of her peaceful accession to the throne she fell to her knees, exclaiming, "It is the Lord's doing, and it is marvellous in our eyes," words which she caused to be stampted upon her coinage; that when she entered London as queen she kissed, as "the jewel that she still loved best," the English Bible presented to her and promised "diligently to read therein"; that in every office at court was placed "a Bible, chronicle, or the like"; that she commemorated the destruction of the Spanish Armada by a medal engraved, "The Lord sent his wind, and scattered them."

At any rate, through her long reign the Bible flourished as never before. Ninety editions of the Geneva version (the Breeches Bible, in which Adam and Eve made breeches of fig leaves) appeared, and forty editions of other versions. After a thousand years in England the Bible had suddenly become a best seller. It reached the common people as no other book had ever done. Says Green, the historian:

> So far as the nation at large was concerned, no history, no romance, hardly any poetry save the little-known verse of Chaucer, existed in the English tongue when the Bible was ordered to be set up in churches. Sunday after Sunday, day after day, the crowds that gathered round the Bible in the nave of St. Paul's, or the family . . . at home, were leavened with a new literature. Legend and annal, war song and psalm, state-roll and biography, the mighty voices of prophets, the parables of Evangelists, stories of mission journeys, of perils by the sea and among the heathen, philosophic arguments, apocalyptic visions, all were flung broadcast over minds unoccupied for the most part by any rival learning.[45]

This mighty fertilization of English thought changed greatly the character of the people.

> The Bible was as yet the one book which was familiar to every Englishman; and everywhere its words, as they fell on ears which custom had not deadened to their force and beauty, kindled a startling enthusiasm. The whole moral effect which is produced nowadays by the religious newspaper, the tract, the essay, the missionary report, the sermon, was then produced by the Bible alone; and its effect in this way, however dispassionately we examine it, was simply amazing. The whole nation became a church.[46]

No one could enter England without sensing the change. Two years after Elizabeth's death Grotius remarked of England, "Theology rules there." Casaubon, called to the court of James, ruefully agreed. "There is a great abundance of theologians in England," he said; "all point their studies in that direction."

This energetic reading of the Bible changed English diction, resulting temporarily in that "strange mosaic of Biblical words and phrases which colored English talk," and in a permanent addition to its vocabulary. New words were upon men's lips. It seems incredible that there was ever a time when "beautiful" was not in the English language, but Tyndale was one of the first, perhaps the very first, to use it in a book. "Peacemaker" was his, too, and "long-suffering," "brokenhearted," and "stumbling block." By a happy blunder, he brought us "scapegoat." His biting phrase, "filthy lucre," loaded that unhappy word with such a weight of disgrace as it has not in four centuries been able to shake off, although its close relative, "lucrative," to this present day wraps the purple and fine linen of eminent respectability around its plump and well-fed form.

Coverdale, too, excelled in initiating new and lasting word linkings. "Loving-kindness," "tender mercy," "blood guiltiness," "noonday," "morning star," and "kindhearted" seem now inevitably joined, but they all came from Coverdale's Bible.

Tyndale's common-sense translation of the Bible, steering a middle course between the "zizanias" of the ultra-classicists and the "moon'ds" of the hyper-Anglicists, and becoming the core of all future translations of the Bible (including the King James), ultimately revolutionized English prose and verse rhythms. New cadences were in men's ears. Slowly the ponderous vocabulary and the long, rolling sentences of a heavy, Latinized style gave way before the terse simplicity of biblical diction and biblical sentence structure. The English language was now ready for modern authorship.

9. Shakespeare and Company

"That's Shakespeare's house, isn't it?" . . .
"Yes." . . .
"Did he write . . . ?"
"Oh, yes, he writ."
"What was it?"
"Well, . . . I think he wrote for the Bible."

—JOHN L. TOOLE[47]

WHEN the tumult and the shouting of the tempestuous sixteenth century had ceased, when its wranglings and its janglings had died away, when Henry with his assorted wives and their ill-assorted children had all been borne to quiet graves, it became evident that in the midst of the turmoil a new literature had been created.

Literary criticism had arisen, with the Bible as one of its patterns. To Sir Philip Sidney the oldest and most excellent types of poetry "were they that did imitate the inconceivable excellencies of God. Such were David in his Psalms, Solomon in his Song of Songs, in his Ecclesiastes, and Proverbs, Moses and Deborah in their hymns, and the writer of Job. . . . Against these none will speak that hath the Holy Ghost in due holy reverence." [48] Gabriel Harvey was equally appreciative "of the land that floweth with milk and honey. For what festival hymns so divinely dainty as the sweet Psalms of King David . . . or what sage gnomes so profoundly pithy as the wise proverbs of King Solomon. . . . Such lively springs of streaming eloquence and such right-Olympical hills of mounting wit I cordially recommend to the dear lovers of the Muses." [49]

The literature of English maritime discovery had arisen, with Richard Hakluyt as its great pioneer. He never forgot the day he visited his older cousin in the Middle Temple. About the room were fascinating books on cosmography, and a map. Seeing the lad's interest, his cousin obligingly pointed out seas and rivers, empires and territories, discussing their significances and discoursing upon trade, commerce, and traffic. Then taking down his Bible and turning to Psalm 107, he commanded, "Read." Like stirring organ music the majestic words swept the boy's soul:

> They which go down to the sea in ships and occupy the great waters, they see the works of the Lord, and his wonders in the deep.

Before he left the room Richard Hakluyt had found an aim in life; years later, when Hakluyt's *Voyages* appeared, his dream had taken tangible form and substance.

Religious bickerings gave rise to a locust swarm of hard-hitting pamphlets, such as John Lyly's "Pappe with an Hatchet," issued in the Martin Marprelate controversy as "a sound boxe of the eare, for the idiot Martin to hold his peace, seeing the pitch will take no warning." It was merciless fighting: "Rip up my life, discipher my name, fill thy answer as full of lies as of lines, swel like a toade, hisse like an adder, bite like a dog, & chatter like a monkey. . . . And so farewell, and be hanged, and I pray God ye fare no worse," [50] cried Lyly, and John Penry, though he denied authorship of the Martin tracts, and though his known writings are unlike them, was hanged for them.

Macaulay designates political speech of the time as "the eloquence of men who had lived with the first translators of the Bible, and with the authors of the Book of Common Prayer," and among these orators Ben Jonson rates Sir Francis Bacon as best. Abraham Cowley likens him in his relation to the new learning, to Moses standing upon Mount Pisgah, looking over the Promised Land to which he had brought his people.

It was this Bacon, eloquent, brilliant, cynical, capable as few men have been of compressing much thought into few words, who wrote the *Essays,* thereby bringing into English literature a new form. They were heavily laden with Scripture. Who that knows literature can ever forget his "*What is truth?* said jesting Pilate; and would not stay for an Answer." What garden lover could spare "God *Almightie* first planted a Garden. And, indeed, it is the Purest of Human Pleasures"? And it was this Bacon the worldling who said:

> The first Creature of God, in the workes of the Dayes, was the Light of the Sense; The Last, was the Light of Reason; And his Sabbath Worke, ever since, is the Illumination of his Spirit. First he breathed Light, upon the Face, of the Matter or Chaos; Then he breathed Light, into the Face, of Man; and still he breatheth and inspireth Light, into the Face of his Chosen.[51]

"Solomon saith" became almost his shibboleth, whenever he wished to clinch a point.

Such were the beginnings of modern English nondramatic prose.

Poetry rose from a nap of two centuries, stretched and for a century busied itself turning gorgeous biblical tapestries into English poetical patterns. Renditions especially of the Psalms, Ecclesiastes, and the Song of Songs "virtually gushed from the pens of English poets." That secular poetry felt the same influence is abundantly evidenced by Spenser's *Shephardes Calender*. Hidden under its seemingly innocuous pastoral form is as trenchant a criticism of the religious abuses of his day as ever animated *Piers Plowman*. But it is in the stupendous mosaic of his *Faerie Queene* that the powers of this "superb decorator" reach their prime. It opens with a young knight clad in that armor of God which Paul recommended to the Ephesians, riding forth against dragon error in protection of maiden truth. In the first two books of the poem approximately four hundred references to the Bible have been located,[52] while in all Spenser's works four hundred separate passages, ignoring repetitions, taken from forty-nine books of the Bible, have been found.[53] But it is in his *Epithalamion* that the influence of the Bible appears most clearly. As his bride approaches, he suddenly casts aside the gorgeous pagan imagery in which he has decked the marriage song, and exults in words inspired by the Psalmist,

> Open the temple gates unto my love,
> Open them wide that she may enter in;

while for his wedding march he beseeches,

> And let the roring organs loudly play
> The praises of the Lord in lively notes.

But greatest of all sixteenth-century literature was its drama. Recent research has revealed that much more of Elizabethan drama than has been realized was biblical. "For as godless a lot as their critics make them out, the Elizabethan dramatists displayed unexpected interest in things scriptural and pious." [54] School plays, puppet plays, closet drama, secular stage drama—all used biblical themes in profusion: the prodigal son, Jephthah, Abraham, Lot, Esther, Pontius Pilate, Joshua, Judas, Samson, Nebuchadnezzar, Tobias, Job, David, Bathsheba, Absalom.

One controversialist who turned morality plays into diatribes against Catholics was Bishop Bale; "bilious Bale," his enemies nicknamed him, and not without cause, for his eleven "comedies" upon the life of Christ are but dismal things. His God detests man: "In my syghte he is more venym than the spyder." In Bale's play Noah, realizing God's testiness, wisely refrains from irritating him: "With thee to dispute it were inconvenient."

It was a much abler playwright, that wild "atheistical" young man, Christopher ("Christbearer") Marlowe, who called Moses a juggler and incurred considerable danger because he remarked that if he were to write a new religion it would be superior to the Christianity he observed about him. He it was who wrote the streamlined morality, *Dr. Faustus,* wherein a supertalented youth trades his soul for a crowded share of those things which the Renaissance cherished.

It was rare Ben Jonson, scholarly Ben Jonson, who wrote *The Devil Is an Ass, The Alchemist,* and *Bartholomew Fair,* taking in the two last an exceedingly ample revenge upon the Puritans for their savage attacks upon the stage. In *The Alchemist* the whining, canting, Puritan teacher, Tribulation Wholsome, and his overzealous helper, Ananias, are foul fish indeed. But it was in *Bar-*

tholomew Fair that the full sting of his lash was felt. Here was a caricature of puritanism so robust that even after the Restoration it was frequently presented at court by royal command, and so realistic that a rustic Puritan taken to see it thought it real and waxed furious over the disgrace visited upon the Puritan elder, Zeal-of-the-Land Busy. This "noble hypocritical vermin" is "of a most lunatic conscience and spleen, and affects the violence of singularity in all he does," especially in his nonsensically repetitious canting conversation:

I will remove Dagon there, I say, that idol, that heathenish idol, that remains, as I may say, a beam, a very beam,—not a beam of the sun, nor a beam of the moon, nor a beam of a balance, neither a house-beam, nor a weaver's beam, but a beam in the eye, in the eye of the brethren; a very great beam, an exceedingly great beam, such as are your stage-players, rimers, and morrice-dancers, who have walked hand in hand, in contempt of the brethren, and the cause; and been borne out by instruments of no mean countenance.[55]

Greater than Marlowe, and greater than Jonson, was Shakespeare, in the First Folio edition of whose plays are 55 biblical proper names in addition to names used in oaths, names of the Deity, names of characters in the plays, and generalized terms. In his plays are 149 passages from Matthew, 138 from the Psalms, 64 from Genesis, 42 from Job, and lesser numbers from other biblical books. In more than twelve hundred uses,[56] Shakespeare quotes from or alludes to 18 books of the Old Testament, 6 of the Apocrypha, and 18 of the New Testament.[57]

Shylock the Jew would be expected to know how Jacob outsmarted his uncle Laban in the matter of the latter's sheep, but he also, though a Jew, knows well the New Testament story of the Gadarene swine. If a close knowledge of the Scriptures should lead one to heaven, then rascally Falstaff stands an excellent chance of evading hell. Scriptural allusions drip from his glib tongue.

He is poor as Job but not so patient (*II Henry IV,* I, ii, 127; Jas. 5:11). He is not afraid of Goliath with a weaver's beam because life itself is a swift-moving shuttle (*Merry Wives,* V, i, 23; I Sam. 17:7). He surely knows by experience the story of the prodigal (*II Henry IV,* II, i, 146; Luke 15:11). If Adam fell in the state of innocency, what should poor Jack Falstaff do in the days of villainy? He has more flesh than other men and therefore more frailty (*I Henry IV,* III, iii,

172; Gen. 3:6, Rom. 7:18). Sometimes he is guilty of leaving the fear of God on the left hand (*Merry Wives,* II, ii, 23; Rom. 3:18). If however mere fat makes a man hated, Pharaoh's lean kine are to be loved (*I Henry IV,* II, iv, 481; Gen. 41:19). He and Harry may repent, but it will not be in ashes and sackcloth, but in new silk and old sack (*II Henry IV,* I, ii, 198; Jonah 3:6). He has irreverent knowledge of Lazarus and the dogs that licked his sores (*I Henry IV,* iv, ii, 25; Luke 16:20), and of Dives burning in hell (*Ibid.,* III, iii, 33; Luke 16:23). He understands that as he that handles pitch is defiled, so the company a man keeps affects his morals (*Ibid.,* II iv, 4:21; Ecclus. 13:1). Henry's goodness comes from his association with him, for a tree is known by its fruit (*Ibid.,* II, iv, 436; Matt. 12:33). It is God who gives men a spirit of persuasion (*Ibid.,* I, ii, 152; I Kings 22:21). Men themselves, however, must rouse up fear and trembling (*II Henry IV,* IV, iii, 14; Phil. 2:12). If he has an enemy the man is an Ahitophel (*Ibid.,* I, ii, 35; II Sam. 15:31). If men are saved by merit, no hole in hell is hot enough for him (*I Henry IV,* I, ii, 109; Jas. 2:24, Luke 16:23). A man who has plenty of gold-pieces is possessed of a legion of "angels" (*Merry Wives,* I, iii, 54; Mark 5:9). Falstaff can even make sport of Paul's lofty injunction to owe no man anything but love (*I Henry IV,* III, iii, 144; Rom. 13:8). Sometimes, in fine, his scripture quotations are themselves, like Mrs. Ford's scriptural remark about him, quite unquotable (*Merry Wives,* II, i, 60; Jonah 2:10). Falstaff's whole character may be known by the Scripture he uses and by the way he uses it. But, once more, in the closing scripture citation Shakespeare passes an unrelenting judgment upon the profane and surfeited fool and jester whose character he has created (*II Henry IV,* V, v, 51; Ps. 73:7-9 and esp. 20).[58]

There are other ways not so obvious in which Shakespeare and his contemporaries drew ultimately from the Bible. When, for example, in *Henry VIII,* Cranmer modestly hesitates to stand sponsor for the infant Elizabeth and the king jestingly accuses him of trying to save his spoons, the allusion is to the now-treasured and rare apostle spoons which godparents once gave as reminders to godchildren—four if the donor was poor; twelve, one of each of the apostles, if he was richer—forerunners of modern souvenir spoons.

This borrowing of scriptural ideas for common objects was not peculiar to the Elizabethan period. A jesse (branched candlestick, from its similarity to the shape of genealogical tables—"a root out of Jesse") was earlier. Later usages include "jericho" (privy) and "jeroboam," a wine bottle holding eight to twelve quarts, reminiscent of that mighty man of valor who caused Israel to sin. A "rehoboam" was even greater and more regal, for it equaled in capacity two jeroboams. A "jorum" was a large drinking vessel commemorating that biblical Joram who brought with him vessels of silver, vessels of gold, and vessels of brass. In clothing, the seventeenth century brought in "pantaloons" from good St. Pantaleone; "josephs" were once reminiscent of the long coat left in the clutches of Potiphar's wife; and a nineteenth-century tailor initiated "benjamins," the topcoat which the twentieth century shortened to "benny." Clergymen's well-starched "bands" were once carried in bandboxes, so named for what they contained.

The Shakespearean age was, however, unique in one important respect. It was England's first crowding, opulent age of varied and full-statured secular authorship. It is particularly significant that in this formative stage modern literature leaned so heavily upon the Bible. Newly risen arts, however, frequently develop, alongside their more solid achievements, extravagances of thought and expression which are often amusing, sometimes pathetic, but always fascinating. England's experience was no exception.

10. Altars and Angel Wings

Oh, we are ridiculous animals; and if angels have any fun in them, how we must divert them. —HORACE WALPOLE[59]

NATIONS in the throes of cultural revampings should at frequent intervals be subjected to heavy doses of gusty laughter. Perhaps starry-eyed experimenters might thus be kept within bounds and a sense of proportion preserved. During England's literary renaissance, close crammed as it was between two religious upheavals (the break from Rome and the rise of Puritanism), the neglect of widespread laughter was a major disaster, leaving for a time both literature and religion defenseless against faddists.

When in 1589 it was solemnly announced that "the Lozange is a most beautiful figure. . . . the Fuzie is of the same nature but that he is sharper and slenderer," [60] not nearly enough people laughed, and the minor fad of emblem poetry was merrily on its way. Admitting that his new-fangled fripperies, which he claimed to have learned in Italy from a returned traveler to the Orient, would at first seem "nothing pleasant" to English judgments, but asserting that time and usage would make them acceptable enough, "as it doth in all other guises be it for wearing of apparell or otherwise" (a remark which must not be interpreted as favoring nudism), the innovator calmly suggested the various figures—lozenges, fusees, triangles, squares, cylinders, spires, spheres, eggs—into which poems might be written, and the positions—upright, sidewise, upside down, split and stacked (hourglass-fashion)—into which they might be placed.

Soon the literary foplings were aflutter, busily concocting versified wineglasses, bows and arrows, truelove knots, and even, as Ben Jonson remarked, "A pair of scissors and a comb in verse." [61] The pious sighed out their souls in altars, crosses, and angel wings.

"Heading the list of English word-torturers stands so good and great a man as George Herbert. We quote two specimens and then pass on with our eyes veiled, to avoid gazing too intently on a good man's shame." [62] First there is a tear-cemented altar poem:

THE ALTAR

A BROKEN ALTAR, Lord, thy servant rears,
Made of a heart, and cemented with tears;
Whose parts are as thy hand did frame;
No workman's tool hath touch'd the same.
A HEART alone
Is such a stone,
As nothing but
Thy power doth cut.
Wherefore each part
Of my hard heart
Meets in this frame,
To praise thy name:
That, if I chance to hold my peace,
These stones to praise thee may not cease.
O let thy blessed SACRIFICE be mine,
And sanctify this ALTAR to be thine.[63]

And then there is a pair of rather stiff angel wings:

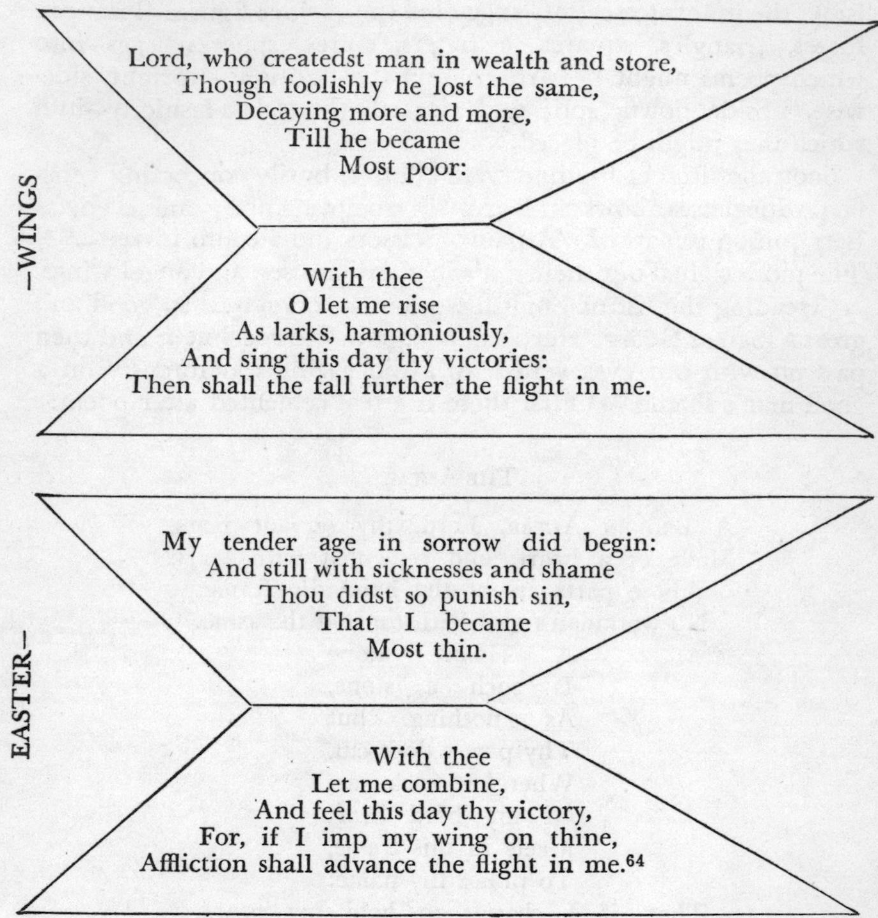

EASTER—WINGS

Lord, who createdst man in wealth and store,
Though foolishly he lost the same,
Decaying more and more,
Till he became
Most poor:

With thee
O let me rise
As larks, harmoniously,
And sing this day thy victories:
Then shall the fall further the flight in me.

My tender age in sorrow did begin:
And still with sicknesses and shame
Thou didst so punish sin,
That I became
Most thin.

With thee
Let me combine,
And feel this day thy victory,
For, if I imp my wing on thine,
Affliction shall advance the flight in me.[64]

Even so tuneful a singer as Robert Herrick fell into the snare:

This Crosse-Tree here
Doth JESUS *beare,*
Who sweet'ned first,
The Death accurs't.
Here all things ready are, make hast, make hast away;
For, long this work wil be, & very short this Day.
Why then, go on to act: Here's wonders to be done,
Before the last least sand of Thy ninth houre be run;
Or e're dark Clouds do dull, or dead the Mid-dayes Sun.
Act when Thou wilt,
Bloud will be spilt;
Pure Balm, that shall
Bring Health to All.
Why then, Begin
To powre first in
Some Drops of Wine,
In stead of Brine,
To search the Wound,
So long unsound:
And, when that's done,
Let Oyle, next, run,
To cure the Sore
Sinne made before.
And O! Deare Christ,
E'en as Thou di'st,
Look down, and see
Us weepe for Thee.
And tho (love knows)
Thy dreadfull Woes
Wee cannot ease;
Yet doe Thou please,
Who Mercie art,
T'accept each Heart,
That gladly would
Helpe, if it could.
Meane while, let mee,
Beneath this Tree
This Honour have
To make my grave.[65]

Yet more intricate was the triple-cross poem concocted by some now unknown genius:

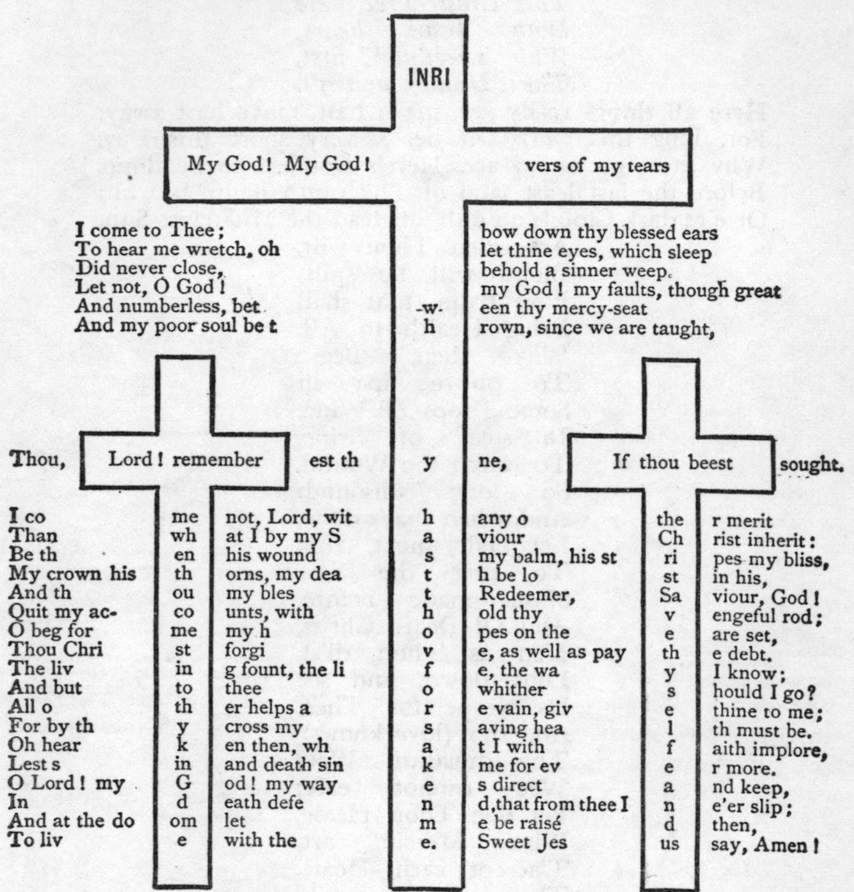

St. John's College, Oxford, carefully preserved a picture of Charles I, containing all the psalms written into the lines of the face and hairs of the head, of which the reserved Addison once wrote:

When I was last in Oxford I perused one of the whiskers; and was reading the other, but could not go as far in it as I would have done, by reason of the impatience of my friends and fellow travellers, who all of them pressed to see such a curiosity.[67]

The fad left remnants in Addison's own sophisticated day.

I have since heard that there is now an eminent writing-master in town who has transcribed all the Old Testament in a full-bottomed periwig; and if the fashion should introduce the thick kind of wigs which were in vogue some few years ago, he promises to add some two or three supernumerary locks that shall contain all the Apocrypha. He designed this wig originally for King William, having disposed of the two books of Kings in the two forks of the foretop, but that glorious monarch dying before the wig was finished, there is a space left in it for the face of any one that has a mind to purchase it.[68]

The modern equivalents of these monstrosities are portraits pounded out on typewriters, poems shaped like Christmas trees, and vests like that of the late Alexander Woollcott, who was once reported to be

wearing a new waistcoat, given him by Mrs. Theodore Roosevelt, Jr., embroidered with nosegays and monsters, and cross-stitched with a verse from *Psalms: They are enclosed in their own fat: with their mouth they speak proudly.*[69]

Alongside fantastic form flourished fantastic imagery, as a part of the fad for the baroque which swept over Europe. John Donne was one of England's greatest metaphysical poets and one of her most eloquent preachers, yet he wrote,

Whilst my Physitians by their love are growne
  Cosmographers, and I their Mapp, who lie
Flat on this bed, that by them may be showne
  That this is my South-west discoverie
. . . . . . As West and East
In all flatt Maps (and I am one) are one,
So death doth touch the Resurrection.[70]

His "The Litany" makes the Apostles "thy illustrious zodiac," and himself a temple of the Holy Ghost, "but of mud walls and condensed dust." "Of the Progress of the Soul" finds the body to be "a poor inn, a Province pack'd up in two yards of skin."

Donne was not alone in using tormented imagery. Brilliant George Herbert, for eight years Orator of Cambridge University, and devoted Anglican priest, cried out:

O let me, when thy roof my soul hath hid,
O let me roost and nestle there.[71]

Elsewhere he asks how man can preach God's word, since man is but "a brittle crazy glass," which, however, God can anneal and thus make into a window. Deity, when not transforming men into art glass, is busy manufacturing chronological bracelets for his wife!

The Sundays of man's life,
Threaded together on time's string,
Make bracelets to adorn the wife
Of the eternal glorious King.[72]

God enjoys nothing more than man's groans.

All *Solomon's* sea of brass and world of stone
Is not so dear to thee as one good groan.

The groans are most unusual. They

. . . are quick, and full of wings
And all their motions upwards be;
And ever as they mount, like larks they sing:
The note is sad, yet music for a King.[73]

After this grotesque choral medley, one is not surprised to find that, in preparation for the Incarnation,

The God of power, as he did ride
In his majestic robes of glory,
Resolved to light; and so one day
He did descend, undressing all the way.[74]

At the Resurrection,

Christ left his grave-clothes, that we might, when grief
Draws tears, or blood, not want a handkerchief.[75]

In Richard Crashaw's verse, Satan "fries himself" in hell, which is his shop of flames; Mary's tear is "a moist spark" and a "watery diamond." That this tear may not make its bed in the dust, Crashaw will bring a pillow "stuffed with down of angel's wing."

> At my feet the blubb'ring mountain,
> Weeping, melts into a fountain,
> Whose soft, silver-sweating streams
> Make high noon forget his beams,[76]

is Crashaw's idea of attractive wording for the Twenty-third Psalm! Wherever Christ goes

> He's follow'd by two faithful fountains;
> Two walking baths, two weeping motions;
> Portable, and compendious oceans,[77]

which are Mary Magdalene's streaming eyes. For this unparalleled aqueousness Mary gets only a milkmaid's reward:

> Upwards thou dost weep;
> Heaven's bosom drinks the gentle stream.
> Where the milky rivers creep,
> Thine floats above and is the cream.[78]

Equally notable is the flaming heart of St. Teresa, which is so ultravivid in its fervor that it lures even "a seraphim" into tourist sight-seeing:

> This is the mistress flame, and duteous he
> Her happy fireworks, here, comes down to see:[79]

Perhaps, after all, the figure is appropriate, for fireworks received much of their early publicity in religious celebrations, and in England one of the early pieces was "a cunning peece of fire work framed in forme like to ye Arke of Noy." Roman candles, Pharaoh's serpents (Exodus 7:9-12), and Catherine wheels (reminding of the manner of St. Catherine's martyrdom) are yet standard parts of the fireworks sellers' stock in trade.

At last England once more learned to laugh. Whereas in the seventeenth century Sir Thomas Urquhart had gravely traced his family history through his father back to Adam and through his mother to Eve, finding that in each case he was the one hundred and fifty-third in descent,[80] in the nineteenth century Thomas

Moore could prove his own descent by the quip, "Noah had three sons, Shem, Ham, and one More." [81] Sydney Smith could rule, "A bishop should be given to hospitality, and never be without a smoked little boy in the bacon rack, and a cold missionary on the side board." [82] In America Oliver Wendell Holmes could invent amusing pseudo history:

> Why, at the last Auto-da-fe, in 1824 or '25, or somewhere there,—it's a traveller's story, but a mighty knowing traveller he is,—they had a "heretic" to use up according to the statutes provided for the crime of private opinion. They couldn't quite make up their minds to burn him, so they only *hung* him in a hogshead painted all over with flames.[83]

Emblem verses, penmanship stunts, metaphysical poetry, and genealogical gullibilities were, after all, rather harmless eccentricities, which sometimes served as the channels for deep piety. England would have been happier than history proved her to be had her extravagances of thought and action taken no more sinister turns than these.

THE BIBLE BRINGS THE GOOD AND BAD RESULTS OF QUARRELING

11. Thwack-coate Lane

We are God's chosen few,
All others will be damned;
There is no place in heaven for you,
We can't have heaven crammed!

—JONATHAN SWIFT[1]

ENGLAND grew not only poetically extravagant; it grew also extravagantly pugnacious. Words became bludgeons. Books were bitterly written "to be sold at the signe of the crab tree cudgell in thwack-coate lane." [2]

In this extravaganza of hatred the theater took many sound drubbings, successors of those given it by Tertullian in the days of the early Church Fathers. Protestants, finding that for reasons of state they were barred from using plays for propaganda, speedily discovered that drama was wholly without authority in Holy Writ and therefore to be uncompromisingly condemned. In 1577, one year after England's first theater was built, Thomas White fulminated: "The cause of plagues is sinne, if you look to it well; and the cause of sinne are playes; therefore the cause of plagues are playes." [3] John Northbrooke insisted that Satan possesses no speedier way nor fitter school in which to work and teach his desire than theaters are. Anthony Munday is credited with nicknaming the theater the Chapel of Satan where hell breaks loose. "Beware, therefore, you masking players, you painted sepulchres, you double dealing ambidexters," thundered Philip Stubbes in 1583. Biblical plays, he thought, abused God. "Intermingle not his blessed word with such profane vanities." Secular plays to his mind dishonored God and nourished vice, "both of which are damnable. So that whether they be the one or the other, they are quite contrary to the word of grace, and sucked out of the Devil's teats to nourish us in idolatry, heathenry and sin." [4]

Those going to houses frequented by players "go to Venus' Palace, and Satan's Synagogue, to worship devils, and betray Jesus Christ." People were flocking to theaters "thick and threefold" while churches were bare and empty. "Away therefore with so infamous an art!"

The early seventeenth century saw no abatement, particularly of the antagonism to the use of scriptural themes in plays. "Must the holy Prophets and patriarchs be set upon a Stage, to be derided, hist, and laughed at?" [5] The origin and vogue of mystery and miracle play had been forgotten or repudiated, so far as these bitter critics were concerned. Drama was now thrice damned: it was devilish, it was pagan, and it was popish.

> The ungodly Plays and Interludes so rife in this nation: what are they but a bastard of Babylon, a daughter of error and confusion, a hellish device (the Devil's own recreation to mock at holy things) by him delivered to the Heathen, from them to the Papists, and from them to us? . . . Now they bring religion and holy things upon the stage: no marvel though the worthiest and mightiest men escape not, when God himself is so abused.[6]

In 1632 William Prynne issued—to be sold at the Blue Bible Bookshop—his Gargantuan book *Histriomastix*. He was not entirely without firsthand knowledge of drama—he had been enticed to attend four plays in his youth, and he knew that Shakespeare's plays were shamelessly "printed in the best Crowne paper, far better than most Bibles." Fortified by this somewhat sketchy personal acquaintance with the subject, he wrote an eleven-hundred-page book against plays and players, piling up authorities ancient and modern so profusely that Laud asserted it would take at least sixty years to read all the works cited.

He ran afoul of royalty. Three years earlier, French-born Queen Henrietta Maria had dared invite a company of French actresses to perform in London, thus transgressing the English habit of having women's parts played by boys. The shameless hussies had been "hissed, hooted, and pippen-pelted from the stage," as Prynne gleefully noted. In the table of contents he referred to actresses as "notorious whores." When the book came from the press, the queen and her court women were themselves rehearsing a play. It looked as if his reference had a personal application. Prynne was punished most savagely. A sentence of life imprisonment was recalled, but he was expelled from Lincoln's Inn, deprived of his Oxford degree, fined five thousand pounds, and sent to the pillory. Both ears were lopped off, and he was branded "S. L." (for seditious libeler), letters which he sardonically insisted stood for *Stigmata Laudis* (marks of praise). Attacks upon the stage diminished rather suddenly.

After a few years the Puritans prevailed, and theaters were closed. When, after the Restoration in 1660, two opened again upon a monopolistic basis, such strong antagonism had been built up against God's appearing in a play—a commonplace in the mystery and miracle plays—that the prohibition still stands. Not until the twentieth century were biblical plays readmitted to the English stage.

But the theater was not alone in suffering from the saturnalia of jangling. The language itself was degraded. An age in which a Dean of Canterbury's sermon could parody, "Our Pope, which art in Rome, hellish be thy name," [7] and the head of a Cambridge college, seeing a student reading a Catholic mathematician's discussion of Euclid, could angrily command, "By all means leave off this author and read protestant mathematical books," [8] could not fail to develop "a pretty little vocabulary of abuse."

"Jack-in-the-box" was reputedly born of jeers at the consecrated Host in its sacred vessel, and "hocus-pocus" arose as a parody on the *Hoc est corpus* (This is my body) at the moment of transsubstantiation. "Pernicious," "faction," and "factious" upon the tongues of angry Catholics acquired almost the force of actual profanity.

Their opponents retaliated in kind. Tyndale, Latimer, and Coverdale hurled "dunce" (from Duns Scotus), "monkery," "popery," "Romanist," and "Babylonish." So insulting had "Roman," "Romanist," and "Romish" become by the beginning of the seventeenth century that when a Spanish marriage for Charles I was proposed, diplomats were forced to scurry around for a more courteous term in which to negotiate. The one invented, "Roman Catholic," still has a more courteous connotation than the others.

"Libertine," the name of a sect of freedom-loving Anabaptists, unjustly received its present unsavory connotation, as Protestants lustily quarreled among themselves. "Precise" and "puritan" have not yet crept entirely from under the shadow of those days, nor has "reprobate," the Calvinistic term for those rejected of God and therefore doomed to such misery as is somewhat lightly described by a modern author:

> Picture the Hell of my Aunt Sally:
> A pit of flame in a thirsty valley,
> With black walls sheer to the gates of glory,
> And red imps telling a bed-time story;
> A ring of demons with spear and trident,
> With eyes malicious and voices strident,
> Flaying babies and toasting sinners
> To the hellish wailing of violiners;
> . . . .
> And gamblers groaning and drinkers yearning,
> And the smell of artists and actors burning,
> And dancers dancing on fiery griddles
> To the devil's drums and the devil's fiddles,
> While the devil skips and the devil hollers
> For more hot pitch and more spiked collars.[9]

"Bigoted," "bigotry," and "malignant" yet bear the scars of battlings by the saints. "Vindictive" finally came to be used approvingly of God himself, so that there is still more than a trace of grim humor in the modern jests, "The Universalists believe that all men will be saved, but we hope for better things," [10] and

"I hope, madam, you believe in total depravity."
"Oh, parson, what a fine doctrine it would be, if folks only lived up to it." [11]

Milton coined "prelatry," "goosery," and "fustianist." "Sectarian," "cant," and "fanatic" (whence baseball "fan") all bear unpleasant associations. Nor was the warring always verbal—witness the audience reaction to one of George Fox's preachings:

& when I began to speake they fell upon mee, & ye clarke uppe with his bible as I was speakinge & hitt me in ye face, yt [that] I bleade exceedingely in ye steeple-house & soe ye people cryd letts have him out of ye church (as they caled it); & when they had mee out they exceedingely beate mee & threw mee over a hedge: & after dragged mee through a house Into ye street stoneinge & beatteinge mee: And they gott my hatt from mee which I never gott againe (& I was all over besmeared with bloode) [12]

The battered Quaker continued to preach to his tormentors the words of life "& showed to ym ye fruites of there teachers & howe they dishonored Christianity."

In 1660 the Restoration gave yet another blow to the language. King Charles and his followers brought from France the spirit of mockery and vented it upon the Puritans.

To this period belong the verbs to *burlesque,* to *banter,* to *droll,* to *ridicule;* nouns like *travesty, badinage,* and adjectives like *jocose* or *teasing* in their modern use; while *prig* was borrowed from rogues' cant to describe a Puritan or nonconformist minister.[13]

"Gossip," "pious," "demure," and "silly"; "prim," "ogle," and "officious" were other words permanently injured.

While this vocabulary of vituperation flourished, there rose and fell also the most grotesque fashion of personal names that England ever knew. "At the Reformation such a locust swarm of new names burst upon the land that we may well style it the Hebrew Invasion." [14] Three factors aided this spread of Old Testament names. The rupture with Rome had made New Testament names unpopular, as many of them were the names of Roman Catholic saints. Printing the English Bible had made Old Testament names more familiar to the general public. The Puritan temper was attuned to the Old Testament sternness. Parents ruthlessly affixed to their helpless offspring such names as Abimelech, Habakkuk, Hezekiah, Melchizedek, Pelatiah, Shadrach, Zebulon, and Zerubbabel.

"Cromwell," said Cleveland, "hath beat up his drums clean through the Old Testament, you may know the genealogy of our Saviour by the names of his regiment. The muster master hath no other list than the first chapter of Saint Matthew." [15] As controversies increased even these became too tame. Zealots flaunted their faith in the names of their children. Be-Stedfast Elyarde, Faint-not Dighurst, Fear-not Rhodes, Flie-fornication Andrews, Glory-be-to-God Penniman, Good-gift Gynnings, Hew-Agag-in-pieces Robinson lived, died, and were ceremoniously buried. Job-raked-out-of-the-ashes, found deserted on the ash pile in the lane leading to Sir John Spencer's back gate, mercifully died the day after baptism, but Stand-fast-on-high Stringer, Swear-not-at-all Ireton, and Obadiah-bind-their-kings-in-chains-and-their-nobles-in-irons Needham all lived. The Barebone family, which gave name to a notable session of Parliament, included Praise-God Barebone, Fear-God Barebone, Jesus-Christ-came-into-the-world-to-save Barebone, and If-Christ-had-not-died-for-thee-thou-hadst-been-damned Barebone, the last of whom was familiarly known as Dr. Damned Barebone.

Such stupefying nomenclature has mercifully died out, except for crackpots, Negroes, and kings. G. K. Chesterton mentions "an old gentleman with long grey whiskers, living in the suburbs; whose name, it appeared, was King Solomon David Jesus. . . . The monarch explained that his title had been given him by an actual voice speaking out of the sky."[16] Among Negroes one finds Pism C. Jackson, named for Psalm C, and the pastor's son, Matthew Mark Luke John Acts of the Apostles Son of Zebedee Garden of Gethsemane Hill. As for royalty, there is the much-besainted Edward Albert Christian George Andrew Patrick David Windsor, former King of England. Grace names—Charity, Faith, Hope, Mercy, and Prudence—are apparently on the way out, being replaced, the New York Library reports, by names of movie stars.

From the bitter wrangling of the Puritan years came still another notable result—an increase in scholarship. Since one cannot be an able quarreler without a thorough grounding in the subject under dispute, there arose such a tide of listening and studying as England and America have never surpassed. More than half the books published in London in 1620 were religious in theme.

Much of the Bible was memorized, not only by ministers, but also by laymen and children. One preacher took fifteen years expounding straight through the Bible, then started again and took ten more years. A second gave 152 lectures upon the Fifty-first Psalm. A third drew 145 expository sermons from the seventeenth chapter of John, and wrote 657 pages upon the first chapter of Second Corinthians. A fourth in four volumes of commentary failed to finish thirteen chapters of Hosea. A fifth took nearly three thousand quarto pages for Ezekiel, and a sixth almost five thousand folio pages for Job.

> The medieval conception of the authority of Aristotle and scholasticism was shattered. It was transferred in all its ingrained strength and with infinitely increased brooding awe to the Bible. . . . Psychologically, there were developed enormous industry in learning, endurance in listening to preachers and teachers, tenacious memory, and the power of visualizing and concentrating the thoughts on Bible

heroes, Bible stories, Bible language and Bible aspirations. Scripture students were indefatigable workers. Bishop Morton was at his studies before four o'clock in the morning, even after he was eighty years of age. Matthew Poole rose at three or four o'clock, ate a raw egg at eight or nine, another at twelve and continued his studies till late in the afternoon. Sir Matthew Hale, for many years, studied sixteen hours a day. For several years John Owen did not allow himself more than four hours' sleep. . . . In short, the scholarship and learning of this period, by their direct bearing upon the Bible, permeated and transfigured the national life in a rare degree, giving it, in spite of all its excesses and deficiencies, a strenuousness, sobriety, and, on the whole, a sincerity, probably never so largely sustained, by book learning, in any age, and rarely in any country.[17]

12. A Famous Forth-faring

Religion stands on tip-toe in our land
Ready to pass to the American strand.

—GEORGE HERBERT[18]

ANOTHER major effect of England's quarreling was the Puritan migration to America. Although the Honorable Bardwell Sloat, in B. E. Wolf's comedy, *The Mighty Dollar,* mangled his facts when he boasted that his "ancestors came over in the *Cauliflower* and landed at Plymouth Church," the actual arrival of the Puritans proved to be of major importance in world affairs.

Not that they first brought biblical ideas to America; that had been done long ago, when Christ-Bearer (Christopher) Dove (Columbus), sailing in a ship called *Holy Mary* (*Santa Maria*), reached land which he called Holy Saviour (San Salvador),

. . . and shining in his armor
With royal banners borne around the Cross
Columbus landed, and upon his knees
Gave thanks to God.[19]

His disillusioned followers nicknamed the new soil Mosquitoland, but biblical thought concerning it so persisted that the Bishops' Bible, issued in 1568, carried a marginal note to Psalm 45:9—

Ophir is thought to be the Ilande in the West Coast, of late founde by Christopher Colombo, from which at this day is brought most fine gold.

The composition of the first Jamestown colony in 1607 showed an astounding disregard of the conditions to be encountered. Of one hundred and five members but twelve were laborers and four carpenters. Yet despite all other pressing needs, they erected a church immediately.

Wee did hang an awning (Which is an olde Saile) to three or four trees to shaden us from the Sunne; our Walles were rales of wood; our seats were unhewed trees, till we cut planks; our Pulpit, a bar of wood, nailed to two neighboring trees. . . . This was our Church till we built a homely thing, like a barne, set upon Cratchets, covered with rafts, sedge and earth.[20]

Here, five weeks after landing, the First Families of Virginia partook of communion. The legal penalty for not attending church was loss of a week's provisions; for a second offense, whipping; for a third, death. Death also was the penalty for a third conviction for profane swearing or blasphemy against the Trinity or the king. If their books indicate accurately their interests, Virginians leaned strongly toward religion. Everybody owned the Bible—frequently no other book. About half the private libraries recorded before 1700 contained fewer than fifty volumes, but from 25 to 40 per cent of the titles were of religious works.[21]

The Puritans, then, were not the first to introduce the Bible to America; nor did they sow the land with biblical place names, though thickly sown it now is. Salem they named, and Sharon, in Massachusetts. Other groups were less sparing: there are no less than eleven "Beulahs," nine "Canaans," eleven "Jordans," and twenty-one "Sharons."

Adam is sponsor for a town in West Virginia and an island in the Chesapeake, and Eve for a village in Kentucky. There are five post offices named Aaron, two named Abraham, two named Job, and a town and a lake named Moses . . . eight Wesleys and Wesleyvilles, eight Asburys and twelve names embodying Luther. . . . And in Arkansas and New York there are Sodoms.[22]

Utterly repugnant to the Puritan conscience would have been the thronging saint names—St. Louis, St. Paul, San Antonio—which so besprinkle the present map of America. California, farthest removed from Puritanism geographically, reeks with nomenclative saintliness, from its capital—named for the Holy Sacrament (Sacramento)—to its largest city, once basking under the resounding title of "The Pueblo of Our Lady the Queen of the Angels of Porciúncula" but now withered to a mere "the Angels" (Los Angeles).

From the latter city one may hurtle, like Jehu, past Holy Forest (Hollywood), San Buenaventura's town (now Ventura), and Santa Barbara, or through the valley of Christ's Grandfather (San Joaquin), past the rivers of Our Lady of Mercy and of the Three Holy Kings (Merced and Kings rivers), to the city of St. Francis (San Francisco), where he can find streets named for Adam and for Eve. If he prefers to turn southward from Los Angeles he can pass San Gabriel's town and waterless river, cross the Santa Ana River (once called The Sweet Name of Jesus of the Earthquakes),[23] go past San Juan Capistrano and San Luis Rey missions to the city of that St. James—San Diego—whose name gave us the opprobrious epithet, "Dago." He may remain nearer home and loll on Santa Monica's beach, or embark from Peter's port (San Pedro) for St. Catherine's island (Santa Catalina).

Tourist once thronged the Angelus (Angel's Message) Temple to hear Aimee Semple MacPherson (Beloved St. Paul the Parson's Child) preach, or read about her, under the cellophanic disguise of Sister Minnie Tekel Upharsin Smith, in Eric Knight's hilarious nonsense novelette, *The Flying Yorkshireman.* Down near the Salton Sea they may gape at King Solomon, date tree husband de luxe, which annually pollenates some four hundred otherwise dateless wives.

But Californians have no monopoly upon the flavor of sanctity. They may stow their Samson brand luggage aboard a Holy Faith (Santa Fe) train and travel eastward, through Colorado with its Town of Trinity (Trinidad), its Blood of Christ mountains (Sangre de Cristo), and its *Rivière de Purgatoire,* now the prosaic Picketwire, to Kansas, with its wheat raised by tractors made of Bethlehem steel, and formerly milled into Moses' Best Flour, sacked in bags gaudy with babe, basket, and bulrushes. They may turn southward through the Bible Belt to the state discovered on Easter Sunday, *pascua florida,* or northward to New York, there to buy "strictly fresh Father Divine poultry and vegetables in season," brought by truck from various heavens, after being packed by, possibly, Faithful Sparrow, Righteous J. Truth, or Faith Hope

Charity. Returning homeward, they may visit the Great White Throne in Zion National Park.

It is clear that had the Puritans never landed in America, the land would yet be polka-dotted with biblical names. But they did land—"seventy-four English Puritans and twenty-eight women," as one chronicler discriminatingly put it—men and women "interested in forests, furs, fish, and faith."

They agreed to consider the Bible as their constitution "until they had time to frame a better one." Death was the penalty for blasphemy or the worship of any but the true God. Whoever denied that any book of the Bible was the infallible Word of God might be whipped forty lashes and fined forty pounds; a second offense might bring banishment or death. Their school code began, "It being one chief project of that old deluder Satan to keep men from a knowledge of the Scriptures. . . ." John Cotton cited marginal biblical references for each law he proposed, as did Michael Wigglesworth for each point in *The Day of Doom,* which became the most popular long poem of the age, selling eighteen hundred copies within a year, and ten other editions within a century. Profanity was a decided luxury in old Massachusetts, the penalty being ten shillings per oath unless the swearer vented "more oaths than one at a time, before he removed out of the room or company where he so sware," in which case he obtained a wholesale rate of twenty shillings' total. The release of pent emotions must have been notable for Richard Praye on the day in which he was fined ten shillings for cursing, ten for swearing, twenty for wife beating, and forty for contempt of court.[24]

The Puritans were harsh with the harshness which still characterized England, where in 1634 Cotton Mather's grandfather Richard was refused restoration into the Church of England because he had preached without wearing a surplice. "It had been better for him if he had gotten seven bastards," snarled one of the examiners in condemning this heinous breach of behavior. Because Roger Chillingworth wrote that the Bible, and the Bible alone, was the religion of the Protestants, his own physician hurled into Chillingworth's grave his book, shouting, "Rott with the rotten; let the dead bury the dead."

Against this English background *The Simple Cobler of Aggawam in America* seems harsh but not strange when it says:

He that is willing to tolerate any unsound Opinion, that his owne may also be tolerated, though never so sound, will for a need hang God's Bible at the Devill's girdle.[25]

This intolerance drove John Eliot to the Indians, whom he and others believed descended from the lost tribes of Israel. Having told them that they were children of the devil, Eliot found them eager to know of their new-found ancestor, and asking embarrassing questions:

Whether ye devil or man was made first?
Whether there might not be something, if only a little, gained by praying to ye devil?
Why does not God, who has full power, kill ye devil that makes all men so bad?
If God made hell in one of the six days, why did he make it before Adam had sinned?
If all ye world be burned up, where then shall hell be? [26]

No man now living can read Eliot's Indian Bible, but the word "mugwump," which he used for "duke" in Genesis 36, has entered English.

The puritanic harshness extended even to music. Sternhold and Hopkins psalmbooks, rough as they were, yet offended some of the Puritans, who wondered if too much effort at smoothness had not been made at the expense of accuracy. So the first full volume issued in America was *The Bay Psalm Book,* whose lines clanked, as one critic phrased it, like an engine with gravel in its bearings. The translators were well pleased with its roughness. "God's Altar needs not our pollishings: Ex. 20," they explained in the preface. Apparently others felt as they did, for *The Bay Psalm Book* not only served America well for more than a century but was pirated into England, for eighteen editions there and twenty-two in Scotland.

"Not one of the Puritans was capable of laughter," [27] asserts a modern historian; no one could possibly claim that they were not capable of grueling labor. Increase Mather studied sixteen hours a day. His son, Cotton, preached four hundred sermons annually, wrote in several languages almost four hundred books and pamphlets, and found time to jot in his diary that he must "think up some exquisite and obliging Wayes" in which to abate his ten-year-old Sammy's "Inordinate Love of Play."

Puritan theology was equally merciless. To Jonathan Edwards children were "young vipers, and infinitely more hateful than vipers" in God's eyes. As for adults,

> The God that holds you over the pit of Hell, much as one holds a spider, or some loathsome insect, over the fire, abhors you and is dreadfully provoked.[28]

The redeemed gloat endlessly and sadistically over the torments of the damned:

> When the saints in glory, therefore, shall see the doleful state of the damned . . . when they shall see the smoke of their torment, and the raging of the flames of their burning, and hear their dolorous shrieks and cries, and consider that they in the meantime are in the most blissful state, and shall surely be in it to all eternity; how will they rejoice! . . . How joyfully will they sing to God and the Lamb, when they behold this.[29]

It must never be forgotten, however, that, despite their intolerance, the Puritans were the experimenting liberals of their day. In an age in which many important towns in England had yet no printing press, and in which Governor Berkeley was thanking God that there was no press in Virginia, the Puritans in America were busily printing. Of 157 titles issued by the press at Cambridge between its founding, in 1638 and 1670, 63 were religious, as were probably 19 others issued in Indian.[30] While elsewhere education was for the select few, New England embarked upon popular elementary education and established a broad-based higher education. The winds of freedom blew when Increase Mather said in a Harvard presidential address:

> Yet I would have you hold fast to that one truly golden saying of Aristotle: *Find a friend in Plato, a friend in Socrates* (and I say a friend in Aristotle), *but above all find a friend in TRUTH."* [31]

The Puritan love of education is seen clearly in the welcome accorded the "Little Bible of New England," *The New England Primer*. For a century and a half this little book, with its

In Adam's fall,
We sinned all,

dominated American education, selling in a sparsely settled land an astounding seven million copies before 1840.[32] Editions varied greatly as publishers thriftily reused materials on hand. A three-decker crown on the almanac's Man in the Zodiac made him "The POPE, or Man of Sin." Once the queen's picture was from the block used for the backs of playing cards. In the 1776 edition the portrait of King George was relabeled "John Hancock."

One thing, however, was most emphatically not in any *New England Primer*—the cross at the beginning of the first line which had been so prominent in older English primers. It was not by accident that the crisscross line was missing. John Endicott in 1634 had slashed the cross of St. George from the English flag at Salem as a relic of Antichrist, and the military leaders had ordered such ensigns laid away, since so many soldiers would not follow a flag with the cross visible. Morton's *New England's Canaan* tells of a minister who brought over

> a great bundell of Horn books with him and careful he was (good man) to blott out all the crosses of them for feare least the people of the land should become Idolaters.[33]

So sensitive were the people that the lines which explained the letter *J* in the earliest surviving primer,

Sweet Jesus he
Dy'd on a tree

were too much a reference to the cross, so Job was substituted, with

Job feels the rod
Yet blesses God.

Papistical saints were removed from an older poem,

Matthew, Mark, Luke and John,
Bless the bed that I lie on,
And blessed guardian Angel keep
Me safe from danger while I sleep.

I lay me down to rest me
And pray the Lord to bless me;
If I should sleep, no more to wake,
I pray the Lord my soul to take,[34]

which in its newer form has far outlasted even *The New England Primer:*

Now I lay me down to sleep,
I pray the Lord my soul to keep;
If I should die before I wake
I pray the Lord my soul to take.

The Puritan served his day and passed on, but this tiny prayer from *The New England Primer* lingers like the chiming of far-off bells in the minds and hearts of men.

13. Prose Classic

A bibulous man is one who freely quotes from the Scriptures. —ANONYMOUS[35]

"MUST! Is 'must' a word to be addressed to princes?" Queen Elizabeth was seventy, and dying, but her proud old heart rebelled against being told that she must go to bed. "Little man, little man," her words lashed out, "thy father, if he had been alive, durst not use that word; but thou art grown presumptuous because thou knowest that I shall die." [36]

But death has a "must" even for queens, and stricken Elizabeth finally went to bed, where, no longer able to speak, she kept the aged, bone-weary Archbishop of Canterbury at his interminable praying by a twitch of her imperious wrist as at half-hourly intervals he paused. At last the inexorable hand lay still; the woman who had shrewdly led England to greatness was unconscious; at three A.M. she died.

Seven hours later sickly, stiff-necked, Scottish James, "the wisest fool in Christendom," was proclaimed King of England. As he rode to London, Puritans handed him a petition for church reform. James rushed in where Elizabeth had feared to tread; he called a conference of the warring factions, lost his temper, and in two minutes "sealed his own fate and that of England forever."

Berating the Puritans for seeking a more democratic form of church government, "which agrees with monarchy as well as God and the devil," he grimly warned, "I will make them conform themselves, or else hurry them out of this land, or do worse." [37] He hurried the pilgrim fathers to America, his son to the block, and England to the Commonwealth.

One good, however, came of the tragically mismanaged conference—the plan for the so-called King James, or Authorized, Bible. Fifty-four learned translators were selected, and suggestions sought from all qualified scholars in the nation; this must be the best Bible the united scholarship of England could produce. And the scholarship of England, sharpened by a generation of earnest theological squabbling, was just then very great. The result was accuracy added to an unparalleled felicity of style—a felicity which two centuries later led Father Faber, after forsaking this version for that of the Roman faith, to write:

> Who will say that the uncommon beauty and marvellous English of the Protestant Bible is not one of the great strongholds of heresy in this country? It lives on the ear like a music that can never be forgotten, like the sound of church bells, which the convert scarcely knows how he can forego. Its felicities seem often to be almost things rather than words. It is part of the national mind, and the anchor of the national seriousness.[38]

The Bible, after it had been more than a thousand years in England, was now translated into English, printed in English, and a best seller; it had become and has since remained England's greatest prose masterpiece. For fifty years the common people had loved the Geneva Version; it took forty years for the new one to replace this. Thereafter, so far as the generality of English-speaking people was concerned, the King James Version was the Bible "just as God gave it," its lightest word law, and its every comma sacrosanct. Its cadences became the warp and woof of common thought. From all lips now fall its phrases: "apple of his eye," "army with banners," "birds of the air," "broken reed," "clear as crystal," "decently and in order," "fat of the land," "handwriting on the wall," "highways and hedges," "holy of holies," "labor of love," "lick the dust," "loaves and fishes," "many mansions,' "peace on earth," "powers that be," "pride of life," "salt of the earth," "soft answer," "still small voice," "thorn in the flesh," "weighed in the balance," "whited sepulchers," "widow's mite," "windows of heaven," "wings of the morning." Its personages have become types—a Daniel, a doubting Thomas, a good Samaritan, an Ishmael, a Joseph, a Judas, a Lazarus, a Methuselah, a Samson, a Solomon.

Adam has proved a godsend to namers of books, giving such titles as: *Adam's Ancestors, Adam's Apples, Adam's Breed, Adam Cargo, Adam Chasers, Adam the Creator, Adam's Daughters, Adam's Diary, Adam and Eve, Adam and Eve and Pinch Me, Adam and Two Eves, Adam's Evening, Adam and Evelyn in the Garden of Edenbridge, Adam's Fifth Rib, Adam's First Wife, Adam's Garden, Adam's Great-Great-Grandfather, Adam's Profession and Its Conquest by Eve, Adam's Rest.* Nor is Adam alone; the whole of this prose classic has been ransacked for attention-catching book titles: *A Certain Rich Man, And Fear Came, As a Man Thinks, The Bent Twig, Children of the Market Place, The Dwelling Place of Light, East of Eden, A Far Country, The Fruit of the Tree, Giants in the Earth, The House Divided, The Inside of the Cup, Lamb in His Bosom, Many Inventions, The Mote and the Beam, My Son, My Son! Outside Eden, Prodigal Parents, Raleigh's Eden, The Seven Pillars of Wisdom, The Street Called Straight, These Twain, Uncertain Trumpet, The Woman Thou Gavest Me, The Years of the Locust.* One recent display showed more than a thousand successful modern books and plays whose titles were scriptural quotations.

Common words soon changed meanings. "Talented," from the parable of the talents, appeared. The Land of Nod, "slumberland," forms a pretty pun on Genesis 4:16. Readers unfamiliar with the meaning of "meet" in Genesis 2:18—"I will make him a help meet [suitable] for him"—fused the two words into "helpmeet," which then shifted to "helpmate," and was twisted by a newspaper columnist to "helpspend."

But greater than phrase, allusion, title, or word growth has been the unprecedented effectiveness of the King James Version in forming the thought and literary style of succeeding writers. Ignoring for the time being the Miltons, Bunyans, and Blakes, let us hear first George Saintsbury, critic, who selected the Song of Solomon 8:7, 8, "as the best example known to me of absolutely perfect English prose—harmonious, modulated, yet in no sense trespassing the limits of prose and becoming poetry." [39] As a companion piece of literary perfection he chose the charity passage of the First Epistle to the Corinthians.

Lord Grenville considered the finest passage Edmund Burke ever wrote—perhaps the finest in the English tongue—to be in his "Address to the King," beginning, "What, gracious sovereign, is the empire of America to us, or the empire of the world, if we lose our own liberties?" This same scriptural base was used in Benjamin Jowett's terse "What shall it profit a man if he gain a telescope and lose his sight?" [40]

Rich cadences sigh and sob through Thomas De Quincey's supple prose. The sixty-third chapter of Isaiah shapes his opening in "The Trial and Death of Joan of Arc":

> Who is she that cometh from Domremy? Who is she in bloody coronation robes from Rheims? Who is she that cometh with blackened flesh from walking the furnaces of Rouen?

"It had happened," he wrote in *"Suspiria de Profundis,"* "that among our vast nursery collection of books was the Bible, illustrated with many pictures. And in long, dark evenings, as my three sisters with myself sat by the firelight round the guard [fender] of our nursery, no book was so much in request amongst us. It ruled us and swayed us as mysteriously as music." [41]

At twenty-eight Robert Burns had an exciting adventure, which he hastened to report to one of his correspondents: "I have taken tooth and nail to the Bible and am got through the five books of Moses and half way in Joshua," he exulted; "it is really a glorious book." [42] Forthwith he sent out and bought a copy, ordering it bound with the binder's utmost magnificence.

As soon as baby John Ruskin was able to read, his inflexible mother began that rigid regimen of daily Bible study and reading which she did not relax until he went to college, of which he recorded in old age:

> I have next with deeper gratitude to chronicle what I owed to my mother for the resolutely consistent lessons which so exercised me in the Scriptures as to make every word of them familiar to my ear in habitual music . . . she began with the first verse of Genesis, and went straight through, to the last verse of the Apocalypse; hard names, numbers, Levitical law, and all; and began again at Genesis the next day.[43]

"And truly," continued this prolific writer on many subjects, "though I have picked up the elements of a little further knowledge—in mathematics, meteorology, and the like, in after life—and owe not a little to the teaching of many people, this maternal installation of my mind in that property of chapters, I count very confidently the most precious, and on the whole, the one *essential* part of all my education." [44]

"I do not know exactly how many quotations from the Bible can be found in his writings," confessed one of Ruskin's biographers, "I once counted up to forty-eight hundred and then gave in, with a considerable area yet unexplored." [45] All his life long, images from the Bible flooded Ruskin's mind.

Did you ever hear, not of a Maud, but a Madeleine, who went down to her garden in the dawn, and found One waiting at the gate, whom she supposed to be the gardener? Have you not sought Him often; sought Him in vain, all through the night; sought Him in vain at the gate of that old garden where the fiery sword is set? He is never there; but at the gate of *this* garden He is waiting always—waiting to take your hand—ready to go down to see the fruits of the valley, to see whether the vine has flourished, and the pomegranate budded. There you shall see with Him the little tendrils of the vines that His hand is guiding —there you shall see the pomegranate springing where His hand cast the sanguine seed;—more: you shall see the troops of the angel keepers that, with their wings, wave away the hungry birds from the pathsides where He has sown, and call to each other between the vineyard rows, "Take us the foxes, the little foxes, that spoil the vines, for our vines have tender grapes." Oh—you queens—you queens; among the hills and happy greenwood of this land of yours, shall the foxes have holes and the birds of the air have nests; and in your cities shall the stones cry out against you, that they are the only pillows where the Son of Man can lay His head? [46]

"Bring me the book," commanded Sir Walter Scott, in his final illness.

"What book?"

"Need you ask? There is but one," replied the sturdy veteran of many books of his own penning; and his son-in-law brought the Bible, turned to the fourteenth chapter of John, and read.[47]

"Cursed be Sallie," pipingly raged the infant Thomas Babington Macaulay against the maid who had disarranged the pebble boundaries of his play garden; and then the passionate, childish voice went on, "for it is written 'Cursed be he that removeth his neighbor's landmark.' "[48] What could poor Sallie reply? Steeped in the Bible from childhood, Macaulay found its words and rhythms ever at his instant command. How terrible is his measured indictment of Barère:

> Whatsoever things are false, whatsoever things are dishonest, whatsoever things are unjust, whatsoever things are impure, whatsoever things are hateful, whatsoever things are of evil report, if there be any vice, and if there be any infamy, all these things, we knew, were blended in Barère.[49]

As Robert Louis Stevenson wrote Alan Breck's sword song for *Kidnapped,* the Song of Lamech (Genesis 4) ran through his mind "like the lilt of a song through the brain of a boy."

Charles Dickens wrote a *Life of Christ* for his children, packed a Bible in the trunk of his departing son, and called the parable of the prodigal son the most touching story in the literature of the world.

"The most completely sweet and cultured letter ever sent by one gentleman to another," Samuel Taylor Coleridge rated Paul's letter to Philemon.[50]

"And there is one immortal work that moves me still more—" confessed Sir Rider Haggard, writer of superthrillers, "a work that utters all the world's yearning anguish and disillusionment in one sorrow-laden and bitter cry, and whose stately music thrills like the voice of pines heard in the darkness of a midnight gale, and that is the book of Ecclesiastes."[51]

Rudyard Kipling bought a fountain pen in Jerusalem, named it Jael, and hammered the Philistines mercilessly with it.[52] Even the critic who jeered at these two last with

> When the Rudyards cease from Kipling
> And the Haggards ride no more,

was but paraphrasing Job's longing cry,

> There the wicked cease from troubling
> And the weary are at rest.

Hall Caine reports having "read the four gospels over carefully, not less than one hundred times, and copied them out with my own hand at least four or five times."[53]

"For years no style seemed to me natural but that of the Bible," confessed Lord Dunsany.[54]

So all-inclusive has been the influence of England's prose masterpiece that in 1937 Laurence Housman wrote:

> Not Shakespeare nor Bacon, nor any great figure in English literature that one could name, has had so wide and deep an influence on the form and substance of all the literary and poetic work which followed during the next two centuries, as has the English Authorized Version of the Old and New Testaments.[55]

In 1935 F. K. Stamm had put the case even more dramatically:

> One morning, so runs an old story, England woke up and found that the Bible was gone. Not only had the book itself been lost, but all traces of its influence and every note of its music had disappeared from life.
>
> The result was appalling. People did not know what the great writers were talking about. Shakespeare was almost unintelligible. Ruskin's works resembled an ancient tapestry. Everyday speech stammered and faltered. A change passed over the whole tone and temper of the nation. Life became hectic and vulgar. . . . Some fine high quality had taken its departure from life.[56]

This was but repeating in other words what Sir Arthur Quiller-Couch had told his students at Cambridge twenty years before, as he lectured "On the Art of Writing":

> The Authorized version, setting a seal on all, set a seal on our national style, thinking and speaking. It has cadences homely and sublime, yet so harmonizes them that the voice is always one. Simple men—holy and humble men of heart like Isaak Walton or Bunyan—have their lips touched and speak to the homelier tune. Proud men, scholars,—Milton, Sir Thomas Browne—practice the rolling Latin sentence; but upon the rhythms of our Bible they, too, fall back. . . . The precise man Addison cannot excel one parable in brevity or in heavenly clarity: the two parts of Johnson's antithesis come to no more than this "Our Lord has gone up to the sound of a trump: with the sound of a trump our Lord has gone up." The Bible controls its enemy Gibbon as surely as it haunts the curious music of a light sentence of Thackeray's. It is in everything we see, hear, feel, because it is in us, in our blood.[57]

14. Streamlining Satan

"Neat, but not gaudy," as the devil said when he painted his tail pea green. —VINCENT S. LEAN[58]

"THERE were once seven churches here, but all save this were torn down by Oliver Cromwell in the days of William the Conqueror," [59] asserted a village crone whose history was slightly hazy. Life in seventeenth-century England must have been equally confused and confusing. James I, strange contradiction of shrewdness and folly, of learning and ignorance, of piety and unscrupulousness, could flatteringly dedicate a book on religion "To the honour of our Lord and Saviour Jesus Christ, the Eternal Sonne of the Eternal Father, the onely THEANTHROPOS, Mediatour and Reconciler of Mankind, in Signe of Thankefulness," and with equal heartiness shield his followers in shameless crimes. He could call his favorite "Steenie," from a resemblance to pictures of the martyr Stephen, and unblushingly head a scandal-ridden court.

His son Charles, unreliable and unwise, goaded his people until they slew him. Cromwell's psalm-singing Ironsides took brief control. A few years more and, the monarchy restored, the government swung back to gay licentiousness.

Sir Thomas Browne was inditing his *Religio Medici,* and at the same time ascribing ear-burnings to guardian angels, who touched one's right ear if the remark was favorable, the left if unfavorable. He discussed also whether the serpent which tempted Eve had a human face, whether women actually have fewer ribs than men, and whether Adam and Ave, created instead of born, had navels—a question which leaped to life in 1939 when the magazine *Life* republished William Blake's drawings of Adam and Eve, precipitating a barrage of letters giving biological pointers to the editors. Abraham Cowley was writing *Davideis* and defending the use of biblical materials in poetry. In the midst stood Milton, the everlasting battleground. Samuel Johnson declared that his *Paradise Lost* was one of those books one admires, lays down, and forgets to take up again, never wishing it longer than it is. Macaulay was enthusiastic:

> Though there were many clever men in England during the latter half of the seventeenth century, there were only two great creative minds. One of these minds produced the *Paradise Lost.*[60]

Alexander Pope took a middle ground:

> Milton's strong pinion now not Heav'n can bound,
> Now, Serpent-like, in prose he sweeps the ground,
> In Quibbles Angel and Archangel join,
> And God the Father turns a School-divine.[61]

Tennyson thought him the mighty "organ voice of England," but a later critic sneers that he was "a psychopathic Puritan" in whom "humane studies were swamped in a Biblical brawl" until, "by the time he came to write *Paradise Lost* and *Paradise Regained,* he was a disgruntled Puritan trying to remember that he once was a poet." [62]

Milton looked forward to the writing of poetry with the same fervent consecration with which he would have entered a priesthood. From his school days onward he formed a habit of reading each morning from the Bible, usually in Hebrew; "then he contemplated." His use-frayed Bible shows the most worn pages to be those of Ecclesiasticus, John, and most of the New Testament after John.[63] In his judgment the Scriptures were incomparable: "There are no songs to be compared to the songs of Zion, no orations equal to those of the Prophets, and no politics equal to those the Scriptures can teach us.[64]

At fifteen he versified two of the psalms; at twenty-one his "birthday gift for Christ" was the "Ode on the Morning of Christ's Nativity." Upon reaching the ripe old age of twenty-three he mused:

> All is, if I have grace to use it so,
> As ever in my great Task-Master's eye.

At twenty-nine, in *Lycidas,* he suddenly placed St. Peter in a procession of pagan mourners!

> Last came, and last did go
> The pilot of the Galilean Lake;
> Two massy keys he bore of metals twain
> (The golden opes, the iron shuts amain).
> He shook his mitred locks, and stern bespake

that bitter denunciation of the clergy which Ruskin was later to use so eloquently in *Of King's Treasures.*

In his thirty-sixth year he worked upon his third divorce pamphlet, *Tetrachordon,* based upon passages from Genesis, Deuteronomy, Matthew, and First Corinthians. At forty he versified nine additional psalms; at forty-five, eight more. *Paradise Lost,* outlined when he was thirty-four, written largely between his fiftieth and fifty-fifth years, was published when he was fifty-nine; *Paradise Regained* and *Samson Agonistes,* at sixty-three. Of the more than five hundred biblical citations in his English prose, fewer than half those before his blindness coincide with the standard text, showing that he quoted largely from memory; after his blindness, when his amanuensis checked more carefully, four fifths so agreed.[65]

For more than a century and a half his Latin *De Doctrina Christiana,* lost among the state papers of England, lay hidden. Its discovery, with its reference to more than seven thousand biblical passages[66] (fifty-two crammed into a passage thirty-three lines long), gave a pathetic glimpse into Milton's mind. Unless it was written before *Paradise Lost,* the man who spent his life reading the Bible, "contemplating," justifying the ways of God to man, "died no longer believing the omnipotence of his Creator, the Divinity of his Saviour, and the native immortality of mankind." [67]

Milton made at least three important literary contributions. He gave us a notable stock of new words, mostly in *Paradise Lost*—"words like *dimensionless, infinitude, emblazonry, liturgical, ensanguined, anarch, gloom, irradiance, Pandemonium, bannered, echoing, rumoured, impassive, moonstruck, Satanic.*" [68] Next, he fixed the newly found biblical rhythms more firmly into English prose style.

> All through, even if half whelmed by the over sentencing, there rings the wonderful prose cadence which we never find in English—not even in Malory—till the early translators of the Bible got it somehow from their originals and infused it into our literature forever.[69]

Then, steeped as he was in the classical learning of the Renaissance, he fused, as no earlier English writer had done, classical form and biblical substance, molding them so freely by his own independence of mind that he revolutionized English thought concerning biblical things.

"More people have their ideas about heaven and hell from Milton than from the Bible, though they do not know it." [70] Gabriel, for example, first blows his judgment horn at Milton's behest. This fusion of the classical with the biblical was most important: by it he gave English thought a new heaven, a new earth, and a new hell.

Milton's Paradise, we know, while founded chiefly upon the vision of the Heavenly City of John, includes also details which came to him from elsewhere in the Old and New Testaments, and not only the canonical Michael and Gabriel, the Raphael and Uriel of the Apocrypha and Enoch, and the seven angels which in Zechariah and the Revelation "run to and fro through the whole earth" with the "dominions," "thrones," "powers" of vaguer Biblical references, but they have incorporated in themselves—in addition to a wealth of post-Biblical angelology—many of the qualities of classical gods and heroes. The battle between Satan and Michael had its origin, indeed, less in Scripture than in the Iliad.[71]

Milton created the home life of Eden, making it a place where human beings faced problems of growing complexity. His Adam and Eve may have been, as charged, "a typical Puritan *menage* of the period, of whom a French critic has said, 'Good heavens! —Make them put on their clothes at once! Such nice people would immediately have invented trousers and prudery,' " [72] but it must be remembered that even the most incorrigible of the Puritans had their moments. Samuel Sewall resolutely wrung deep spiritual lessons from the way his chickens gobbled up the Indian corn he fed them, but he also wrote in his diary, "I saw Six Swallows together flying and chippering very rapturously." [73]

Adam may be overpompous and prone to make after-dinner speeches; Eve may suffer at Milton's hand the penalty of his own unhappy relations with his series of wives. Nevertheless they are psychologically real. They grow and develop from their experiences. Henceforth men may write of Eden as a place and Adam and Eve as people, because Milton made men's minds familiar with them.

Nathaniel Hawthorne and his bride, dreaming in the Old Manse, may use the pretty fiction that they are the Primal Honeymooners, though "it is one of the drawbacks upon our Eden that it contains no water fit either to drink or to bathe in," and there are "callers, who preposterously think that the courtesies of the lower world are to be responded to by people whose home is in Paradise. . . . We have so far improved upon the custom of Adam and Eve, that we generally furnish forth our feasts with portions of some delicate calf or lamb." [74] These mundane drawbacks Hawthorne removes in "The New Adam and Eve," by placing the pair in the wreckage of a lost world, letting them sample civilization, and see that it was mostly bad.

Mark Twain depicts Adam on a park bench in New York City, dreamily watching humanity drift by, and at sight of a baby buggy remembering the first child: "Let me see. . . . It is three hundred thousand years ago come Tuesday." [75] Seldom are the amusing and the poignant so skillfully blended as in his "Eve's Diary" and "Extracts from Adam's Diary." Here are Primal Man and Primal Woman, blunderingly trying to understand each other and themselves. Eve, eager, inquisitive, intuitive, thrills to companionship and beauty: "There's storms of sociable birds, and hurricanes of whirring wings; and when the sun strikes all that feathery commotion, you have a blazing up of all the colors you can think of, enough to put your eyes out."[76] Womanlike, she scorns Adam's slow-wittedness, but loves him—she wonders why. She even encourages him to sing, because he likes to do so, though his voice is catastrophic. "It sours the milk, but it doesn't matter; I can get used to that kind of milk." Adam, in turn, traverses vast ranges of emotion from his early, irritated "This new creature with the long hair is a good deal in the way. It is always hanging around and following me about. I don't like this; I am not used to company. I wish it would stay with the other animals," [77] to his heart-wrung epitaph at Eve's grave: "Wheresoever she was, there was Eden."

But most spectacular of all Milton's achievements was his remodeling of the devil. Satan and his cohorts were no newcomers to English literature. They had appeared in Anglo-Saxon *Genesis* and the *Harrowing of Hell.* In medieval plays they became commonplace comic relief—shaggy, masked, menacing, shouting, tumbling in and out of smoking Hellmouth, forking doomed souls to destruction. In medieval legends they draped souls on burning trees, dipped them in caldrons of snow, ice, blood, and snakes, broke them on burning wheels, boiled them in pitch. In *Gammer Gurton's Needle* Diccon frightened Hodge out of his wits when he placed him in a magic circle and mumbled a rigmarole to evoke the devil. With a Latin invocation the priest in Chapman's *Bussy D'Ambois* raised the prince of devils amid thunderclaps. With a Latin charm, too, Marlowe's Dr. Faustus called Mephistopheles to his ill-starred aid. Shakespeare's Othello, when Iago was led in prisoner, glanced down to see if he had a cloven hoof. In Jonson's *The Devil Is An Ass* Satan chortled when one of the lesser fiends begged a vacation from hell that he might do some notable evil exploit upon earth; the disillusioned imp quickly discovered that human beings knew far more deviltry than he, and by evening he was glad to be rescued back into the safety of hell.

Milton modernized Satan and made him a gentleman.

> He is at once the Satan of the book of Job, and Lucifer, the star of the morning, of the book of Isaiah, the fallen angel of the non-canonical book of Enoch with whom there fell a tenth part of heaven . . . he is descended now from Aeschylus, now from Sophocles, now from Seneca. Yet he is still more than these originals. This is no figure such as Dante's, unmoving, frozen with the wings of his negation into the lake of ice, but a moving, changing, developing human being. The study of Satan's degeneration is one of the great triumphs of the world. Milton has added to literature one of its greatest figures, but he has done something else as well. More than one Protestant . . . still believes in his heart that the Satan of Milton is the "true" Satan and turns back to Scripture to feel a sense of loss.[78]

In introducing to us a proud chief, gigantic in size, beautiful in person, daring and commanding in spirit, Milton presented a superman whom we found fascinating. The man who set out to justify the ways of God to man, by a quirk of psychology, succeeded best in making the devil likable. "The reason Milton wrote in fetters when he wrote of Angels and God, and at liberty when of Devils and Hell, is because he was a true Poet, and of the Devil's party without knowing it," commented poet William Blake[79]—a remark which doubtless would have irritated Milton greatly.

Since Milton's time we have had two devils, the one of folklore and humor, as in Barham's *Ingoldsby Legends* and Coleridge's schoolboy incantation:

> The devil is tying a knot in my leg!
> Matthew, Luke, and John, unloose it I beg!—
> Crosses three we make to ease us,
> Two for the thieves and one for Christ Jesus! [80]

The other is the new, Miltonic hero.

15. On Going a Journey

Blessed are the meek, for they shall irritate the earth.

—ANONYMOUS[81]

THE WORLD'S best travel book was written by a man in jail. Macaulay said that one of the two most imaginative minds in England penned *Paradise Lost.* He continued, "The other the *Pilgrim's Progress.*" While John Bunyan wrote sixty things, he is a man of one book, or at most four books—*Pilgrim's Progress, Grace Abounding, The Holy War,* and *The Life and Death of Mr. Badman.*

Pilgrim's Progress, called by the London *Times* "the world's best supplement to the Bible," has had an unparalleled career. Truth with the bit in its teeth, it overran the jeering opposition which any Puritan book was sure to receive from the dominant anti-Puritans of the day. Any book by an illiterate tinker—especially one in a highly controversial field—while it might be read in multiplying numbers by the middle class and the poor, would inevitably invite the withering scorn of cultivated critics, especially in an age in which criticism was brutal and merciless. This critical harshness fell upon the author of *Pilgrim's Progress* in such ample measure that William Cowper, his great admirer, writing a century later, refrained from mentioning the name of the begetter of this runaway best seller:

> Ingenious dreamer, in whose well-told tale
> Sweet fiction and sweet truth alike prevail;
> Whose humorous vein, strong sense, and simple style
> May teach the gayest, make the gravest smile;

Witty, and well employ'd, and like thy Lord
Speaking in parables his slighted word;
I name thee not, lest so despised a name
Should move a sneer at thy deserved fame.[82]

But the book was too much for the critics. An estimated hundred thousand copies were sold during the author's life. Ninety-two editions were issued within a century, "and then the publishers left off counting." The greatest boast which Sterne's Tristram Shandy could make of his own popularity was that his life and opinions would "be no less read than the *Pilgrim's Progress,* itself." By the early part of the twentieth century it was in at least one hundred and eight languages. The critics capitulated and decided that it was a masterpiece, making it "perhaps the only book about which the educated minority has come over to the opinion of the common people." [83] The significance of this achievement is great. "It is worth remembering that out of Puritanism, which is regarded as a narrow creed and life, came the only book since the reformation, which has been accepted by the whole of Christendom." [84]

The idea of life as a journey was not new to English literature. In A.D. 627, when King Edwin of Northumbria conferred with his advisers as to following his father-in-law, Ethelbert, into Christianity, an old councilor expressed the opinion of the majority in words of still-poignant beauty:

The present life of man, O king, seems to me, in comparison of that time which is unknown to us, like to the swift flight of a sparrow through the room wherein you sit at supper in winter, with your commanders and ministers, and a good fire in the midst, whilst the storms of rain and snow prevail abroad; the sparrow, I say, flying in at one door, and immediately out at another, whilst he is within, is safe from the wintry storm; but after a short space of fair weather, he immediately vanishes out of your sight, into the dark winter from which he has emerged. So this life of man appears for a short space, but of what went before, or what is to follow, we are utterly ignorant. If, therefore, this new doctrine contains something more certain, it seems justly to deserve to be followed.[85]

Others utilized the idea of spiritual journeying. Piers Plowman agreed to lead the bewildered multitude on a pilgrimage toward eternal truth. The Arthurian knights rode the quest of the Holy

Grail, unattainable except to the pure in heart. Spenser made his *Faerie Queene* a gorgeous tapestry of settings-forth in search of righteousness. But it was Bunyan who wove the theme into a story so vivid that even staid Quaker John Greenleaf Whittier once exclaimed, "The infidel himself would not willingly let it die." [86]

Bunyan was a stubborn journeyer through life, as the authorities well knew when they ordered his arrest:

> Yet one John Bunnyon of youre said Towne Tynker hath divers times within one month last past in contempt of his Majties Good Lawes preached or teached at a Conventicle Meeting, or Assembly under color or ptence of exercise of Religion in other manner than according to the Liturgie or practise of the Church of England.[87]

"I have determined, the Almighty being my help and shield," wrote the tinker, fearless of all the might that England could muster against him, "yet to suffer, if frail life might continue so long, even till the moss shall grow on mine eyebrows rather than thus to violate my faith and principles." [88]

When such a man clashes with the law, little can be done but cram him into jail; so to jail Bunyan journeyed, and there devoured the Bible until he became "a peripatetic index to the Scriptures. He had so drunk in the King James' translation, word and phrase, so soaked his very fibre in it, that he could not speak save Biblically." [89] Thence came that easy marching style which Coleridge calls a "bandying of texts and half-texts, and demi-semi-texts, just as memory happened to suggest them, or chance brought them before Bunyan's mind." [90]

While he read and acknowledged the power of a few other books, he insisted that the Bible and concordance were his only library, that while he respected the scholarship of learned, godly men, he preferred the Bible, and with it was better furnished than if without it he had all the libraries of both great English universities. "What God makes mine by the evidence of his Word and Spirit," he said, "that I dare make bold with"; and again, "I have not for these things fished in other men's waters."

Had Bunyan been less ignorant than he happily was, he would have been amazed at the kinships and implications of his book. He would have been shocked at the linking of it with that earlier, lying journey-book, *The Travels of Sir John Mandeville,* with its carefully described routes to the earthly Jerusalem. He would have been scandalized to learn that he was carrying on the tradition, type names and all, of the popish morality plays, and that his book was akin to the Spanish picaresque, or rogue, stories. He would have stared uncomprehendingly had he been told that it was to be one of the ancestors of the English novel, and that he had developed a prose style remarkably distinctive and effective. He never would have understood the Roman Catholics' printing their own edition, with Giant Pope left out, but Giant Protestant not substituted.

He had learned from the Bible one thing: vividness. "Bunyan is almost the only writer that ever gave to the abstract the interest of the concrete." [91] His readers recognized Pliable, Faithful, Worldly-Wiseman, and others as their friends, neighbors, and in-laws.

The people moving in and out of his story are the people everyone knows in his own community—Mr. Legality; Judge Hate-good; the tall fellow Talkative; poor Little-Faith, Sincere, who was held up by three gangsters in Dead Man's Lane; that very brisk youngster, Ignorance; Mrs. Diffidence, who rules her ogreish husband Despair; good, timid, troublesome Mr. Fearing, and his plaintive invalid nephew, Feeblemind; that nature's gentleman, Mr. Greatheart.[92]

This definiteness enabled Bunyan to create a new geography. To Jeremiah's land of the shadow of death (Jer. 2:6) he adds that the valley is dark as pitch, on the right hand is a deep ditch, and on the left a quagmire, that it extends past the mouth of hell and is thronged with hobgoblins, satyrs, and dragons. From Psalm 62:9 he got a phrase, "lighter than vanity," and created a Fair so memorable as to give a title to Thackeray's novel and to a twentieth-century magazine. Another magazine took his "House Beautiful" as its name. The City of Destruction, the Slough of Despond, the Delectable Mountains, all are well-known places.

In 1906 Theodore Roosevelt, searching for a supremely vivid word, coined from *Pilgrim's Progress* the stinging term "muck-raker." At Roosevelt's death, Kipling, seeking a title for his requiem, called it "Greatheart."

Slowly, through the centuries, the critics began to praise. Swift found the book entertaining and informing. Samuel Johnson, who did not like to read books through, confessed that *Pilgrim's Prog-*

ress was one of the two or three books he did wish were longer. Samuel Taylor Coleridge found therein theology painted in exquisitely delightful colors. Agnostic Robert Blatchford, listing his favorite books, paused at *Pilgrim's Progress:*

I fear I cannot approach the *Pilgrim's Progress* with the same critical calm with which I approached *Urn Burial.* I was turned of forty years, and somewhat of a writer and student myself when Sir Thomas Browne was introduced to me, but Bunyan was the friend and teacher of my childhood; the *Pilgrim's Progress* was my first book. It was for me one of the books to be "chewed and digested," and in my tenth year I knew it almost by heart.

I used at times, when the baby was restless, to ride it upon my knees, and recite to it passages out of Bunyan, or to sing to it the verses—they are but feeble poetry—from that wonderful book, to tunes of my own composing. . . .

Criticism of Bunyan's work is beyond me, I might as well try to criticize the Lord's Prayer, or "The House That Jack Built," or "Annie Laurie." Bunyan's English is tinker's, and soldier's and preacher's English. It is the English of the Bible of the Ironsides, and of the village green. Therefore all who write for the people shall do well to study Bunyan.[93]

Remarked H. R. Haweis:

Next to the Bible the *Pilgrim's Progress* is probably the book which has exercised more influence over the religion of England than any other . . . it supplied what Milton's *Paradise Lost* failed to give—some account of the ethics of the soul. . . . Perhaps few of those many who believe that the Bible is their sole spiritual guide realize the extent to which they see the Old Testament through Milton's eyes, and believe in the gospel according to Bunyan. . . . Bunyan supplied that imaginative touch . . . without which no religious message seems to win the masses. . . . Bunyan made Evangelicism romantic.[94]

"Lastly," wrote Robert Louis Stevenson, "I must name the *Pilgrim's Progress,* a book that breathes of every beautiful emotion." [95] Irresponsible prankster Eugene Field treasured his grandfather's copy: ". . . it has brought me solace and cheer a many times." [96]

Other writers have built on its foundation. In Nathaniel Hawthorne's "The Celestial Railroad" Mr. Smooth-It-Away has helped throw a bridge across the Slough of Despond by casting into it some editions of books of morality; volumes of French philosophy and German rationalism; tracts, sermons, and essays of modern clergymen; extracts from Plato, Confucius, and various Hindu sages, together with a few ingenious commentaries upon texts of Scripture—all of which by some scientific process, has been converted into a mass like granite.[97]

Crossing the swaying causeway by coach, the passenger buys a ticket at the station erected on the former site of the little wicket gate, our old friend Christian now supposedly being ticket agent, though an imposture is charged by the less gullible. The burdens so heavy to the earlier pilgrim are snugly deposited in the baggage car. Apollyon is Chief Engineer. After a gruesome trip through the Valley of the Shadow of Death—past the cavern where German Giant Transcendentalism has replaced Giants Pope and Pagan—and a long stopover at the City of Vanity, that the tourists may visit the Fair and buy souvenirs, the passengers reach the final river, so near the heavenly city that they hear celestial music and catch the glint of angel wings, only to be ferried, alas, to a different and darker destination.

In lighter vein, Robert Burdette followed Hawthorne's railroad pilgrimage with "The Brakeman at Church," wherein denominations are described in trainman's terminology: Mission church—branch road; Episcopal—limited express, extra fare; Universalist—broad-gauge. Everybody travels on a pass; Presbyterian—narrow-gauge, straight track; Free Thinkers—scrub road, dirt road bed, and no ballast; Methodist—lots of steam; Congregational—comfortable and well managed; Baptist—the river road, single track, "Takes a heap of water to run it, though." [98]

But ironic indeed has been the later fate of the *Pilgrim's Progress*. After convincing the critics that it was a masterpiece, the common people have moved on and left both the *Pilgrim's Progress* and the critics stranded. Moncure Conway was shocked when the youth of his day laughed (at a stage performance of the book) at Christiana's lamentations about her soul, and scorned with contempt Christian's abandonment of his family in the City of Destruction. "It occurred to me," he said, "that the newer generation has, happily, known too little of the catechetical cavern in which their fathers were affectionately prisoned, to realize the splendor of Bunyan's many-colored torch for imaginations which but for it had been eyeless." [99]

At any rate, the critics now vigorously agree that it is one of the world's masterpieces; and the common people sedulously leave it unread.

16. Horse Laughs and Hot Gizzards

Policy consists in serving God in such a manner as not to offend the devil. —THOMAS FULLER[100]

"IF A HORSE sneers after he coughs," reports the New English dictionary, "he is not broken winded." If the same is true of human beings, late seventeenth- and early eighteenth-century Englishmen were respiratorily sound, for they were adept sneerers. "Hot Gospelers," they labeled religious zealots, and delighted to do them dishonor. Merry monarch Charles joyed at the dramatic drubbings which were given the "superlunatical hypocrites" droning dry graces "as long as thy table-cloth" in Ben Jonson's revived *Bartholomew Fair,* with its Puritan caricatures—Zeal-of-the-Land Busy, Win-the-Fight Littlewit, and Dame Purecraft.

Still more scurrilous, and consequently still more popular, was the rough-and-tumble poem *Hudibras,* wherein—lifting the title from Sir Huddibras of the *Faerie Queene,* a man "more huge in strength than wise in works," and the action from *Don Quixote*—Butler pilloried the Puritans, whose tub-thumpings irritated him. "Their spiritual gizzards are too warm," he argued,

For zeal's dreadful termagant
That teaches saints to tear and rant.[101]

Their noisy meetings,

When Gospel-trumpeter, surrounded
With long-eared rout, to battle sounded,
And pulpit, drum ecclesiastic,
Was beat with fist, instead of stick,

made their preachers' leather-lunged argumentativeness seem

As if Divinity had catched
The itch, on purpose to be scratched.[102]

Obeying Numbers 15:38—"Speak unto the children of Israel . . . that they put upon the fringe of the borders a ribband of blue"—the Covenanters had adopted that color in opposition to the royal red; so Butler jeered of their religion, " 'Twas Presbyterian true blue," not foreseeing that their steadfastness would for the future make "true blue" a badge of honor, just as Simon Pure, the sneered-at Quaker in Mrs. Centlivre's *A Bold Stroke for a Wife,* was to make that phrase a superlative of merit. Hudibras' attendant, Squire Ralpho—counterpart of Cervantes' Sancho Panza—was "learned for salvation" by "gifts" or "new light," and, having been a tailor, had seen hell, "hell" being in tailor's slang the scrap box for discarded bits of cloth.

Meanwhile, a much greater poet than Butler, John Dryden, was facilely veering with the political breezes. At Cromwell's death he had lauded the fallen leader unreservedly:

His name a great example stands, to show
How strangely high endeavour may be blest,
Where piety and valour jointly go.[103]

Two years later Dryden hurled Cromwell and all his crew into Cimmerian darkness; England had all along, he said, been yearning for the now restored Charles and had been kept from recalling him only by those lunatics of Cromwell's gang:

While our cross stars denied us Charles's bed
Whom our first flames and virgin love did wed.
For his long absence Church and State did groan;
Madness the pulpit, faction seized the throne.
. . . .
Thus banished David spent abroad his time,
When to be God's anointed was his crime.[104]

Charles proved a very worldly David indeed, but Dryden liked the allusion, and twenty-one years later he resurrected it for political propaganda. Though the term "propaganda" (from the Catholic board of missions—*Congregatio de Propaganda Fide*) had not yet entered English, Dryden used the method with consummate skill and made English literature for the first time a major factor in political controversy. With all England jittery over the prospect of Catholic James's succeeding Protestant Charles, and with the

Earl of Shaftesbury in the Tower for attempting to turn the succession to Charles' illegitimate son, the Duke of Monmouth, Dryden hurled into the explosive situation his "Absalom and Achitophel." Getting off to a Hollywoodian sex-thriller beginning, wherein the king's sexual promiscuities were brilliantly extenuated,

> In pious times, ere priestcraft did begin,
> Before polygamy was made a sin;
> When man on many multiplied his kind,
> Ere one to one was cursedly confined;
> When nature prompted, and no law denied
> Promiscuous use of concubine and bride;
> Then Israel's monarch after Heaven's own heart,
> His vigorous warmth did variously impart
> To wives and slaves; and, wide as his command,
> Scatter'd his Maker's image through the land,[105]

Dryden likened Charles to King David, Queen Catherine to Michal, the Duchess of Portsmouth to Bathsheba, Monmouth to Absalom, Shaftesbury to Achitophel, etc. France became Egypt; Brussels, Gath; Scotland, Hebron; and London, Jerusalem. Under this imposing array of biblical personages and places, Dryden discussed contemporary politics to the widespread interest of the public—the poem selling with unprecedented swiftness.

When Shaftesbury was freed from the Tower, Dryden struck again with "The Medal: a Satire against Sedition," in which he lampooned Shaftesbury for sitting for the medal his followers issued in celebration:

> Five days he sat, for every cast and look,
> Four more than God to finish Adam took.

He followed with a slash at the populace, which

> This side today, and that tomorrow burns;
> So all are God-a'mighties in their turns.[106]

Having written *"Religio Laici"* to defend the position of the Church of England, he changed his opinion and wrote "The Hind and the Panther," in which he defended even more brilliantly the position of the Roman Church. Herein the two beasts, representing the two faiths, learnedly discussed transubstantiation, infallibility, church authority, and kindred points of disagreement, while various nonconformist groups received barbed attention. Among these were the Independents, "The bloody bear, an independent beast"; the Quakers, "the quaking hare"; the Atheists, "the buffoon ape"; and "the bristled Baptist boar." As for the chanting priests and praying nuns expelled at the Reformation,

> Such feats in former times had wrought the falls
> Of crowing chanticleers in cloister'd walls.
> Expelled for this, and for their lands, they fled;
> And Sister Partlet, with her hooded head,
> Was hooted hence, because she would not pray a-bed.[107]

Matthew Prior and Charles Montague mocked Dryden's poem in "The Hind and the Panther Transvers'd to the Story of the Country-Mouse and the City-Mouse." Dryden's opening lines,

> A milk-white hind, immortal and unchanged,
> Fed on the lawns, and in the forest ranged,

became

> A milk-white mouse, Immortal and unchanged,
> Fed on soft Cheese, and o'er the Dairy ranged.[108]

Two years after Dryden's death, Daniel Defoe's "Shortest Way with the Dissenters" raised a hullabaloo. Burlesquing the intolerance of High-Church extremists, he proposed that whoever was found at a conventicle be banished and the preacher hanged. Both sides were deceived; the bigots applauded, the dissenters trembled. When the hoax was discovered, Defoe was widely condemned. He was sentenced to pay two hundred marks, to stand in the pillory thrice (where he was applauded by the populace), to be imprisoned during the queen's pleasure, and to furnish bond for good behavior for the next seven years. His pamphlet was ordered burned.

Jonathan Swift likewise wielded a terrible cat-o'-nine-tails. "Good God," he cried in old age when he reread *A Tale of a Tub,* "what a genius I had when I wrote that book!" Under the allegory of the coats which three brothers—Peter (Romanists),

Jack (Presbyterians and other dissenters), and Martin (Lutherans and Anglicans)—had inherited from their father, Swift lashed fanaticism and superstition. Religion, he conceded, ought not to be ridiculed, yet "surely the corruptions of it may." He noted certain "oratorical machines," first of which was the pulpit, made preferably of Scottish (Calvinistic) wood, very narrow, pillory-like, and hence "a mighty influence upon human ears." If somewhat decayed, so much the better, for then they gave light in darkness, and their cavities were filled with worms, thus symbolizing "the two principal qualifications of the orator, and the two different fates attending upon its works."

A father (God) gave each of his triplet sons a new coat (the Christian religion) and a copy of his will (the Bible), in which they would find how to wear the coats to best advantage. For seven years they cared for the garments well as they joined in seeking their fortunes, and "travelled through several countries, encountered a reasonable quantity of giants, and slew certain dragons."

Then they fell into worldiness; "they drank, and fought, and whored, and slept, and swore, and took snuff." A sect arose which worshiped an idol (tailor) who had a goose for an ensign, at the side of whose altar (table) hell (the scrap box) yawned. "Is not religion a cloak . . . and conscience a pair of breeches, and so an apt conjunction of lawn and black satin we entitle a bishop?" [109]

Finally Peter began to insist upon pre-eminence, buying up a large new continent (purgatory), projecting a sovereign remedy for the worms (penance and absolution) and a whispering office (confessional), where by talking to an ass's ears all who were hypochrondiacal or troubled with the colic might ease themselves. He also projected an insurance office (indulgences) and a famous universal pickle (holy water)—"for Peter would put in a certain quantity of his powder pimperlimpimp" (consecration of holy water), "after which it never failed of success."

The two brothers, tiring of his arrogance and huge lies, broke with him and tried to get rid of all the gold lace added to their coats—Martin by careful means, Jack by yanking. Martin's begging his brother not to damage his coat put Jack into a rage, and he flounced off to new lodgings, becoming "a person whose intellectuals were overturned."

In his argument concerning "The Abolishing of Christianity in

England," Swift satirically pleads that he is urging only the retention of nominal Christianity, "the other having been for some time wholly laid aside by general consent." If this is not kept, wits will have nothing to make fun of; men will lose the stimulation of the forbidden unless others are "hired, to bawl one day in seven against those methods most in use . . . on the other six."

I do very much apprehend that, in six months time after the act is passed for the extirpation of the gospel, the Bank and East India stock may fall at least one *per cent.* And since this is fifty times over more than ever the wisdom of our age thought fit to venture for the preservation of Christianity, there is no reason we should be at so great a loss, merely for the sake of destroying it.[110]

In *Gulliver's Travels* the Lilliputians war over High Heels and Low Heels (High Church and Low Church), and whether eggs shall be broken at the big end or the little end, with the Big-Endians (Catholics) forbidden to hold office. To the Horses, curious concerning war,

I answered, . . . Difference in opinion hath cost many millions of lives: for instance, whether flesh be bread, or bread be flesh; whether the juice of a certain berry be blood or wine; whether whistling be a vice or a virtue; whether it be better to kiss a post or throw it into the fire; what is the best color for a coat . . . and whether it should be long or short, narrow or wide.[111]

As the eighteenth century developed, formal correctness came into fashion. Alexander Pope, "wicked wasp of Twickenham," had caught Dryden's knack of trouncing and might, as in *The Dunciad,* still lay a heavy parodying hand upon offenders:

Lift up your Gates, ye Princes, see him come!
Sound, sound, ye Viols; be the Cat-call dumb! [112]

But in general a light whiplash replaced head-cracking clubs. Had church music grown tinkling and trivial? Let Pope flick the flanks of the offenders:

And now the Chapel's silver bell you hear,
That summons you to all the Pride of Pray'r:
Light quirks of Music, broken and uneven,
Make the soul dance upon a Jig to Heav'n.

Had ecclesiastical art become unduly undraped and fleshly?

> On painted Ceilings you devoutly stare
> Where sprawl the saints of Verrio and Laguerre.

Had preachers grown mealy mouthed, like that dean who, preaching at court, threatened eternal punishment in "a certain place which 'tis not good manners to mention here"? Pope's rapier enters so subtly that one at first is scarce aware of the depth to which it has been driven:

> To rest, the cushion and soft dean invite,
> Who never mentions hell to ears polite.[113]

Not even females are to be exempt from the dagger of his wit. If it be true, as alleged, he says, that women have no character at all, then whether they beautifully cry with Magdalene's loosened hair and lifted eye or smilingly shine like St. Cecilia, surrounded "with simp'ring Angels, Palms, and Harps, divine," is all one to Pope. None shall escape.

> Whether the Charmer sinner it, or saint it,
> If folly grows romantic, I must paint it.[114]

Truly the spacious days of resounding religious brawlings were at last delicately departing.

THE BIBLE SURVIVES THE LUKEWARM YEARS

17. Crusoe's Converts

Going to church doesn't make you a Christian any more than going to a garage makes you an automobile.

—BILLY SUNDAY[1]

MEANWHILE the English novel was preparing to be born. Seventeenth-century Bunyan had demonstrated that the terseness of biblical prose could give a hitherto unsuspected vigor to English narrative and that the struggle of man with himself and his environment was interesting to multitudes of people. Man's pilgrimage through this world, with its sloughs of despond, its doubting castles, its vanity fairs, its tense contests with giant despairs and mighty Apollyons—of such things novels are created. In the early eighteenth century *Gulliver's Travels* and *Robinson Crusoe,* with their strong illusion of reality, brought the novel still nearer birth.

Daniel Defoe's pious Presbyterian parents, hoping that he would enter the ministry, had early set him to copying parts of the Bible and taking notes on sermons. These things formed a lifelong background to his writings, though in a different way from what his parents had expected, for this Daniel, too, acquired the habit of getting into all the lions' dens of trouble in his vicinity. Pillories and prisons he knew, for he could not resist penning unpalatable truths.

"This is *playing Bopeep* with God Almighty," he rapped out against those dissenters who, for the sake of holding high office, attended, on required occasions, the state church. Ruined by the clamor against his misunderstood satire, "The Shortest Way with the Dissenters," he became a journalistic Ishmael, a government spy, and a chameleonlike writer on both sides of controversial subjects. When Low-Church Bishop Hoadley, preaching before George I, unleased the Bangorian controversy by his sermon on the relation between church and state, Defoe secretly wrote articles to spur further strife, then other articles deploring the current quarreling among Christians.

His journalistic flair for sensing what would sell caused him to write numerous religious pamphlets—a manual on religious courtship, one on spiritual and physical preparation against the plague raging at Marseille, if it should cross the Channel, and a clever political history of the devil.

Then a literary miracle occurred. At fifty-eight this ruined hack writer, this double-dealing journalist, this religious controversialist, produced one of the world's wisest and most tolerant books in the whole field of applied Christianity, *Robinson Crusoe.*

Those who have forgotten the portions of the book which deal with religion, or have read editions from which the religious portions have been omitted, remember Robinson Crusoe as a happy-go-lucky vagabond interested primarily in eating regularly. His religion was indeed at first almost nonexistent, being merely the inherited fringe which no modern man could hope to escape. A few stock exclamations, a few oaths, an ejaculatory prayer when danger threatened—this was the sum and substance of it. Without asking God's blessing or his father's, "in an ill hour, God knows," the itching-footed youngster took ship, thereby setting in motion the events which led to his shipwreck.

This is related with such an air of actuality that the only thing in the whole book hard to believe is the assertion—recorded in the first edition, but changed thereafter—that he took off his clothes, swam out to the wreck, and filled his pockets with ship biscuits. In one of the salvaged boxes he discovered "three very good Bibles" and some other books, including "two or three Popish prayer-books," which he took ashore—doubtless to the scandal of many English readers in an age when Catholics were barred from English universities and from officeholding. But the books lay undisturbed in their box, since Crusoe was too careless to bother with them. "All this while I had not the least serious religious thought, nothing but the common, 'Lord, have mercy upon me!' and when it was over, that went away, too." [2]

Finally, deeply affected during illness by a nightmare of judgment, he cried out, "Lord, be my help, for I am in great distress" —his first prayer for many years. Then he ate, the food being, so far as he could remember, the first upon which he had ever asked God's blessing.

Taking one of the Bibles from the chest and opening it casually, he began to read, "Call on me in the day of trouble, and I will deliver thee, and thou shalt glorify me." The words made a tremendous impression, giving him hope of deliverance. Gradually, however, they came to signify not so much escape from the island as escape from his haunting sense of sin. Soon he regularly read the Book thrice daily, joyfully admiring God's providence which had so happily shown him a new way of life in the wilderness. "Thus I lived mighty comfortably."

The coming of the man Friday brought a disturbing problem: Friday was a heathen. This must be remedied at once.

> I began to instruct him in the knowledge of the true God. I told him that the great Maker of all things lived up there, pointing up towards heaven; that He governs the world by the same power and providence by which he had made it; that He was omnipotent . . . and thus, by degrees, I opened his eyes.[3]

Friday easily accepted God but, like John Eliot's Indians, was greatly puzzled about the devil. If God was mightier than the devil, why did he not at once kill him, and thus put an end to his villainies? This stumped Crusoe for a time, but he finally answered to his own and Friday's satisfaction, after which they dwelt together in great content.

> As to all the disputes, wranglings, strife, and contention which has happened in the world about religion, whether niceties in doctrines, or schemes of church government, they were all perfectly useless to us, as, for aught I can yet see, they have been to all the rest of the world.[4]

Strong words to cast into an England which for two centuries had been bitterly wrangling over religion!

When Crusoe rescued Friday's father and a Spaniard he had three subjects in his realm, and three varieties of religion. Friday was a Protestant, his father a pagan, and the Spaniard a Roman Catholic. This last fact became a threatening one with the rescue of other Spaniards. Dared Crusoe return to civilization with a Catholic crew? Would the Spaniards not, being in the majority, head the ship for a Catholic port, to his utter destruction?

> I had rather be delivered up to the savages, and be devoured alive, than fall into the merciless claws of the priests, and be carried into the Inquisition.[5]

Finally matters were adjusted, and Crusoe returned home, having left a considerable settlement upon his island.

But he could not conquer his wanderlust and was in time once more afloat, determined to find how his colony was faring. Meeting a ship in distress, he found among the survivors a French Catholic priest, a very excellent man. For Defoe to place such a person in his tale was a fourfold affront to many Englishmen. Catholics were discriminated against; priests were detested—especially French priests. Defoe not only put such a man into his book, but made him a model of virtue and tolerance. It was not by chance that he sinned thus against English prejudices.

> It is true that this man was a Roman, and perhaps it may give offence to some hereafter if I leave anything extraordinary upon record of a man, whom, before I begin, I must, to set him out in just colours, represent in terms very much to his disadvantage in the account of Protestants; as, first, that he was a Papist; secondly, a Popish priest; and, thirdly, a French Popist priest.

Nevertheless, continued Crusoe gravely,

> he was a grave, sober, pious, and most religious person; exact in his life, extensive in his charity, and exemplary in almost everything he did.[6]

When they reached Crusoe's colony the priest quietly and privately pointed out to him the devastation wrought in the lives of his subjects by the lack of religion, and the scandal of their living unmarried with the native women they had acquired, urging him to remedy the situation and preferring to see the Protestant religion spread rather than none exist. Crusoe was impressed.

> I was amazed to see so much true piety, and so much sincerity of zeal, besides the unusual impartiality in his discourse, as to his own party or church, and such true warmth for the preserving people . . . from transgressing the laws of God, the like of which I had indeed not met with anywhere.[7]

Believing that he had before him a spirit of true Christian zeal, Crusoe invited the priest himself to undertake the work, which he did with great joy and tact. Calling the Englishmen together, he urged them to instruct their savage mates in religion, that, they being Christianized, he might regularize their impromptu unions by marriage, for he would have no hand in joining Christians and savages—nay, was forbidden by God's word from so doing.

The men were eager to have the marriages performed, but they shied from talking religion to their consorts.

" 'Lord, sir,' says Will Atkins, 'how should we teach them religion? . . . Folks must have some religion themselves before they pretend to teach other people.' "

The priest was clever. "Can you not tell your wife . . . ?" he asked quietly, and under guise of the question he outlined the points he wished Atkins to present.

When Atkins finally agreed to broach the subject, the priest remarked shrewdly to Crusoe, "I doubt not but when he comes to talk religion to his wife, he will talk himself effectually into it."

How does all this comfort you, Crusoe curiously inquired, since according to your tenets these people, all outside your church, are and can be nothing but heretics?

> Sir, I am a Catholic of the Roman Church, and a priest of the order of St. Benedict, and I embrace all the principles of the Roman faith . . . nevertheless . . . I will by no means limit the mercy of Christ so far as to think that He cannot receive you into the bosom of His church, in a manner to us unperceivable, . . . and I hope you will have the same charity for us.[8]

Soon Atkins returned, reporting ruefully:

> I have been talking about God and religion to my wife, in order, as you directed me, to make a Christian of her; and she has preached such a sermon to me as I shall never forget while I live.[9]

Inquiry elicited the wife's utter inability to imagine a powerful God who would not long ago have struck down her husband for his exceeding wickedness.

Wife: What! He no hear you swear, curse, speak the great damn?
Will Atkins: Yes, yes, He hears it all.
Wife: Where be then the muchee great power strong? [10]

Finally, driven to the end of his tether by her artless but earnest questioning, Will Atkins fell down upon his knees and prayed.

Wife: What you put down the knee for? What you hold up the hand for? What you say? Who you speak to? What is all that?

On the earnest catechizing went, until at last the pagan woman expressed a desire to worship God, at which they knelt and prayed together. After further instruction she was considered ready for baptism, which the priest performed in a manner not offensive to non-Catholics.

As the time approached for Crusoe and the priest to leave the island, they rejoiced that religion was thriving, but as they left two colonies, one Catholic and one Protestant, they feared that trouble might ensue.

So we divided it—he to speak to the Spaniards, who were all Papists, and I to the English, who were all Protestants; and we . . . made them promise that they would never make any distinction of Papist or Protestant in their exhorting the savages to turn Christians, but teach them the general knowledge of the true God, and of their Saviour Jesus Christ; and they likewise promised us that they would never have any differences or disputes one with another about religion.[11]

So Robinson Crusoe took final farewell of his island, which has become a favorite port of call for fireside travelers of all ages.

Douglas Jerrold, Thackeray's great colleague on *Punch,* parodied the book with his *Miss Robinson Crusoe,* in which Crusoe's Bible is replaced by the *Complete Art of Cookery,* and Miss Crusoe and Miss Friday worry, not about theology, but about corsets and hose, problems destined for wide prominence in the twentieth century. Jerrold's parody died, but Defoe's book continues to flourish. At least one minister of religion has felt "that he had learned more of his duty to God, his neighbor, and himself, from *Robinson Crusoe* than from all the books, except the Bible, that were known to his youth." [12]

Fiction had long had incident. *Pilgrim's Progress* and *Robin-*

son Crusoe gave to it characters which—in a rudimentary way, at least—grew and developed as a result of forces brought to bear upon their lives, and in both cases the character-changing force was the Bible.

With character development, the novel was ready to be born. Twenty-one years after Robinson Crusoe appeared in literature, Samuel Richardson inadvertently wrote the book that is frequently called the first novel.

18. Pamela's Predicament

Had not a bishop announced that his duty was "to preach the Gospel and put down Enthusiasm"?

—SAMUEL F. DAMON[13]

CRITICS often assume that the novel was born in an age in which literature had lost the Bible. "During the so-called Augustan Age, covering the last quarter of the seventeenth century, and the first three quarters of the eighteenth, English literature shows comparatively little influence of the Bible,"[14] they glibly say, and point perhaps to the famous cautious prayer, "O God, if there be a God, save my soul, if I have a soul."

No literature dominated for twelve centuries by any book could possibly have lost that book suddenly. Eighteenth-century English literature did not lose the Bible. Defoe, as we have seen, was saturated with biblical thinking; at the close of his days he sadly compared himself to Jeremiah preaching to a heedless generation. In his last letter to his son-in-law he wrote:

> I would say, (I hope) with comfort, that 'tis yet well. I am so near my journey's end, and am hastening to the place where the weary are at rest, and where the wicked cease to trouble; be it that the passage is rough, and the day stormy, by what way soever He please to bring me to the end of it, I desire to finish life with this temper of soul in all cases. *Te Deum Laudamus.*[15]

Jonathan Swift's contact with the Bible began early, his nurse having taught him so assiduously that he is said to have been able to read any chapter before he was three years old. So instinct with biblical directness was his scathing pen that even *Gulliver's Travels* has been called his "gospel of hatred, his testament of woe."

Sir Richard Steele, despite his own erratic life, wrote with carc *The Christian Hero,* "a standing testmony against himself."

When Addison invited his friends to come see how a Christian could die, he left unfinished his *Evidences of Christianity,* but he had paraphrased some of the psalms and had pictured his Sir Roger de Coverley as personally presenting Bibles to his neighbors as marks of special approbation. Addison felt the Bible to be a tremendously formative force in English literature, commenting in one of the *Spectator* papers:

> It happens very luckily that the Hebrew idioms run into the English tongue with a particular grace and beauty. Our language has received innumerable elegancies and improvements from . . . Holy Writ. They give a force and energy to our expressions, warm and animate our language, and convey our thoughts in more ardent and intense phrases than any that are to be met with in our own tongue.[16]

So potent were the many lay sermons sprinkled through the *Spectator* papers that John Wesley, talking many years later about the origin of Methodism, pointed out how

> God raised up Mr. Addison and his associates to lash the prevailing vices and ridiculous and profane customs of the country, and to show the excellence of Christianity and Christian institutions. The *Spectators,* written with all the simplicity, elegance, and force of the English language, were everywhere read, and were the first instruments in the hands of God to check the mighty and growing profanity and call men back to religion and decency and common sense. Methodism, in the order of God, succeeded and revived and spread Scriptural and experimental Christianity over the nation. And now what hath God wrought! [17]

Pope wrote his "Messiah"; composed "The Dying Christian to His Soul"; attempted in his "Essay on Man" to vindicate the ways of God, and affixed at its end "The Universal Prayer"; besides weaving into much of his other verse a many-threaded biblical allusiveness. For Isaac Newton he wrote an epitaph:

> Nature and Nature's laws lay hid in Night:
> God said, "Let Newton be!" and all was light.[18]

John Wesley's first hymnal had been off the press for three years.

Such was the literary world into which the English novel was born. What of the latter half of the century, the years in which it grew into maturity?

Dr. Samuel Johnson was woof-woofing, "Sir, a woman preaching is like a dog's walking on his hind legs. It is not done well; but you are surprised to find it done at all";[19] or again, to a remark that God made Scotland, "Certainly, but we must always remember that He made it for Scotchmen; and comparisons are odious, Mr. Strahan, but God made hell."[20] But the old bear was not always so savage, as one of his friends noted in describing his last days.

We had a most affecting conversation on the subject of religion, in which he exhorted me, with the greatest warmth of kindness, to attend closely to every religious duty, and particularly enforced the obligation of private prayer and receiving the sacrament. He desired me to stay that night and join in prayer with him; adding that he always went to prayer every night with his man Francis. He conjured me to read and meditate upon the Bible, and not to throw it aside for a play or novel. He said he himself had lived in great negligence of religion and worship for forty years, that he had neglected to read his Bible, and had often reflected what he could hereafter say when he should be asked why he had not read it.[21]

Stenographer-at-large Boswell was liberally larding his *Hypochondriack* efforts with Pope, Shakespeare, and the Bible, and justifying his assiduous eavesdropping upon Johnson's conversation with words from Archbishop Secker:

Rabbi David Kimchi, a noted Jewish commentator, who lived about five hundred years ago, explains that passage in the First Psalm, *His leaf also shall not wither,* from Rabbins yet older than himself, thus: That even the idle talk, so he expresses it, *of a good man ought to be regarded;* the most superfluous things he saith are always of value.[22]

Sheridan was writing at the bottom of the *School for Scandal,*

Finished at last; thank God!
R. B. SHERIDAN.

And the still-frightened prompter, knowing that the fifth act had reached the theater but five days before the opening date, was adding beneath Sheridan's signature,

Amen!
W. HAWKINS.[23]

Goldsmith was writing like an angel and talking like poor Poll; the Vicar of Wakefield was going his artless way.

Burke was reading his usual chapter from Isaiah before delivering his orations.

Toplady was composing the "Rock of Ages," reputedly on the back of a playing card.

This was the literary environment in which the English novel came to fruition, and it was not a Bible-deserted environment. Nor was the novel a stranger to the Bible.

According to the title page of the book, Richardson's *Pamela* (1740), was "published in order to cultivate the principles of Virtue and Religion in the minds of the youth of both sexes," thus giving initial bent to the English novel, whose heroines for two centuries have been "girls with the doctrine of St. Paul in their veins; its frail ones were those whose inoculation did not 'take.' . . . Modesty, then, preserves chastity like paint; 'Save the surface and you save all.' "[24]

The parsons in Fielding's novels, Lewis' *The Monk,* Goldsmith's *The Vicar of Wakefield,* and the undercurrent of Methodism in Smollett's *Humphrey Clinker,* all show clearly the influence of religion upon the early novel.

From Sir Thomas Browne's *Religio Medici,* Jeremy Taylor's *Holy Living* and *Holy Dying,* sermons of Hall, Berkeley, Young, Tillotson, and others, and "the daily reading of the Old and New Testaments, books which were to his liking as well as necessary to his profession,"[25] scalawaggish parson Laurence Sterne shaped the potpourri of Scripture-laden allusions, chucklings, innuendoes, bawdinesses, moralizings, and sermonizings of that teasingly irresponsible book, *The Life and Opinions of Tristram Shandy, Gentleman,* wherein Shandy claims that

> of all the several ways of beginning a book which are now in practice throughout the known world, I am confident my own way of doing it is the best—I'm sure it is the most religious—for I begin with writing the first sentence—and trusting to Almighty God for the second.[26]

"The muleteer was a son of *Adam,*" says Shandy; "I need not say a word more." Again, "A daughter of *Eve,* for such was the widow Wadman, and 'tis all the character I intend to give of her." His father hesitated to take his wife to church, to "place his rib and self in so many tormenting lights and attitudes in the face of the whole congregation." "Now my father had a way, a little like that of Job's (in case there ever was such a man—if not, there's an end of the matter)," comments the son, cheerfully. And again, "And was not (I forget his name) who had more discretion than both, town-clerk of Ephesus?"

While Trim and Shandy's Uncle Toby were laboring to save the life of a stricken soldier—

> A-well-o'-day,—do what we can for him, said *Trim,* maintaining his point,—the poor soul will die:—He shall not die, by G—, cried my uncle *Toby.*—The ACCUSING SPIRIT, which flew up to heaven's chancery with the oath, blush'd as he gave it in; and the RECORDING ANGEL, as he wrote it down, dropped a tear upon the word, and blotted it out forever—[27]

His Majesty was reported to have inquired, "And what name has the republic fixed upon for the Dauphin?"

"Shadrack, Meshech Abednego," replied the minister.

"By Saint *Peter's* girdle, I will have nothing to do with the *Swiss,*" cried *Francis* the First, pulling up his breeches and walking hastily across the floor.[28]

While waiting for the widow Wadman's answer to his marriage proposal, Uncle Toby calmly picked up her Bible and immersed himself in the fascinating siege of Jericho.

So well had Sterne caught the scriptural cadence that men, seeking "God tempers the wind to the shorn lamb," often look for it in the Bible but find it in Sterne's *Sentimental Journey.*

> She . . . had travel'd over all Lombardy without money—and through the flinty roads of Savoy without shoes—how she had borne it . . . she could not tell—but *God tempers the wind,* said Maria, to the shorn lamb.
>
> Shorn indeed! and to the quick, said I.[29]

The momentum of twelve centuries was, however, slowly slackening. In an age of "tea-pot pieties" and "tape-yard infidelities" Puritanism had lost its driving power. The Established Church had grown drowsy. Literary style had become stilted. Bibles were gathering dust. "We saw but one Bible in the parish of Cheddar," wrote Hannah More in 1791, "and that was used to prop a flowerpot." She suggested to Sir Joshua Reynolds that he get someone to write an oratorio about Samuel, so that people would know the origin of his painting of the child Samuel.

In an effort to make the Bible genteel, William Mace (1729) translated James 2:3: "If you should respectfully say to the suit of fine clothes, Sit you there, that's for quality." In 1754 a London fruit seller translated the first chapter of Genesis:

1. AELOHIM, beginning, created *lucide* and *illucide* matter.
2. And the *illucide,* void of Co-adjunct Cohesion, was unmodified, and distinguishableness was nowhere upon the face of Chaos: and the Ruach of AELOHIM emanated over the periphery of the fluctuation.[30]

Dr. Edward Harwood attempted "to clothe the genuine ideas and doctrines of the apostles with that propriety and perspicuity in which they themselves, I apprehend, would have exhibited them, had they now lived and written in our language." He hoped that this "attempt to diffuse over the sacred page the elegance of modern English would induce persons of a liberal education and polite taste to peruse the sacred volume," which was "now, alas, too generally neglected." His parable of the prodigal son began:

A gentleman of splendid family and opulent fortune had two sons. One day the younger approached his father, and begged him in the most importunate and soothing terms to make a partition of his effects betwixt himself and his elder brother—the indulgent father, overcome by his blandishments, immediately divided all his fortunes betwixt them.

His Sermon on the Mount reeked with gentility.

Happy are those who are endowed with true humility—for such are properly disposed for the reception of the gospel.

Happy are those who lament with unfeigned contrition the vices and errors of their past lives—for they shall be comforted with the cheering promises of the gospel.

Happy are those who are possessed with a mild and inoffensive disposition—for they shall be enriched with the greatest happiness this world can furnish.

Happy are those whose minds are inflamed with a sacred ardour to attain universal virtue—their enlarged and generous desires shall be satisfied.[31]

God's message to the Laodiceans became, "Since . . . you are now in a state of lukewarmness, a disagreeable medium between two extremes, I will, in no long time, eject you from my heart with fastidious contempt." Nicodemus became "this gentleman," Damaris "a lady of distinction," and the daughter of Herodias "a young lady who danced with inimitable grace and elegance." Paul's cloak left at Troas became a portmanteau.

As Dr. Harwood modestly admitted, this edition of the New Testament leaves the most exacting velleity without ground for quiritation!

But even gentility of diction was in some cases insufficient. In the novel which gave "Monk" Lewis his nickname, the monk found the young woman, Antonia, reading her Bible in her bedroom. How, he wondered, could she read the Bible and still be so abysmally ignorant of sex as she obviously was? Upon inquiry he discovered that her prudent mother, feeling that no reading was more improper for the female breast than the unrestricted Bible, with its plainness of speech and bluntness of thought, had with her own hand copied out the book, altering or omitting all improper passages.

Such niceness had men's minds acquired that even profanity grew dainty.

19. Hell's Bells

"You're a dingle dangle," Knox shouted with his voice rising shrilly, "you're a low-down dingle dangle."

Baldy burst out laughing. "Now what in hell's a dingle dangle?"
—ALBERT MALTZ[32]

FOR centuries Englishmen had been famed for the forthrightness and frequency of their oaths. Since, "like hosiery and philanthropy, swearing follows fashion," it had registered the changing manners of men's thoughts. "By the Splendor of God" was William the Conqueror's oath. "By St. Luke's Face" was his son's. Henry II swore by God's eyes, John by God's tooth, and Richard III by St. Paul. The habit grew. In the *Vision of Piers Plowman,* Gluttony confessed that he had sworn needlessly nine hundred times.

As Chaucer's pilgrims made their imaginary journey down to Canterbury, notwithstanding the sacred goal of their journey they thoughtlessly invoked most of the saints in the calendar; they swore by Christ and his body and his wounds until the irreverent Host's "For God's bones" and "By God's dignity" drove the earnest parson to protest, "What aileth the man so sinfully to swear?" [33]

So notable were some medieval swearers that their descendants inherited commemorative surnames. Alicia Godbode, John Godme-fetch, Basilia Godsowle, and others are recorded. "The French, themselves no mean practitioners of the art, professed themselves shocked by the license in language of their neighbors, and their favorite name for the Englishman was Jean Goddano." [34] "You think when you have slain me you will conquer France," Joan of Arc, chained in her prison cell, is reported to have told the earls of Warwick and Stafford, "but that you will never do. Though there were a hundred thousand Goddammees more in France than there are, they will never conquer that kingdom." [35]

As late as the nineteenth century Lord Byron could sneer:

Juan, who did not understand a word
  Of English, save their shibboleth, "God Damn!"
And even that he had so rarely heard,
  He sometimes thought 'twas only their "salam,"
Or "God be with you!"—and 'tis not absurd
  To think so: for half English as I am
(To my misfortune) never can I say
  I heard them wish "God with you," save that way.[36]

In Gilbert and Sullivan's rollicking comedy Captain Corcoran crowed:

Bad language or abuse
I never, never use.
Whatever the emergency;
Though "bother it!" I may
Occasionally say,
I never use a big, big D!

But the crew was skeptical.

> MEN: What, never?
> CAPTAIN: No, never!
> MEN: What, *never?*
> CAPTAIN: Hardly ever!
> MEN: Hardly ever swears a big, big D.[37]

But English profanity had not always been limited to the big, big *D;* in her day good Queen Bess could make "cuss-words sizzle like apples in an oven." In Shakespeare's *King Henry IV*, Part I, Hotspur calls his wife to task for her anemic vocabulary:

> Swear me, Kate, like a lady as thou art,
> A good mouth-filling oath, and leave "in sooth,"
> . . . .
> To velvet-guards and Sunday-citizens.

"When a gentleman is disposed to swear, it is not for any standers-by to curtail his oaths," fumes Cloten in *Cymbeline,* irked because "a whoreson jackanapes must take me up for swearing, as if I borrowed mine oaths of him and might not spend them at my pleasure." In other plays Mrs. Page swears by the dickens, Pistol by Cadwallader and all his goats, and Hamlet the Dane by St. Patrick.

But Puritanism detested swearing. A law in 1605 forbade, by a penalty of ten pounds, profanity upon the stage. Still it continued to flourish in England so unrestrainedly that William Howel could write in 1628:

> This infamous custom of swearing, I observe, reigns in England lately more than anywhere else; though a German, in highest puff of passion, swears by a hundred thousand sacraments, the Frenchman by the death of God, the Spaniard by His flesh, the Irishman by His Five Wounds, though the Scot commonly bids the Devil hale his soul, yet for variety of oaths the English roarers put down all. Consider well what a dangerous thing it is to tear in pieces that Dreadful Name, which makes the vast fabric of the world to tremble.[38]

A change was not far distant. When Cromwell's Ironsides came upon the scene, "Not a man swears but he pays his twelve pence." [39]

After the Restoration the triumphant Cavaliers took pains to irritate the Puritans by studied looseness of speech.

The new breed of wits and fine gentlemen never opened their mouths without uttering ribaldry of which a porter would now be ashamed, and without calling on their maker to curse them, sink them, confound them, blast them, and damn them.[40]

Even after the revolution of 1688 profanity continued to be a common exercise of English lungs, whether in male or female breasts. Sarah, Duchess of Marlborough, calling upon an eminent judge and finding him absent, departed so sulphurously that the servant failed to get her name and could only report that "she swore like a lady of quality." Swift ironically agreed that adequate profanity was a mark of gentility.

A footman may swear, but he cannot swear like a lord. He can swear as often, but can he swear with equal delicacy, propriety and judgment? [41]

He ruled that "oathes well chosen are not only very useful expletives to matter, but great ornaments of style," and urged his male readers

that they would please a little to study variety. For it is the opinion of our most refined swearers, that the same oath cannot, consistently with true politeness, be repeated above nine times in the same company, by the same person, and at one sitting.

When Commodore Trunnion, in Smollett's *Peregrine Pickle,* learned that he was in imminent danger of being married, he retreated to his hammock, where he muttered oaths for twenty-four hours without pausing. Sterne's Tristram Shandy not only swore fluently but invited his readers' collaboration:

It then presently occurr'd to me, that I had left my remarks in the pocket of the chaise—and that in selling my chaise, I had sold my remarks along with it, to the chaise-vamper.

I leave this void space that the reader may swear into it any oath that he is most accustomed to—— For my own part, if ever I swore a *whole* oath into a vacancy in my life, I think it was into that --------******, said I.[42]

"When Ernulphus cursed—" said Shandy, "no part escaped him. —'Tis true there is something of a hardness in his manner—and, as in Michael Angelo, a want of *grace*—but then there is such a greatness of *gusto!*" [43] And it was precisely greatness of gusto which swearing was now losing. Whereas an Elizabethan had sworn impromptu, he hardly knew how or why, Augustan playwrights could jeer at the nice refinements of oratorical blasphemy which they burlesqued.

ACRES: . . . If I can find out this Ensign Beverly, odds triggers and flints! I'll make him knoe the difference o't.

ABSOLUTE: Spoke like a man! But pray, Bob, I observe you have got an odd kind of a new method of swearing——

ACRES: Ha! ha! you've taken notice of it— 'tis genteel, isn't it?— I didn't invent it myself though; but a commander in our militia— a great scholar, I assure you— says that there is no meaning in the common oaths, and that nothing but their antiquity makes them respectable . . .— so that to swear with propriety, says my little Major, the "oath should be an echo to the sense"; and this we call the "oath referential," or "sentimental swearing"— ha! ha! ha! 'tis genteel, isn't it?

ABSOLUTE: Very genteel, and very new, indeed— and I dare say will supplant all other figures of imprecation.

ACRES: Aye, aye, the best terms will grow obsolete.— D——s have had their day.[44]

Profanity grew mincingly artificial. "Zounds" (God's wounds) became "oons"; "God's blood" became "adsblud"; "God" became "Gad," "Egad," "Gadsobs," "Gadsocks," or "Odzooks." "By the Mass" became "Mess.' The horrendous "Gads daggers, beets, blades, and scabbards" arose. By 1826 swearing had so fallen into disrepute that at least one man could comment, "The only oath which I can recollect of lately meeting with, in circles that have any pretension to fashion, is *by Jove*." [45] A hundred years later, in 1927, Robert Graves, in *Lars Porsena, or the Future of Swearing and Improper Language,* lamented the "notable decline of swearing and foul language in England." Others agreed.

Gone are the echoing oaths of a day when swearing was an art. Those swashbuckling phrases went with swashbuckling deeds. "By the bones of Saint Michael! I will spit thee to thy cringing gizzard!" There was a mouth-filling and classic threat for you! In these days, when automatic revolvers have replaced fencing swords, there isn't time to say it. Gone are the cloud-splitting denunciations of militant churchmen. . . . What a humiliating spectacle is the word *damn!* Once a powerful invective, conveying all the righteous anger of the church, now a miserable subterfuge of the playwright if he needs a laugh in a tense situation; now a commonplace that a French translator of English idiom found he could render only by the word *tres*.[46]

In America, however, it is alleged that swearing is increasing.

There is no doubt that the habit of profane swearing . . . has greatly increased among all classes of society in the twentieth century. . . . The telephone has surely spread the habit of cursing. As Figaro says, "To get your telephone connection is no longer an achievement; it is a career." Learning to play the typewriter has also loosened the tongue. . . . But golf has done more for swearing than any other modern employment; it has made taciturn gentlemen as efficient as teamsters. . . . Nearly all men, and women, too, must swear tacitly in their thoughts, else how explain such easily acquired efficiency.[47]

Others attribute the rising tide of American profanity to the world war—which leaves unexplained the falling tide in England. At least one critic attributes it to the increase of books by women novelists. Perhaps it is partially explained by America's traditional liking for vividness in all language, its efforts to keep the language from going to sleep.

Since, however, the Puritan heritage is still powerful in American thought, the psychologic stress set up by the desire to swear and the hesitancy to do so has been especially strong, resulting in a great mass of denatured oaths.

The human impulse to swear is held in check by religious or social prohibitions. The usual compromise is a word or phrase that suggests rather than states, that at once approaches the forbidden and shies away from it . . . a curious exhibition, indeed, of the human desire to sin combined with want of courage.[48]

For this reason,

in place of the more blasphemous forms of oaths, various conventional substitutes have developed and persisted in popular usage: for "God" the expressions *by gad, by golly, by gum, by Jove* . . . for "Jesus" the shortened form *gee and jeeze,* and the longer *Jerusalem, gee whillikins, gee whizz;* for "Christ" *cripes, Jiminy Christmas, for crying out loud;* for "Lord" *lor, lawdy, law sakes*. . . .[49]

To these should be added "jeepers creepers."

Two models of virtue are Hollywood and the cheap magazines. In Hollywood,

> *God* must be used circumspectly, and *Gawd* is under the ban. So are *Lord* ("when used profanely"), *Christ, hell, hellcat, Jesus, Geez.* . . . Even the word *virtuous* is to be avoided.[50]

In the pulp magazines,

> Hairy chested as they are, these Pulp he-men are alike in their careful avoidance of strong language. Heroes in the trenches can, under stress of excitement, exclaim "Cripes!" but must not let slip either gee or geez, which are forbidden as blasphemous. The oldest of the western story magazines has never had its pages sullied by a Damn.[51]

These prohibitions are not so drastic as they seem, since meaning is secondary, or even unnecessary, in profanity. All one needs "is a good big mouthful of crackling consonants," as was realized by the newspaper columnist who threatened:

> Am going to think me up some innocent new cuss words to yell out during double feature movies. "Abradembazoolum! Dantiphonesabellum! Vrum! Zibrokipides!" [52]

Herein lies a partial explanation of the ease with which one blurts out profanity in English:

> It is certainly a misfortune that in our English speech so many of our words for deity and for the popularly supposed acts of enraged deity begin with gutturals or dentals. In moments of excitement, in play or anger or pain or fear the throat contracts and the teeth shut; consequently any expression that tears its way through is bound to begin with those same gutturals or dentals.[53]

The results attributed to this vary widely. One man says: "The ease with which one swears in English is what has made it the great commercial language of the world." [54] Another charges profanity with being the cause of world-wide economic depressions. A leading American magazine reported in 1938 concerning an International Conference on Swearing, held at Budapest:

A sensation was created at the meeting when a delegate attempted to prove that the economic depressions were the results of the widespread use of bad language. After heated debate, the conference rejected this point of view on the ground that there were no *statistical* data for its support.[55]

20. Wigs to Wigwams

Puritanism, believing itself quick with the seed of religious liberty, laid, without knowing it, the egg of democracy.
—JAMES RUSSELL LOWELL[56]

AMERICA and England have gradually developed a marked difference in religious vocabulary.

The English have an ecclesiastical vocabulary with which we are almost unacquainted, and it is in daily use, for the church bulks much larger in public affairs over there than it does here. Such terms as *vicar, canon, verger, prebendary, primate, curate, nonconformist, dissenter, convocation, minster, chapter, crypt, living, presentation, glebe, benefice, locum tenens, suffragan, almoner, tithe, dean* and *pluralist* are to be met with in the English newspapers constantly, but on this side of the water they are seldom encountered. Nor do we hear much of *mattins* (which has two t's in England), *lauds, lay-readers, ritualism* and the *liturgy*. The English use of *holy orders* is also strange to us. . . . The English, to make it even, get on without *Holy-rollers, Dunkards, hard-shell Baptists, Seventh Day Adventists* and other such American alarmers of God, and they give a *mourners' bench* the austere name of *penitent-seat* or *form*.[57]

Among other Americanisms are "anxious seat," "camp meeting," "circuit rider," "come-outer," "experience-meeting," "foot-wash," "donation party," "pounding," "pastorium," "to pastor," "to missionate," "to get religion," "to fellowship," and "to shout."

This rift between English and American thinking is not new, nor is it confined to religious matters. "In the four quarters of the globe, who reads an American book, or goes to an American play, or looks at an American picture or statue?" asked English Sydney Smith in 1820. Equally might Americans, throughout a surprisingly large part of the colonial period, have asked, "Who in America reads English books?" Not one quotation from Shakespeare has been found in colonial literature before 1700. A Boston bookshop inventoried in 1700 contained 2,504 volumes, but no English literature except "3 Pilgrims Progress with cuts." Only 2 per cent of the volumes dealt with the classics, while 75 per cent were concerned with religion, of which 1,459 volumes were catechisms. In 1723, almost a century after its founding, the Harvard College library contained one volume of Shakespeare, newly acquired, at least some of Milton's work, but nothing by Addison, Dryden, Steele, or Swift. Eighty-six per cent of its books were religious.

This predominance of books on religion permeated American life. Samuel Sewall's favorite courting gifts were bound sermons and psalmbooks. When Widow Winthrop kept him dangling, he summoned his pastor son to come pray with him, "more especially concerning my Courtship"; thus fortified, he sallied forth, "having Dr. Sibb's Bowels with me to read," the full title of which was *Bowels Opened; or a Discovery of the Union Between Christ and the Church.* He read two sermons therefrom ere his adored one appeared. Wigs wrecked his love-making. The widow hinted that he needed a wig; he replied that God had supplied him hair since infancy, and he would not change custom now. She turned one of his own gifts against him: "She commended the book I gave her, Dr. Preston, the Church Marriage; quoted him saying 'twas inconvenient keeping out of a Fashion commonly used."[58] He was adamant and lost the lady.

This entangling of wigs and religion was no sudden stubbornness; thirty years earlier Sewall had resented Cotton Mather's sermon in which he smelled an approval of wigs:

> I expected not to hear a vindication of Perriwigs in a Boston Pulpit by Mr. Mather. . . . The Lord give me a good Heart and help to know, and not only to know but also to doe his Will; that my Heart and Head may be his.[59]

Nor was Sewall alone; ministers preached against them:

> FIRSTLY: Adam, so long as he continued in innocency, did wear his own Hair, and not a Perriwig . . .
>
> SECONDLY: When the Son of God appeared in the flesh, he did not, from a dislike of his own Hair, cut it off and wear a Perriwig . . .
>
> THIRDLY: The Children of God will not wear Perriwigs after the Resurrection . . .

Fourthly: We have no warrant in the word of God, that I know of, for our wearing of Perriwigs except it be in extraordinary cases. . . . Elisha did not cover his head with a Perriwig, although it was bald . . . oh, Adam, what hast thou done! [60]

Other fashions were likewise castigated. When hoop skirts arrived the Boston *News Letter* announced: "Just published and sold by the printer hereof, Hoop PETTICOATS, arraigned and condemned by the Light of Nature and Law of God." Wiseacres insisted that the Lord would severely punish this feminine aberration, and they predicted dire disasters, including an Indian massacre: "When an earthquake actually did occur, the inhabitants of at least one Massachusetts town were 'so awakened by this awful Providence that the women generally laid aside their hoop petticoats.' " [61]

But the Puritans, seeking to regulate the minutiae of life, were attempting the impossible. They outlawed ninepins. Men added another and advertised, *"Tenpins* played here"; so it is yet ninepins in England, tenpins in America. They banned Christmas, but their descendants took over from their Dutch neighbors Kriss Kringle (German Christ *kindlein*—Christ child) and Santa Claus, named for that St. Nicholas whose gift of three bags of gold to three poor maids has, according to some, originated the three golden balls which gleam over pawnshop doors. And Americans began using that hellish device, the Christmas tree! Puritans might ever so carefully scrape crosses from hornbooks and primers, but the medieval bells which ousted evil spirits now jingle on teething rings and Santa Claus costumes.

Americans even acquired a made-to-order native saint. As matters grew tense between England and America, and loyalists organized their guilds of St. George, St. Andrew, etc., patriots retaliated by "canonizing" King Tamenund, the Delaware chief (in Cooper's *Last of the Mohicans*), and celebrating his "saint's day," May 12. Among the honoring saintly organizations which so sprang up was one which still exists, "founded on the true principles of patriotism, and has for its motives charity and brotherly love"—Tammany Hall.

The rigid theocracy of which the early Puritans rapturously dreamed proved in the end a vain hope. But after the Mather dynasty had fallen and its age was dust, when the Great Awakening had come and gone, when Jonathan Edwards was silent and George Whitefield's impassioned preaching no longer ran like flame from Georgia to New England, when Americans were cutting the ties of the past in politics and plunging into untried methods of government, they yet clung to the Bible.

"There is a book worth all other books that were ever printed," was Patrick Henry's forthright verdict.

The unanimously elected secretary of the First Continental Congress, Charles Thomson, retired in 1789 that he might devote himself to Bible translation. Having bought by chance at auction a part of the Septuagint, and knowing nothing of the book "save that the crier said it was outlandish letters," and having then studied Greek enough to understand it, and having sought in vain for a complete copy, he passed the same store two years later and almost unbelievably found the remainder in process of being auctioned. Twenty years later he issued the first American translation.

To him Thomas Jefferson, who had prepared for his own use *The Life and Morals of Jesus of Nazareth Extracted Textually from the Gospels in Greek, Latin, French, and English* (now treasured at Washington), wrote of Jefferson's own "wee little book" that "a more beautiful or precious morsel of ethics I have never seen; it is a document in proof that I am a *real Christian*, that is to say, a disciple of the doctrines of Jesus." [62]

Congress, when the break with England shut off Bibles, ordered twenty thousand imported from other sources. And when Robert Aitken succeeded in printing copies in America, upon American-made paper, Congress authorized the use of its name in his advertising.

> Resolved, That the United States in Congress assembled . . . recommend this edition of the Bible to the inhabitants of the United States, and hereby authorize him to publish this recommendation in the manner in which he shall think proper.[63]

Benjamin Franklin, wishing to inculcate a lesson in tolerance, hoaxed his friends by printing in biblical language an old Persian tale and binding it into his Bible as "the fifty-first chapter of Genesis."

8. And Abraham's zeal was kindled against the man, and he arose and fell upon him, and drove him forth with blows into the wilderness.
9. And at midnight God called unto Abraham, saying: "Abraham, where is the stranger?"
10. And Abraham answered and said: "Lord, he would not worship thee, neither would he call upon thy name; therefore have I driven him out from before my face into the wilderness."
11. And God said: "Have I borne with him these hundred and ninety and eight years, and nourished him, and clothed him, notwithstanding his rebellion against me; and couldst not thou, that art thyself a sinner, bear with him one night?" [64]

In similar fashion he wrote "A Parable on Brotherly Love," wherein Reuben bought an ax which his brothers vainly tried to borrow. When it fell into the river, he tried to borrow of his brothers, who had meanwhile bought for themselves. Simeon refused, Levi reproached but agreed to lend, Judah offered before asked.

15. And Reuben fell on his neck, and kissed him, with tears, saying: "Thy kindness is great, but thy goodness in forgiving me is greater. Thou art indeed my brother, and whilst I live, will I surely love thee."
16. And Judah said: "Let us also love our other brethren; behold, are we not all of one blood?" [65]

While still in his teens Franklin had penned for his brother's paper an attack upon the pretensions of place and power:

In old time it was no disrespect for men and women to be called by their own names. Adam was never called Master Adam; we never read of Noah Esquire, Lot Knight and Baronet, nor the Right Honorable Abraham, Viscount Mesopotamia, Baron of Canaan. No, no, they were plain men, honest country graziers, that took care of their families and their flocks. Moses was a great prophet and Aaron a priest of the Lord; but we never read of the Reverend Moses nor the Right Reverend Father in God, Aaron, by Divine Providence Lord Archbishop of Israel. Thou never sawest Madam Rebecca in the Bible, my Lady Rachel; nor Mary, though a princess of the blood, after the death of Joseph called the Princess Dowager of Nazareth. No, plain Rebecca, Rachel, Mary, or the Widow Mary, or the like. It was no incivility then to mention their naked names as they were expressed.[66]

Through life he retained this love of simplicity. When asked to help abridge the Book of Common Prayer, he left of the Catechism only two questions: "What is your duty to God?" and "What is your duty to your neighbor?"

The artificialities of court life abroad led Franklin to suggest ironically a revision of the Bible which would have pleased even Dr. Harwood's genteel taste. He sent the editor to whom he suggested the idea a few revised verses of the first chapter of Job:

Verse 6. And it being *levee* day in heaven, all God's nobility came to court, to present themselves before him; and Satan also appeared in the circle, as one of the ministry.
7. And God said to Satan: You have been some time absent; where were you? And Satan answered: I have been at my country seat, and in different places visiting my friends.
8. And God said: Well, what think you of Lord Job? You see he is my best friend, a perfectly honest man, full of respect for me, and avoiding everything that might offend me.
9. And Satan answered: Does your Majesty imagine that his good conduct is the effect of mere personal attachment and affection?
10. Have you not protected him, and heaped your benefits upon him, till he is grown enormously rich?
11. Try him; only withdraw your favor, turn him out of his places, and withhold his pensions, and you will soon find him in the opposition.[67]

His irony worked better than he dared hope. It entrapped the editor, who printed his suggestion as a bona fide proposal. It later entrapped so great a critic as Matthew Arnold, who wrote, "I well remember how when I first read that I drew a deep breath of relief, and said to myself, 'After all, there is a stretch of humanity beyond Franklin's good sense.' "[68] It entrapped others, one of whom ranted:

Many years later, when age and experience should have taught him better, he . . . took some verses from the first chapter of Job, stripped them of every particle of grace, beauty, imagery, terseness, and strength, and wrote a paraphrase which, of all paraphrases of the Bible, is surely the worst. . . . The plan is beneath criticism. Were such a piece of folly ever begun, there would remain but one other depth of folly to which it would be possible to go down. Franklin proposed to fit out the Kingdom of Heaven with lords, nobles, a ministry, and levee days. It would on the same principle be proper to make another version suitable for republics . . . nor would he have hesitated to make such a version.[69]

Franklin's actual attitude may be seen from his epitaph, the first version of which he wrote when twenty-two:

The body
of
Benamin Franklin, Printer,
(Like the cover of an old book,
Its contents torn out,
And stript of its lettering and gilding,)
Lies food for worms:
Yet the work itself shall not be lost.
For it will, [as he believed] appear once more,
In a new
And more beautiful edition,
Corrected and amended
by
The Author.[70]

It may be seen still more clearly when at eighty-one he rose in the Constitutional Convention and spoke:

> I have lived, sir, a long time, and the longer I live the more convincing proofs I see of this truth, *that* GOD *governs in the affairs of men.* And if a sparrow cannot fall to the ground without his notice, is it probable that an empire can rise without his aid? We have been assured, sir, in the sacred writings that "except the Lord build the house, they labor in vain that build it." I firmly believe this, and I also believe that without his concurring aid we shall succeed in this political building no better than the builders of Babel.[71]

Then the aged Franklin eloquently moved that daily prayers be initiated in the Convention.

In the years between the Mathers and Franklin, a new spirit, a more secular spirit, had come into control in America, but it was not willing to let go of the Bible.

It was John Quincy Adams who said, "The first and almost the only book deserving of universal attention is the Bible. I speak as a man of the world . . . and I say to you, 'Search the Scriptures.' " [72]

THE BIBLE CAPTURES SAINT AND SINNER

21. Damaged Archangels

I'd like to talk to De Lawd. I'd like to find out what He does in His spare moments. —ROY LOVELY[1]

ENGLAND owes much to its occasionally deranged ones, with their interesting sanities and insanities; and some of them owe much to the Bible. Such was Collins, who gave up all other books and carried only the New Testament, answering Johnson's inquiry with, "I have only one book, but that book is the best."

Such was self-styled Alexander the Corrector (Alexander Cruden, who compiled the famous concordance to the Bible), going about London with a sponge with which to erase nasty words from public places.

Such was poor, fear-sick Cowper, nerving himself to endure the torture inflicted by a schoolmate, recognizing the tormentor only by his shoe buckles because he dared not lift his eyes above the bully's knees, yet finding courage in Psalm 118:6—"I will not fear: what can man do unto me?"—and finding after attempted suicide and later release from the madhouse other strength in the same psalm:

> The Lord is my strength and song, and is become my salvation. . . . I shall not die, but live, and declare the works of the Lord. The Lord hath chastened me sore: but he hath not given me over unto death. . . . O give thanks unto the Lord . . . for his mercy endureth forever.

He wrote with his reformed slave-trading pastor the lovely *Olney Hymns,* and with the shadow of madness already upon him composed "God Moves in a Mysterious Way His Wonders to Perform" —an achievement, says James Fields, that angels themselves might envy.

Of them also was that name hidden, brain touched one at Cirencester who wrote:

Could we with ink the ocean fill,
  Were the whole earth of parchment made,
Were every single stick a quill,
  Were every man a scribe by trade;
To write the love of God alone
  Would drain the ocean dry,
Nor would the scroll contain the whole
  Though stretched from sky to sky.[2]

But greatest of all was William Blake. Into an England which scorned enthusiasm and intuition came this "Wesley of the arts" shouting a loud literary and artistic "Amen! Huzza! Selah!" [3]

The Vision of Christ that thou dost see
Is my vision's greatest enemy.
. . . .
Thine loves the same world that mine hates;
Thy heaven doors are my hell gates.
. . . .
Both read the Bible day and night,
But thou read'st black where I read white.[4]

Reading white where others read black is not the best way of persuading others to agree with one, but when one lives in an England where to him

Each field seems Eden, and each calm retreat;
Each village seems the haunt of holy feet,[5]

and where he commonly companions

With angels planted in hawthorn bowers,
With God himself in the passing hours;
With silver angels across my way,
And golden demons that none can stay,[6]

he finds it hard to do otherwise than exclaim, "For everything that lives is Holy!"

Blake was horrified and repelled by the somnolence of eighteenth-century England:

Awake! Thou sleeper on the Rock of Eternity, Albion, awake!
The trumpet of Judgment hath twice sounded: all Nations are
awake,
But thou art still heavy and dull. Awake, Albion, awake! [7]

From childhood, Deity and His Great Ones had been as real to William Blake as the meals he ate.

"The first time you ever saw God," his wife remarked, "was when you were four years old, and He put his head to the window and set you a-screaming." [8] She lived with him forty-five understanding years, and at the end could only remark wistfully, "Mr. Blake has been so little with me. For though in body we were never separated, he was incessantly away in Paradise." [9]

When eight or nine years old, Blake spied Ezekiel under a tree and was soundly thrashed for saying so when he got home. Again it was a tree filled with angels, whose multicolored wings spangled its boughs like stars. Then it was angels strolling among the harvesters. While drawing at Westminster Abbey, he glimpsed Christ and the apostles. Once the mighty building was suddenly astir with majestic procession of monks, priests, choristers, and incense bearers, while ghostly chants and organ music made the vaulted roof tremble. Old and New Testament heroes and long-dead poets were Blake's common contemporaries.

"Yesterday I saw Milton," he might casually observe; "he spoke to me and, in my turn, I tried to tell him he was wrong, but it was no use."

"Who was that you said 'good day' to?" inquired a puzzled companion out for a stroll with him.

"That? Why that was the Apostle Paul." [10]

"Disturb me not," he whispered as a friend found him gazing into vacancy, then drawing busily; "I have some one sitting to me."

"Where?"

"There, his name is Lot, you may read of him in the Scriptures. He is sitting for his portrait." [11]

When Isaiah and Ezekiel dined with him he asked how they dared assert that God spoke to them, and if they did not think they would be misunderstood. The three had an animated session. "After dinner I asked Isaiah to favour the world with his lost works; he said none of equal value was lost. Ezekiel said the same thing of his." [12]

" 'What!' it will be questioned," he once wrote, "when the sun rises, 'do you not see a round disc of fire somewhat like a guinea?' Oh! no, no! I see an innumerable company of the heavenly host crying, 'Holy, holy, holy is the God Almighty.' " [13]

He saw his dying brother's soul ascend to heaven, "clapping its hands for joy," and from it received the process for "illuminated printing" by means of which he gave the world some of its most treasured books. From his heart flowed melodies of unearthly sweetness, and cloudy prophetic books which baffle neat, sane arrangers; from his hand came fluent drawings, engravings, and paintings, such as his "Creation of Eve," and the mighty illustrations for the *Book of Job*. At seventy he died, singing strange new songs he was even then hearing from heaven.

After him came another "archangel a little damaged," Samuel Taylor Coleridge. This self-styled "literary cormorant," with his omnivorous reading and subtle brain, was to many contemporaries the most stimulative mind of his age, a talkative prodigy safely emerged from the youthful Unitarianism during which he had zealously preached in blue coat and white waistcoat, so that not a rag of the Romish Woman of Babylon might be seen upon him. He had thereafter survived German rationalism and now rested eloquently in the bosom of the Established Church. Like Bunyan, he had known Giant Despairs and Doubting Castles:

> Doubts rushed in, broke upon me "from the fountains of the great deep," and "fell from the windows of heaven." The fontal truths of natural Religion, and the book of Revelation, alike contributed to the flood; and it was long ere my Ark touched on an Ararat, and rested. . . . My head was with Spinoza, though my whole heart remained with Paul and John.[14]

No wonder he read *Pilgrim's Progress* twice—once as theologian and once as poet—and called it "incomparably the best compendium of gospel truth ever produced by a writer not divinely inspired."

To Coleridge, Scripture was the light-bearer of progress. "For more than a thousand years the Bible, collectively taken, has gone hand in hand with civilization, science, law—in short, with the moral and intellectual cultivation of the species, always supporting and often leading the way." [15] In his eyes Job was the "sublimest," the Epistle to the Romans "the most profound work in existence." In the Bible he found "words for my inmost thoughts, songs for my joy, utterances for my hidden griefs, and pleadings for my shame and feebleness. . . . In the Bible there is more that *finds* me than I have experienced in all other books put together. . . . The words of the Bible find me at greater depths of my being." [16] And, "After reading Isaiah, or St. Paul's Epistle to the Hebrews, Homer and Virgil are disgustingly tame to me, and Milton himself barely tolerable." [17] One has but to read his "Hymn Before Sunrise in the Vale of Chamounix," with its echoes of the Nineteenth Psalm, to realize how his writings sparkle with phrases and turns of thought from the Book.

There came yet another "beautiful and ineffectual angel beating in the void his luminous wings in vain"—Percy Bysshe Shelley. In the callow certainty of school days he published *The Necessity for Atheism* and was promptly expelled from college. In the ripe cocksureness of his twentieth year he wrote *Queen Mab,* with such annotations as, "All that miserable tale of the Devil, and Eve, and an Intercessor, with the childish mummeries of the God of the Jews, is irreconcilable with the knowledge of the stars. The works of his fingers have borne witness against him" [18]—forgetting that if the stars really are the works of His fingers they bear as eloquent testimony for Him as against false notions of Him, thus leaving Shelley's necessity for atheism limpingly stranded.

As a matter of cold sober fact, Shelley was never able to get away from the Bible, nor did he desire to do so. Like Blake, he raged against accepted notions concerning it; but, like Jefferson, he prepared extracts from it, designed to set forth a morality purged from what he considered biblical mythology.

Believing that a good library consists not of many books but of a few well-chosen ones, he was asked by Medwin which he considered such.

> I'll give you my list: The Greek Plays, Plato, Lord Bacon's Works, Shakespeare, the Old Dramatists, Milton, Goethe and Schiller, Dante, Petrarch and Boccaccio, and Machiavelli and Guicciardini, not forgetting Calderon; and last, yet first, the Bible.[19]

The man who could write of the great poets, "Their errors have been weighed and found to have been dust in the balance; if their sins were as scarlet, they are now white as snow; they have been washed in the blood of the mediator and redeemer, Time," [20] had read his Bible lovingly and well.

In her note on *The Revolt of Islam,* Shelley's wife explains that he prepared for a career in poetry by studying the poets of Greece, Italy, and England, and then she says: "To these may be added a constant perusal of portions of the Old Testament—the Psalms, the Book of Job, the Prophet Isaiah, and others, the sublime poetry of which filled him with delight." [21]

In her note on *Prometheus Unbound* Mrs. Shelley adds that the subjects he meditated for lyrical dramas were three—the Prometheus, which he wrote; the story of Tasso, which he wrote in part; and the Book of Job, which he never wrote, but which he never abandoned as a subject. In her note to the 1816 poems she comments that he had read aloud to her that year the New Testament, *Paradise Lost, The Faerie Queene,* and *Don Quixote.*

But it is in her diary that one sees Shelley most clearly.

1820

Saturday, Jan. 1—Read Livy: work. Shelley reads the Bible, Sophocles and the Gospel of St. Matthew to me.

Wednesday, Jan. 12.—Shelley reads the "Tempest" aloud, and the Bible and Sophocles to himself.

Friday, Jan. 14.—Work. Finish the Book of Proverbs. Shelley reads the Bible and Sophocles.

Friday, Jan. 21.—Shelley reads Sophocles, the Bible, and "King John." Finish Proverbs, Ecclesiastes, and Solomon's Song.

Wednesday, Feb. 2.—Shelley returns; he reads Isaiah aloud to me.

Sunday, Feb. 13.—Shelley reads Jeremiah aloud in the evening.

Thursday, Mar. 9.—Percy has the measles. Shelley reads Hobbes, and Ezekiel aloud.[22]

Whatever one may think of Browning's conclusion that Shelley was steadily moving toward the positions of Paul and David and, had he lived, would have ranged himself with the Christians; however bizarre may seem Shelley's own confession to Thomas Love Peacock of his inclination toward becoming a clergyman; and however astounding may be H. J. Massingham's placing him as "one of the ten Christians since Christ," [23] one thing is indisputable—Shelley did not always beat his luminous wings against the Bible.

Roused to fury at the death of Keats, which he attributed to the harshness of critics, Shelley berated them in biblical invective:

It may well be said that these wretched men know not what they do. . . . What gnat did they strain at here, after having swallowed all those camels? Against what woman taken in adultery dares the foremost of these literary prostitutes to cast his opprobious stone?[24]

From Keats's own poor body "the angel soul that was its guest" fled at the age of twenty-five, but not before Keats had had time to see the splendor of God in this life. He wrote to his brother:

I have no doubt that thousands of people never heard of have had hearts completely disinterested: I can remember but two—Socrates and Jesus—Their histories evince it. What I heard a little time ago, Taylor observe with respect to Socrates, may be said of Jesus— That he was so great a man that though he transmitted no writing of his own to posterity, we have his Mind and his sayings and his greatness handed to us by others. It is to be lamented that the history of the latter was written and revised by Men interested in the pious frauds of Religion. Yet through all this I see his splendour.[25]

And that, after all, is the chief business and glory of angels and archangels—to see and to speak the splendor of God.

22. Paeans of Praise

"Sensible men are all of the same religion."
"Pray, what is that," inquired the Prince.
"Sensible men never tell."

—BENJAMIN DISRAELI[26]

SELDOM has greater diversity of authorship arisen than that of the motley crew of individualists known as the English romanticists. Saints and sinners, lairds and plowboys, rakes and moralists, idealists and cynics, thunderers and warblers, jailbirds, madmen, dope fiends, drunkards, tea swillers—all were here, each busily engaged in chasing his own fascinating rainbow. In one thing they united—a fervent paean of praise for the Bible.

Robert Burns, irrepressible tilter of bottles and petticoats, confessed that so strong was the memory of the daily worship in his father's home that he could never hear the words "Let us worship

God" without a feeling of awe stealing over him. "Holy Willie's Prayer" might caricature a canting churchly hypocrite; the "Address to the Unco' Guid or the Rigidly Righteous" might jeer at the pharisaism of the untempted; "The Holy Fair" might exalt Fun at the expense of Superstition and Hypocrisy; the "Address to the Deil" quaintly harangues the not too dignified but thoroughly ignified

> Auld Hornie, Satan, Nick, or Clootie,
> Wha in yon cavern grim and sootie,

busily splashes the brimstone tub, eager to scald poor wretches—these were but Burns's attacks on sham and narrowness.

On the positive side, few pictures of Scottish life excel the scene in "The Cotter's Saturday Night" where, after supper, the family gathers about the father as he leads in the singing of psalms ("Compared with these, Italian trills are tame," says Burns), following which

> The priest-like father reads the sacred page,
> How Abram was the friend of God on high;
> . . . .
> Or Job's pathetic plaint, and wailing cry;
> Or rapt Isaiah's wild, seraphic fire;
> . . . .
> How He, who bore in Heaven the second name,
> Had not on earth whereon to lay His head.[27]

When thirty, Burns emphatically asserted, in a letter to Mrs. Dunlop: "Still I am a very sincere believer in the Bible; but I am drawn by the conviction of a man, not the halter of an ass." [28]

James Hogg, the Ettrick Shepherd, nursed his childish imagination on the metrical version of the Psalms, as repeated to him by his Scottish mother, and his mind mingled biblical characters with her stories of giants, brownies, kelpies, and other creatures of fairyland. "Before he knew his letters he could say Psalm 122, and as he grew older, he learned by heart the greater part of the Psalter. The Bible was, in fact, the herd-boy's only book." [29]

William Wordsworth was not especially prone either to praise the Bible or to use it, yet he perpetrated nearly fifty rather stiffish "Ecclesiastical Sonnets," in which he sketched the religious history of England from Gregory's "Not Angles but Angels" to his own time. As he led his ten-year-old daughter for an evening walk, he mused didactically,

The holy time is quiet as a Nun
Breathless with adoration;

while his mystery-haunted mind assured him that

. . . the mighty Being is awake,
And doth with his eternal motion make
A sound like thunder—everlastingly.

The prattling child was less solemn than he, so he tried to excuse her:

Thy nature is not therefore less divine;
Thou liest in Abraham's bosom all the year;
And worship'st at the Temple's inner shrine,
God being with thee when we know it not.[30]

In his gigantic monument to personal egotism, "The Prelude," he called the Bible "the voice that roars along the bed of Jewish song," and God's "pure Word by miracle revealed."

Prospective bridegroom Walter Scott was puzzling over what inscription to put upon the sundial he was designing for his soon-to-be-established home. Perhaps he remembered the new book that was then the talk of the town, Boswell's *Life of Johnson,* and the glimpse the author had once caught of the motto inscribed upon the Leviathan of Literature's watch. At any rate he selected the same, "The Night Cometh."

"Work while it is day," watch and sundial seemed to say, "for the night cometh when no man can work."

Thirty-three years later, when informed, while on a visit, of the sudden illness of a friend, Scott announced his immediate departure: "This is a sad warning. I must home to work while it is called day, for the night cometh when no man can work. I put that text many a year ago on my dialstone, but it often preached in vain." [31]

In his Bible, Scott had written:

Within that awful volume lies
The mystery of mysteries!
Happiest they of human race,
To whom God has granted grace

To read, to fear, to hope, to pray,
To lift the latch, and force the way,
And better had they ne'er been born,
Who read to doubt, or read to scorn.[32]

The men and women of its pages escaped inevitably into his books: Nimrod and Job into *Rob Roy,* Abraham and Sarah into *Kenilworth,* Leah and Rachel into *The Abbot,* Moses and the widow of Zarephath into *The Monastery,* Ruth and Naomi into *Guy Mannering,* David and his men in the cave of Adullam into *Red Gauntlet,* Naaman, Elisha, and the widow of Tekoa into *The Heart of Midlothian.*

Stressing, as he does, the impact of the Bible upon history, he brings before us vivid glimpses of its power or abuse: in *Marmion,* the great hymn for the dead, the *Dies Irae,* sung in Melrose Abbey; in the fourteenth chapter of *The Abbot,* that grotesque survival of the Middle Ages, irreverent parody of all held sacred, the Abbot of Unreason; in *Old Mortality* the savagery of warfare over religion, thick-larded with Old Testament imagery, "the law which gave the men of Jericho to the sword of Joshua the son of Nun."

So deeply imbedded in Scott's mind were Bible, hymns, and Prayer Book that they survived when memory of all else was gone. Of his last illness, his son-in-law records:

On re-entering the house, he desired me to read to him from the New Testament, and after that he again called for a little of Crabbe; but whatever I selected from that poet seemed to be listened to as if it made part of some new volume published while he was in Italy. He attended with this sense of novelty even to the tale of Phoebe Dawson, which not many months before he could have repeated every line of. . . . On the contrary, his recollection of whatever I read from the Bible appeared to be lively; and in the afternoon we made his grandson, a child of six years, repeat some of Dr. Watt's hymns by his chair, he seemed also to remember them perfectly. That evening he heard the church service, and when I was about to close the book, said, "Why do you omit the Visitation for the Sick?"—which I added accordingly. . . . After this he declined daily . . . but commonly whatever we could follow him in was a fragment of the Bible (especially the Prophecies of Isaiah and the Book of Job) or some petition in the Litany, or a verse of some Psalm, (in the old Scotch metrical version), or some of the magnificent hymns of the Romish ritual, in which he had always delighted but which probably hung on his memory now in connection with the church services he had attended while in Italy. We very often heard the *Dies Irae;* and the very last *stanza* we could make out was the first of a still greater favorite.

"Stabat Mater dolorosa
Juxta Crucem lachrymosa." [33]

Two years after Charles Lamb left Christ's Hospital, Leigh Hunt entered, and he has left us a clue to one source of Lamb's curious and whimsical use of the Bible: "On Sundays, the school-time of the other days was occupied in church, both morning and evening; and as the Bible was read to us every day before every meal, and on going to bed, besides prayers and graces, we rivalled the monks in the religious parts of our duties." [34]

Lamb found in the vividness and concreteness of the Bible "a wealth of reference and allusion to suit his odd mind. Gideon's fleece and the fall of Jericho enrich his essay on *Christ's Hospital;* the she-bear which avenged Elisha adds humor to the *Old Benchers of the Inner Temple;* the story of Jael plays its part in *Imperfect Sympathies; Mackery End in Hertfordshire* . . . is made more beautiful by his use of the story of Jepthah's daughter." [35]

Lamb impishly exclaims in "All Fools' Day":

Gebir, my old freemason, and prince of plasterers at Babel, . . . bless us, what a long bell you must have pulled, to call your top workman to their *nuncheon* on the low grounds of Shinar! Or did you send up your garlic and onions by a rocket?

In the same essay he confesses:

When a child, with childlike apprehensions, that dived not below the surface of the matter, I read those *Parables.* Not guessing at the involved wisdom, I had more yearnings toward that simple architect that built his house upon the sand than I entertained for his more cautious neighbor. I grudged at the hard censure pronounced upon the quiet soul that kept his talent; and (prizing their simplicity beyond the more provident, and, to my apprehension, somewhat *unfeminine* wariness of their competitors) I felt a kindliness that almost amounted to a *tendre,* for those five thoughtless virgins.[36]

"Poor Lamb," remarked Coleridge, aged twenty-six, setting forth to study in Germany, "if he wants any *knowledge,* he may apply to me." The remark was tactless and Lamb was twenty-three. His revenge was both sweet and neat.

I could not refrain from sending him the following propositions, to be by himself defended or oppugned (or both) at Leipsic or Gottingen.

Theses Quaedam Theologicae

I. "Whether God loves a lying angel better than a true man?"
II. "Whether the archangel Uriel *could* knowingly affirm an untruth, and whether, if he could, he would."
III. "Whether honesty be an angelic virtue . . .?"
IV. "Whether the seraphim ardentes do not manifest their goodness by way of vision and theory? And whether practice be not a sub-celestial, and merely human virtue?"
V. "Whether the higher order of seraphim illuminati ever *sneer?*" etc.[37]

Coleridge had sense enough not to retort at these needle jabs; the breach was healed and a friendship resumed which ended only at Coleridge's death.

In William Hazlitt's "On Persons One Would Wish to Have Seen," Lamb craves sight of Judas Iscariot. "I would fain see the face of him, who, having dipped his hand in the same dish with the Son of Man, could afterwards betray him. I have no conception of such a thing; nor have I ever seen any picture (not even Leonardo's very fine one) that gave me the least idea of it."

As the buzz of comment at this choice dies down, one who supposedly is Leigh Hunt takes up the thought: "There is only one other person I can ever think of after this," he says, without mentioning the name that once put on the semblance of mortality. "If Shakespeare was to come into the room, we should all rise up to meet him; but if that person was to come into it, we should all fall down and try to kiss the hem of his garment,"[38] and there the conversation ends; nothing further can be said.

As young Thomas De Quincey and his three sisters sat evenings in the nursery's firelight, ecstatically reading the Bible and peering at its pictures,

the fitful gloom and sudden lambencies of the room by firelight suited our evening state of feelings; and they suited, also, the divine revelations of power and mysterious beauty which awed us. Above all, the story of a just man—man and yet *not* man, real above all things, and yet shadowy above all things—who had suffered the passion of death in Palestine, slept upon our minds like early dawn upon the waters.[39]

By the time he was fifteen De Quincey knew the New Testament in Greek so thoroughly that it was a subtle controversial weapon in his hands, but he never outlived the emotional impact of those early firelit evenings. They blaze in the lines of "Levana and Our Ladies of Sorrow":

The eldest of the three is named *Mater Lachrymarum,* Our Lady of Tears. . . . She stood in Rama, where a voice was heard of lamentation,—Rachel weeping for her children, and refused to be comforted. She it was that stood in Bethlehem on the night when Herod's sword swept its nurseries of Innocents, and the little feet stiffened forever, which, heard at times as they tottered along floors overhead, woke pulses of love in household hearts that were not unmarked in heaven.[40]

They shine over the slowly moving cadences of that verse (Isaiah 11:9) which he felt to be the most melodious of all the Scriptures: "For the earth shall be full of the knowledge of the Lord, as the waters cover the sea."

But although the romantics agreed in loving the Scriptures, they did not always agree in loving each other.

23. The Satanic School

"You forget," said the devil, with a chuckle, "that I have been evolving, too." —DEAN INGE[41]

ROBERT SOUTHEY was so busy supporting his own family and that of his archangelic brother-in-law, Coleridge, that he must content himself with being something a little lower than the angels—a poet laureate.

When George III died the hard-working official poet saw his duty and overdid it. In the resulting "Vision of Judgment," "George is shown ascending to heaven, being received there in state, and accepting the plaudits of the angels, who behave like court flunkies." [42]

In the preface Southey lashed out against certain of his contemporaries:

> Men of diseased hearts and depraved imaginations, who, forming a system of opinions to suit their own unhappy course of conduct, have rebelled against the holiest ordinances of human society, and hating that revealed religion which, with all their efforts and bravadoes, they are unable entirely to disebelieve, labour to make others as miserable as themselves, by infecting them with a moral virus that eats into the soul! The school which they have set up may properly be called the Satanic school: for though their productions breathe the spirit of Belial in their lascivious parts, and the spirit of Moloch in those loathsome images of atrocities and horrors which they delight to represent, they are more especially characterized by a Satanic spirit of pride and audacious impiety, which still betrays the wretched feeling of hopelessness wherewith it is allied.[43]

It was Byron, Shelley, Hunt, and their friends to whom he thus publicly applied the branding iron—especially Byron, of whom he later wrote: "I have sent a stone from my sling which has smitten their Goliath in the forehead. I have fastened his name upon the gibbet, for reproach and ignomy, as long as it shall endure.—Take it down who can!"[44]

Byron furiously retorted with a challenge to a duel (which his second never delivered) and a hard-hitting counterblast—his own "The Vision of Judgment," in which

> Saint Peter sat by the celestial gate:
> His keys were rusty, and the lock was dull,

since so few applicants had appeared of late, and

> The angels all were singing out of tune,
> And hoarse with having little else to do,
> Excepting to wind up the sun and moon,
> Or curb a runaway young star or two.

The recording angel, however, was so overworked listing vices and woes

> That he had stripped off both his wings in quills,
> And yet was in arrear of human ills.

So very busy indeed was he that,

By the increased demand for his remarks;
Six angels and twelve saints were named his clerks.

St. Peter was rudely aroused from a nap by a rather pert young cherub's announcement that George III was dead and coming to judgment.

"And who *is* George the Third?" replied the apostle:
"What George? what Third?"

Thus Byron poured scorn upon the high sonorities wherewith Southey had reverberated the same announcement through heaven and hell. In the ensuing trial to determine the ex-king's proper destination, Satan is suave and gentlemanly; Peter loses his temper; and the archangel Michael quails. Finally the devil Asmodeus arrives, lugging along Southey as a witness:

"Confound the renegado! I have sprained
My left wing, he's so heavy; one would think
Some of his works about his neck were chained.

Southey, invited to testify, insists upon reading some of his own poetry, after three lines of which,

The angels stopped their ears and plied their pinions;
The devils ran howling, deafened, down to hell;
. . . .
Michael took refuge in his trump—but lo!
His teeth were set on edge, he could not blow!

At the fifth line St. Peter knocked the laureate down, and he fell into one of England's lakes.

All I saw further, in the last confusion,
Was, that King George slipped into heaven for one;
And when the tumult dwindled to a calm,
I left him practising the hundredth psalm.[45]

Of the Satanic school Byron might be, but he knew his Bible. "I am a great reader of those books," he noted, "and had read them through and through before I was eight years old; that is to say, the Old Testament, for the new struck me as a task, but the other as a pleasure." [46] Many of the psalms he knew by memory, and when a Methodistically inclined physician sought to convert him, Byron discussed matters with him for hours at a time, frequently correcting the zealot's biblical quotations.

"When I look at the marvels of creation," he said, "I bow before the majesty of Heaven; and when I experience the delights of life, health, and happiness, then my heart dilates in gratitude towards God for all His blessings"; and once more, "I do not reject the doctrines of Christianity; I only ask a few more proofs to profess them sincerely. I do not believe myself to be the vile Christian which so many assert that I am." [47]

Writing concerning his estranged wife, Byron noted that they had discussed religion frequently, and that many of their misunderstandings had arisen from that, although he felt that their views on religion were fundamentally much alike. She in turn wrote to Crabb Robinson:

> Not merely from casual expressions, but from the whole tenor of Lord Byron's feelings, I could not but conclude that he was a believer in the inspiration of the Bible, and had the gloomiest Calvinistic tenets. To that unhappy view of the relation of the creature to the creator, I have always ascribed the misery of his life. . . . It was impossible for me to doubt, that, could he at once have been assured of pardon, his living faith in a moral duty and a love of virtue ("I love the virtues which I cannot claim") would have conquered every temptation. Judge, then, how I must hate the Creed which made him see God as an Avenger, not a Father. . . . "The worst of it is, I *do* believe," he said. I, like all connected with him, was broken against the rock of Predestination.[48]

Upon the flyleaf of his Bible, Byron copied those same verses which Sir Walter Scott had written and placed in his.

When his daughter Allegra was three months old he wrote to his sister that he had resolved to send for Allegra and place her in a convent that she might become a good Catholic, possibly a nun —"being a character somewhat needed in our family." In her third year he insisted: "The child shall not quit me again to perish of starvation and green fruit, or to be taught that there is no deity." When she died, aged five, he wrote the inscription for her gravestone, ending it with, "I shall go to her, but she shall not return to me, 2 Samuel XII, 23."

That Byron did not follow the precepts of the Bible is obvious;

that he was strongly moved by it is just as obvious. He was a libertine; he was also the author of the *Hebrew Melodies,* those appealing bursts of biblical song, including the familiar "The Destruction of Sennacherib"—"The Assyrian came down like the wolf on the fold"—and the noble lines

> A spirit pass'd before me: I beheld
> The face of immortality unveiled.

His *Cain,* with its angry sullen hero filled with a quenchless thirst for knowledge, brought upon him an avalanche of hostile criticism, whereupon he took from Genesis 6:1, 2—"And it came to pass . . . that the sons of God saw the daughters of men, that they were fair; and they took them wives of all which they chose"—and wrote upon the theme *Heaven and Earth.* It was upon the same theme that Thomas Moore wrote *The Loves of the Angels,* paralleling also Byron's *Hebrew Melodies* with his *Sacred Songs.*

One gasps that American Nathaniel Hawthorne was ever placed in the same pillory as Byron, but so placed he was, and for *The Scarlet Letter:*

> And if as yet there be no reputable name, involved in the manufacture of a Brothel Library, we congratulate the country that we are yet in time to save such a reputation as that of Hawthorne . . .
>
> . . . But when a degenerate Puritan, whose Socinian conscience is but the skimmed-milk of their creamy fanaticism, allows such a conscience to curdle within him, in dyspeptic acidulation, and then belches forth derision at the sour piety of his forefathers—we snuff at him, with an honest scorn. . . .
>
> Why . . . should the taste of Mr. Hawthorne have preferred as the proper material for romance, the nauseous amour of a Puritan pastor, with a frail creature of his charge, whose mind is represented as far more debauched than her body? . . . We honestly believe that *The Scarlet Letter* has already done not a little to degrade our literature . . .
>
> The romance never hints at the shocking words that belong to its things, but, like Mephistopheles, insinuates that the arch-fiend himself is a very tolerable sort of person, if nobody would call him Mr. Devil. We have heard of persons who could not bear the reading of some Old Testament Lessons in the service of the Church: such persons would be delighted with our author's story; and damsels who shrink at the reading of the Decalogue, would probably luxuriate in bathing their imaginations in the crystal of its delicate sensuality . . .

"Brook-Farm" itself could never have been Mr. Hawthorne's home, had not other influences prepared him for such a Bedlam.[49]

This is the Hawthorne whose son could not ever remember his going to church, yet whose wife wrote to her mother, "My dearest love waits upon God like a child." [50] It is the Hawthorne we now blame for being "incorrigible in his homiletic expoundings," and whose book we now consider "a didactic piece warning man that his sins will find him out."

Biblically speaking, Edgar Allan Poe has the reputation of being the Peck's Bad Boy of American literature. "Of all our American writers laying claim to place in the first class Poe shows the least influence of the Bible, and apparently needs it most." [51] Finally, however, someone checked his writings and found 622 quotations, allusions, and reflections of style from the Bible or prayer book.[52]

Of a loquacious fellow Poe wrote:

> To hear him talk, anybody would suppose that he had been at the laying of the corner stone of Solomon's Temple—to say nothing of being born and brought up in the ark with Noah, and hail-fellow-well-met with every one of the beasts that went into it. . . . He explains . . . what Noah said, and thought, while the ark was building, and what the people . . . said about his undertaking such a work; and how the beasts, birds, and fishes looked, as they came in arm in arm; and what the dove did, and what the raven did not.[53]

Scheherazade, he reported, "being lineally descended from Eve, fell heir, perhaps to the whole seven baskets of talk, which the latter lady, we all know, picked up from under the trees in the Garden of Eden." [54] The man who accused his friend Longfellow and others of plagiarism has himself been accused of that sin, so closely does his "The City in the Sea" resemble parts of Isaiah, Ezekiel, and Revelation.[55]

"And a mouse is miracle enough to stagger sextillions of infidels"—no greater or more lasting furore has been created in American literature than was started with the appearance in 1855 of Walt Whitman's *Leaves of Grass,* with its strange, uncouth rhythms patterned upon Old Testament cadences. Anathematized by some and deified by others, its author went his unswerving way, likened to Satan in his filth and Christ in his purity.

Whitman rather bumptiously boasted of his freedom from borrowings, but searchers have found in his work 197 allusions, paraphrases, and quotations (including 37 repetitions) from the Bible, in addition to 97 other more generalized ones.[56] At his funeral, passages from the Beatitudes, from Isaiah, and from John were eloquently recited by a notable battery of eulogists.

In his late-written "November Boughs" he had paid high tribute to the Bible:

> How many ages and generations have brooded and wept and agonized over this book! What untellable joys and ecstasies, what support to martyrs at the stake, from it! . . . To what myriads has it been the shore and rock of safety—the refuge from driving tempest and wreck! Translated in all languages, how it has united this diverse world! . . . Of its thousands there is not a verse, not a word, but is thick-studded with human emotion.[57]

Even the anathematized ones have read their Bible with loving care.

24. New World Symphony

> *"Then shall the kingdom of Heaven be likened unto ten Virginians, which took their lamps, and went forth to meet the bridegroom. . . ."*
>
> *"Well, if the Bible says so it must be true. But I never would have believed that there were five foolish Virginians."*
>
> —ANONYMOUS[58]

WHEN the colonial age had gone and the revolutionary period had passed, literature stood for a time with hesitant feet, timidly testing the new conditions. Authors did not know what to write, what their fellow Americans wished to read.

The Puritan distrust of fiction still lingered when Charles Brockden Brown began his Gothic horror tales, so he stressed the fiction that they were fact. When he started his *Literary Magazine and American Register,* he cautiously assured subscribers that he was "the ardent friend and the willing champion of the Christian religion" and would shape his editorial policy accordingly.

Washington Irving and all his brothers promptly deserted the church of their religion-ridden father as soon as they were able.

When I was a child religion was forced upon me before I could understand or appreciate it. I was made to swallow it whether I would or not, and that, too, in its most ungracious forms. I was tasked with it; thwarted with it; wearied with it in a thousand harsh and disagreeable ways; until I was disgusted with all its forms and observances.[59]

But each one affiliated with a more congenial communion, and it was in rich biblical language that Irving wrote in old age:

Seventy years of age! I can scarcely realize that I have indeed arrived at the allotted verge of existence, beyond which all is special grace and indulgence. I used to think that a man at seventy must have survived everything worth living for. That with him the silver cord must be loosed—the wheel broken at the cistern—that all desire must fail and the grasshopper become a burden yet here I find myself unconscious of the withering influence of age. . . .

"Strange that a harp of a thousand strings
Should keep in tune so long." [60]

Fitz-Greene Halleck's mother was wiser than Irving's father. Under her tutelage Halleck acquired a spiritual and literary liking that was lifelong. Before manhood he had read the Bible through several times and taken from it subjects for several poems. In New York he read several chapters almost daily, and upon retirement to Guilford he reread the entire book six times. Upon being then persistently urged to read Swedenborg, he replied:

The more I strive to find, in new books on sacred subjects, food for the soul's health, in the beauty of their prairies, and their lakes and mountains, the more gladly do I return to the old pastures amid which my youth was nurtured, and to the One Book, now many, many centuries old.[61]

Noah Webster, gripped by the tradition of genteel language just outgrown by England, forsook his blue-backed spellers long enough to "improve" the King James Version of the Bible by removing "many words and phrases very offensive to delicacy, and even to decency"—especially words relating to the body. He banned "teat," "belly," "stones," "stink," "suck," "fornication," "whore," and "womb." Verses he could not successfully mend he excluded altogether.

When William Cullen Bryant was fourteen he had been reared on Sunday morning Bible readings and the hymns of Isaac Watts. He had versified part of Job, read the New Testament in Latin, and "knew the Greek Testament from end to end almost as if it had been English." Having browsed too much on the works of Young and Blair, and others of the graveyard school—who in turn had read Job to excess—he became so addicted to mortuary thoughts that he never recovered: to him the nicest thing about June was that it was a fine month for a funeral. When Hillhouse's *Hadad* precipitated discussion of the propriety of mingling fiction and religious fact, Bryant wrote that the Bible was "as free to the poet as to the pulpit orator." At sixty he circulated among his friends nineteen privately printed hymns.

James Fenimore Cooper was an indefatigable reader of the Bible, his wife and he finally adopting the arduous plan of reading a hundred verses together each morning before breakfast. According to his daughter he was stirred especially by the Psalms, Job, Isaiah, Hebrews, James, and Revelation. This liking was forever creeping into his writing.

In *The Last of the Mohicans* that gaunt modern David, surnamed Gamut—"an unworthy instructor in the art of psalmody," he called himself—thought the loading of cattle boats was "like the gathering to the ark"; and of an army officer's horse he exulted:

> Never before have I behold a beast which verified the true scripture war-horse like this; "He paweth in the valley, and rejoiceth in his strength; he goeth on to meet the armed men. He saith among the trumpets, Ha, ha; and he smelleth the battle afar off, and the thunder of the captains, and the shouting."—It would seem that the stock of the horse of Israel has descended to our own time; would it not, friend? [62]

Gamut's own ungainly mare bore the name of Moses' sister, Miriam, and a psalm sorrowfully sung was the requiem for her murdered colt. A psalm, too, was the evening recreation of the fugitives hidden in the cavern guarded by the thunderous waterfall.

In *Home as Found* Cooper ruffled his contemporaries by caustic comments on the multitudinous church rivalries and the "editor of one of our most decidedly pious newspapers," who reputedly says grace over all that goes from his press and returns thanks for all that comes to it, and throws over everything "a beautiful halo of morality and religion, never even prevaricating in the hottest discussion, unless with the unction of a saint." [63] There is another one who plans an editorial on the impropriety of a rational being's kneeling in public worship: "To my notion, gentlemen and ladies, God never intended an American to kneel." [64]

Cooper helped found the American Bible Society, which in its first hundred years poured into the United States seventy million Bibles or parts of Bibles, and sent forty-five million abroad. Four times it has sought to supply every family in the United States with a Bible, and a fifth time every child under fifteen able to read.

"Pitch it out the window and bounce it comes back again," remarked Ralph Waldo Emerson, whose writing is so Bible-laden

that it appears to the reader as if this Joshua of the nineteenth century had received from Jehovah this new charge: This book of the law shall not depart out of thy mouth, but thou shalt meditate therein day and night, that thou mayest give back its words in quotations, its thought in paraphrase, its wisdom in philosophy, its beauty in metaphor and symbolism (Joshua 1:8).[65]

In his writings biblical chapter and verse have been cited for 529 references.[66]

Emerson likened the Bible to an old Cremona, played upon by the devotion of thousands of years until every word and particle is public and tunable; it is "the most original book in the world," "the alphabet of the nations," "an engine of education of the first power." The name of Jesus "is not so much written as ploughed into the world."

Father Taylor thought Emerson's life better than his theology, snorting of the latter, "Emerson knows no more of the religion of the New Testament than Balaam's ass did of the principles of Hebrew grammar," but saying of the former:

Well, if Emerson has gone to hell, all I can say is that the climate will speedily change and immigration set in. He might *think* this or that, but he *was* more like Jesus Christ than any one I have ever known. The devil will not know what to do with him.[67]

Henry Wadsworth Longfellow, never quite able to come to grips with life, wrote a series of "psalms," one of which—"The Psalm of Life"—remains America's most successful failure, scorned by critics and loved by the people. In "Christus, a Mystery," he tried the structural sequence of the medieval mystery plays. Occasionally he found a happy phrase, as (in *Evangeline*) "Blossomed the lovely stars, the forget-me-nots of the angels," or "Wrestled the trees of the forest, as Jacob of old with the angel," or "Rose on the ardor of prayer, like Elijah ascending to heaven."

Oliver Wendell Holmes said of Elsie Venner, "My poor heroine found her origin not in fable or romance, but in a physiological conception fertilized by a theological dogma." [68] "I have a creed," the Autocrat of the Breakfast Table proclaimed, "none better, and none shorter. It is told in two words,—the two first of the Paternoster. And when I say these words I mean them." [69] *The Professor at the Breakfast Table* closes with an invitation to join with him

> in singing (inwardly) this hymn to the Source of the light we all need to lead us, and the warmth which alone can make us all brothers.
>
> Lord of all being! throned afar,
> Thy glory flames from sun and star,
> Center and soul of every sphere,
> Yet to each loving heart how near! [70]

Henry David Thoreau, "Jeremiah of the Western World," could be savage concerning

> this restless, nervous, bustling, trivial Nineteenth Century. . . . What are men celebrating? They are all on a committee of arrangements, and hourly expect a speech from somebody. God is only the president of the day, and Webster is His orator.[71]

Thoreau came to the Bible late, but when he did discover it he could hardly read it for the glory shining upon its pages.

> The New Testament is an invaluable book, though I confess to having been slightly prejudiced against it in my very early days by the church and the sabbath school, so that it seemed, before I read it to be the yellowest book in the catalogue. Yet I early escaped from their meshes. It was hard to get the commentaries out of one's head and taste its true flavor. I think that Pilgrim's Progress is the best sermon which has been preached from this text; almost all other sermons that I have heard, or heard of, have been but poor imitations of this. It would be a poor story to be prejudiced against the Life of Christ because the book has been edited by Christians. In fact, I love

this book rarely, though it is a sort of castle in the air to me, which I am permitted to dream. Having come to it so recently and freshly, it has the greater charm, so that I cannot find any to talk with about it. . . . Such has been my experience with the New Testament. I have not yet got to the crucifixion, I have read it over so many times. I should dearly love to read it aloud to my friends, some of whom are seriously inclined; it is so good, and I am sure that they have never heard it, it fits their case exactly, and we should enjoy it so much together —but I instinctively despair of getting their ears. They soon show, by signs not to be mistaken, that it is inexpressibly wearisome to them. . . . It is remarkable that, notwithstanding the universal favor with which the New Testament is outwardly received, and even the bigotry with which it is defended, there is no hospitality shown to, there is no appreciation of, the order of truth with which it deals. I know of no book that has so few readers. There is none so truly strange, and heretical, and unpopular. To Christians, no less than Greeks and Jews, it is foolishness and a stumbling block. There are, indeed, severe things in it which no man should read aloud more than once. "Seek first the kingdom of heaven." "Lay not up for yourselves treasures on earth." "If thou wilt be perfect, go and sell that thou hast, and give to the poor, and thou shalt have treasure in heaven." "For what is a man profited, if he shall gain the whole world, and lose his own soul?" . . . Think of this, Yankees! "Verily, I say unto you, if ye have faith as a grain of mustard seed, ye shall say unto this mountain, Remove hence to yonder place, and it shall remove; and nothing shall be impossible unto you." Think of repeating these things to a New England audience! thirdly, fourthly, fifteenthly, till there are three barrels of sermons! Who, without cant, can read them aloud? Who, without cant, can hear them, and not go out of the meeting house? They never *were* read, they never *were* heard. Let but one of these sentences be rightly read, from any pulpit in the land, and there would not be left one stone of that meeting-house upon another.[72]

"Have you made your peace with God?" he was asked. "I did not know we had quarreled," he replied.

"Call me Ishmael," begins Herman Melville's *Moby Dick,* and the names in the book are in keeping—Ahab, John, Nathan, Seth, Samuel, Ezekiel, Peter, Bildad, Jonah, Peleg. The whale is Leviathan. Scriptural references scurry half hidden through Melville's sentences:

The act of paying is perhaps the most uncomfortable infliction that the two orchard thieves entailed upon us.

But what thinks Lazarus? Can he warm his blue hands by holding them up to the grand northern lights?

It is a land of oil, true enough: but not like Canaan; a land, also, of corn and wine. The streets do not run with milk; nor in the spring time do they pave them with fresh eggs.

From these glimmering obliquenesses it is evident that Melville's mind was saturated with the Scriptures.

Not so much the actual words and tales of the Bible but its inmost spirit and essence, its grandeur and tragedy, have passed into the mind of Melville. His Ahab is a modern Job with Job's huge insoluble problem tormenting heart and brain and with Job's large utterance. That agony of long ago in the land of Uz is lived out again before us on the deck of his New Bedford whaler.[73]

When at the age of twenty-nine Melville discovered Shakespeare, he cried out in Bible-laden words:

Ah, he's full of sermons-on-the-mount, and gentle, ay, almost as Jesus. I take such men to be inspired. I fancy this Mons. Shakespeare in heaven ranks with Gabriel, Raphael, and Michael. And if another Messiah ever comes he will be in Shakespeare's person.[74]

But Melville's great love was to the Old Testament, in which are embedded two thirds of his 650 biblical references. These include allusions to more than 100 biblical people, Jonah being mentioned most often, then Adam, Jesus, Noah, Solomon, Job, Abraham, Moses, and Paul.[75]

James Russell Lowell, home for a college vacation, hustled a letter off to a friend: "I mean to read next term, if possible, a chapter in my Bible every night. Indeed, I mean to this vacation." Two years later ("now that I am older"—he was twenty) he was doubting the inspiration of the Old Testament prophets. At twenty-three, "I never before so clearly felt the spirit of God in me and around me." At twenty-five, " 'He leadeth me in green pastures.' " At twenty-six, "Christ has declared war against the Christianity of this world and it must go down." At thirty, "The name of God is written all over the world in little phenomena that occur under our eyes every moment." At thirty-nine he finds the religious press "a true sour-cider press with belly-ache privileges attached." At fifty, "I take great comfort in God. I think He is considerably amused with us sometimes, but that He likes us, on the whole, and would not let us get at the match box so carelessly as He does, unless He knew that the frame of His universe was fireproof." At fifty-seven it was: "As I can't be certain, I won't be positive, and wouldn't drop some chapters of the Old Testament, even, for all the science that ever undertook to tell me what it doesn't know." At sixty-six,

In vain we call old notions fudge,
And bend our conscience to our dealing;
The Ten Commandments will not budge,
And stealing will continue stealing.[76]

While white men in the North were slowly puzzling their way into a new and untried secular literature, black folk in the South were letting their emotions well forth into what was destined to become one of their greatest contributions to the world—"Go Down, Moses," "Deep River," and other poignant spirituals.

25. Wailers in the Wilderness

She overflowes so with the Bible, that she spils it upon every occasion, and will not cudgell her Maides without Scripture. —JOHN EARLE[77]

"WORK, for the night cometh," said Dr. Johnson's watch. "Work, for the night cometh," said Scott's sundial.

"I . . . now say to myself," cried Thomas Carlyle; ". . . Produce! Produce! Were it but the pitifullest, infinitesimal fraction of a Product, produce it, in God's name! 'Tis the utmost thou hast in thee: out with it, then. Up, up! Whatsoever thy hand findeth to do, do it with thy whole might. Work while it is called To-day; for the Night cometh, wherein no man can work." [78]

This shock-headed prophet, everlastingly crying at the top of his voice for everybody to listen to the eternal silences, had no enervating softness in his dyspeptic acerbity. "God the Beautiful," said Leigh Hunt reverently, as the quiet stars emerged upon their evening walk. "God the Terrible," Carlyle retorted.

Again, Carlyle flashed forth:

Two men I honor, and no third. First, the toilworn Craftsman that with earth-made Implement laboriously conquers the Earth, and makes her man's . . .

A second man I honor, and still more highly: Him who is seen toiling for the spiritually indispensable; not daily bread, but the bread of Life . . .

Unspeakably touching is it, however, when I find both dignities united. . . . Sublimer in this world know I nothing than a Peasant Saint, could such now anywhere be met with. Such a one will take thee back to Nazareth itself . . .

Our highest Orpheus walked in Judea eighteen hundred years ago; his sphere-melody flowing in wild native tones took captive the ravished souls of men.[79]

"In the poorest cottage," this Sage of Chelsea pointed out, "are books; is one BOOK, wherein for several thousands of years the spirit of man has found light, and nourishment, and an interpreting response to whatever is deepest in him." [80]

"David's life and history, as written for us in those Psalms of his," he proclaimed, "I consider to be the truest emblem ever given of a man's moral progress and warfare here below." [81]

To the Psalms also his beautiful, high-strung wife, ill and weak, struggling to accomplish her daily tasks without repinings or fears, turned in desperation:

Have mercy upon me, O Lord, for I am weak: O Lord, heal me; for my bones are vexed. My soul is also sore vexed: but Thou, O Lord, how long? Return, O Lord, deliver my soul: oh save me for thy mercies' sake (Psalm 6:2-4).[82]

But it is Job which lifts Carlyle to his feet in exultation:

I call that, apart from all theories about it, one of the grandest things ever written with pen. . . . A noble Book; all men's book! It is our first, oldest statement of the never-ending problem—man's destiny, and God's ways with him here in this earth. And all in such free flowing outlines: grand in its sincerity, in its simplicity, in its epic melody, and repose of reconcilement. . . . So *True* everywhere; . . . Such living likenesses were never since drawn. Sublime sorrow, sublime reconciliation: oldest choral melody as of the heart of mankind;—so soft, and great; as the summer midnight, as the world with its seas and stars! There is nothing written, I think, in the Bible or out of it, of equal literary merit.[83]

But greater to him than the Psalms, greater than Job, was the figure of the Man of Galilee. "Look on our divinest Symbol," invited the shaggy prophet, "on Jesus of Nazareth, and his Life, and his Biography, and what followed therefrom. Higher has the human Thought not yet reached." [84]

Tempestuous Walter Savage Landor, whose stupendous scholarship in *Imaginary Conversations* delights critics and dazes readers, bent his proud head before the Bible, "a Book which, to say nothing of its holiness or authority, contains more specimens of genius and taste than any other volume in existence." [85]

Thomas Babington Macaulay knew almost by heart the Bible, *Paradise Lost, Pilgrim's Progress,* and even the eight volumes of *Clarissa*. Gifted with one of the most retentive memories in modern times, he once remarked that if all copies of *Paradise Lost* and *Pilgrim's Progress* were destroyed from the face of the earth, he would undertake to reproduce them from memory.

Whenever he wished to learn a new language—Spanish, Portuguese, German—he began with the Bible, thus learning the main vocabulary and grammar without bothersome reference books. Once he amused himself deciphering a Lapponian New Testament, with the help of a Norwegian dictionary. Reared in an atmosphere surcharged with biblical study, he surpassed all his great contemporaries, except possibly Ruskin, in his use of it.

In parliament, in clubs, in correspondence, in the editor's chair, in the service of the East India Company, in drawing rooms, in the literary offices of the historian, in good-natured banter of his sisters, this atmosphere of the Bible is like an aureole about him.[86]

To him it was indispensable for literary culture. It was the book "which if everything else in our language should perish would alone suffice to show its beauty and power."

"A person," Macaulay remarked, after discussing with Lady Holland the history of the word "talents," "who professes to be a critic in the delicacies of the English language ought to have the Bible at his fingers' ends." [87] Macaulay so had it. Describing the licentiousness which swept England after the Restoration, he put it thus:

The Puritans boasted that the unclean spirit was cast out. The house was empty, swept, and garnished; and for a time the expelled tenant wandered through dry places, seeking rest and finding none. But the force of the exorcism was spent. The fiend returned to his abode and returned not alone. He took with him seven other spirits more wicked than himself. They entered in and dwelt together, and the second possession was worse than the first.[88]

But England's plight, while pitiable, was not hopeless:

England is sleeping on the lap of Delilah, traitorously chained, but not yet shorn of strength. Let the cry be once heard—the Philistines be upon thee; and at once that sleep will be broken; and those chains will be as flax in the fire.[89]

Reviewing Mill's essay on government, Macaulay was merciless:

We are sick, it seems, like the children of Israel, of the objects of our old and legitimate worship. We pine for a new idolatry. All that is costly and all that is ornamental in our intellectual treasures must be delivered up and cast into the furnace—and there comes out this Calf![90]

Christianity is more endangered by alliances with power than by opposition:

Those who thrust temporal sovereignty upon her do but treat her as their prototypes treated her Author. They bow the knee and spit upon her. They cry "Hail!" and smite her on the cheek; they put a scepter in her hand, but it is a fragile reed; they crown her, but it is with thorns; they cover with purple the wounds which their own hands have inflicted upon her, and inscribe magnificent titles over the cross on which they have fixed her to perish with ignominy and pain.[91]

He thought it an extraordinary thing for the admirers of Shaftesbury "to whitewash an Ethiopian by giving him a new coat of blacking."

Another man much in the public eye was John Henry Newman. "I was brought up from a child to take great delight in reading the Bible," he related in *Apologia pro Sua Vita,* wherein he traced the steps which led him to be first an eloquent Anglican minister and leader in the Tractarian movement, then to the authorship of "Lead, Kindly Light," and finally into the Roman Catholic faith. His pellucid prose glows with imagination and emotion. In Gethsemane, in that most awful hour, knelt the Saviour of the world, putting off the defences of His divinity, dismissing His reluctant Angels, who in myriads were ready at His call, and opening His arms, baring His breast, sinless as He was, to the assault of His foe,—of a foe whose breath was a pestilence, and whose embrace was an agony.[92]

He seems an actual onlooker at the feast of the Pharisees:

It was a formal banquet, given by a rich Pharisee, to honour, yet to try, our Lord. Magdalen came, young and beautiful, and "rejoicing in her youth," "walking in the ways of her heart and the gaze of her eyes:" she came as if to honour that feast, as women were wont to honour such festive doings, with her sweet odours and cool unguents for the forehead and hair of the guests.[93]

Heartbreaking is his farewell to the Church of England:

O mother of saints! O school of the wise! O nurse of the heroic! Of whom went forth, in whom have dwelt, memorable names of old, to spread the truth abroad, or to cherish and illustrate it at home! O thou, from whom surrounding nations lit their lamps! O virgin of Israel! wherefore dost thou now sit on the ground and keep silence, like one of the foolish women who were without oil on the coming of the bride-groom? Where is now the ruler in Zion, and the doctor in the Temple, and the ascetic on Carmel, and the herald in the wilderness, and the preacher in the market-place? where are thy "effectual fervent prayers," offered in secret, and thy alms and good works coming up as a memorial before God? [94]

But like a benediction is his quiet prayer:

May He, as of old, choose "the foolish things of the world to con-found the wise, and the weak things of the world to confound the things which are mighty!" May He support us all the day long, till the shadows lengthen, and the evening comes, and the busy world is hushed, and the fever of life is over, and our work is done! Then in His mercy may He give us a safe lodging, and a holy rest, and peace at the last.[95]

John Ruskin was rich; he owned beautiful manuscript Bibles, psalters, and missals—thirteenth- and fourteenth-century ones, and even a precious tenth-century copy, rarity indeed. And with a disregard that would make a collector tear his hair in frenzy, he scribbled over even the rarest, "Well questioned, Jude!" or, "I have always a profound sympathy with Thomas." They were irreplaceable, but they were for use—or so John Ruskin thought.

"Once in his rooms at Oxford," relates a friend, "I remember getting into a difficulty about the correct quotation of some passage. 'Haven't you a concordance?' I asked.

" 'I'm ashamed to say I have,' he said.

"I did not quite understand him. 'Well,' he explained, 'you and I oughtn't to need Cruden.' " [96] Such was the biblical knowledge of this "Elisha to Carlyle's Elijah."

In his late sixties Ruskin recorded that he had had Scott's novels and Pope's *Iliad* for his childhood weekday reading, *Robinson Crusoe* and *Pilgrim's Progress* on Sundays—"my mother having it deeply in her heart to make an evangelical clergyman of me," and having, like Hannah, devoted her son to God before he was born. "Very good women are remarkably apt to make away with their children prematurely, in this manner," he remarked dryly.

> My mother forced me, by steady daily toil, to learn long chapters of the Bible by heart; as well as read it every syllable through, aloud, hard names and all, from Genesis to the Apocalypse, about once a year.

This, while it failed to make a clergyman of him ("He would have been a bishop," his wine-seller father regretted, with real tears in his eyes), had a formative effect upon his literary style.

> Once knowing the 32nd of Deuteronomy, the 119th Psalm, the 15th of 1st Corinthians, the Sermon on the Mount, and most of the Apocalypse, every syllable by heart, and having always a way of thinking with myself what words meant, it was not possible for me, even in the foolishest times of youth, to write entirely superficial or formal English.[97]

Ruskin firmly believed the Bible to be the thought-energizer of all Europe: He said: "What would the intellect of Europe have become without Biblical literature? . . . What literature could have taken its place, or fulfilled its function, though every library in the world had remained unravaged, and every teacher's truest words have been written down?" [98] The rhythms of the Bible play like rich organ music through his own majestic prose, as in his arraignment of England at the close of *Modern Painters:*

So far as in it lay, this century has caused every one of its great men, whose hearts were kindest, and whose spirits most receptive of the work of God, to die without hope:—Scott, Keats, Byron, Shelley, Turner. Great England, of the Iron-heart now, not of the Lion-heart; for these souls of her children an account may perhaps be one day required of her.

She has not yet read often enough that old story of the Samaritan's mercy. He whom he saved was going down from Jerusalem to Jericho—to the accursed city (so the old Church used to understand it). He should not have left Jerusalem; it was his own fault that he went out into the desert, and fell among the thieves, and was left for dead. Every one of these English children, in their day, took the desert bypath, as he did, and fell among fiends—took to making bread out of stones at their bidding, and then died, torn and famished; careful England, in her pure, priestly dress, passing by on the other side. So far as we are concerned, this is the account *we* have to give of them.

So far as *they* are concerned, I do not fear for them;—there being one Priest who never passes by. The longer I live, the more clearly I see how all souls are in His hand—the mean and the great. Fallen on the earth in their baseness, or fading as the mist of the morning in their goodness; still in the hand of the potter as the clay, and in the temple of their master as the cloud. It was not the mere bodily death that He conquered—that death had no sting. It was this spiritual death that He conquered, so that at last it should be swallowed up—mark the word—not in life but in victory. As the dead body shall be raised in life, so also the defeated soul to victory, if only it has been fighting on its Master's side, has made no covenant with death; nor itself bowed its forehead for his seal. Blind from the prison-house, maimed from the battle, or mad from the tombs, their souls shall surely yet sit, astonished, at His feet who giveth peace. . . . I do not know what my England desires, or how long she will choose to do as she is doing now; —with her right hand casting away the souls of men, and with her left the gifts of God.[99]

In Ruskin, as in Macaulay and Newman, the cadences of the West had met the cadences of the biblical East, and the two had been forever wedded together.

What really happened to Ruskin was that the Biblical rhythms were literally beating through his nerves as he grew. His whole organism was tuned up to that vibration until, when he became a man, he was permanently rhythmic.[100]

THE BIBLE ENCOUNTERS CERTAIN DRAGONS

26. Apes and Agonies

Backward, turn backward, oh Time, in your flight,
Make me a monkey again, just for tonight!
—HARRY BENTON[1]

CHARLES DARWIN! A hawk among the theological dovecotes. What a fluttering of wings!

When *The Origin of Species* was published in 1859 an era had come to an end; many people feared that the biblical world had come to an end. Shouted Benjamin Disraeli:

What is the question now placed before society with the glib assurance which to me is most astonishing? That question is this: Is man an ape or an angel? I, my Lord, am on the side of the angels. I repudiate with indignation and abhorrence those new fangled theories.[2]

Carlyle was equally emphatic. "I have no patience whatever," he snarled, "with these gorilla damnifications of humanity."[3]

When Bishop Wilberforce, facing Thomas Huxley with suave and smiling insolence, softly inquired whether it was through his grandfather or his grandmother that he claimed descent from a monkey, Huxley whispered, "The Lord hath delivered him into my hands." Then he rose and said that no man had reason to be ashamed of having an ape for a grandfather; an ancestor one should be ashamed of would be a man of restless and versatile intellect who plunged into scientific debates without knowing the field, and sought to obscure by rhetoric the point at issue, and distract the audience from it by skilled appeals to prejudice. A woman in the audience fainted.

Huxley coined "agnostic" to express his noncertainty, but, though a believer in secular education without theology, he made an eloquent plea for retention of the Bible in the schools:

Take the Bible as a whole; make the severest deductions which fair criticism can dictate . . . and there still remains in this old literature a vast residuum of moral beauty and grandeur. And then consider the great historical fact that for three centuries this book has been woven into the life of all that is best and noblest in English history; that it has become the national epic of Britain, and is familiar to noble and simple from John o' Groat's House to Land's End . . . that it is written in the noblest and purest English, and abounds in exquisite beauties of a merely literary form; and, finally, that it forbids the veriest hind who never left his village to be ignorant of the existence of other countries and other civilizations; and of a great past, stretching back to the farthest limits of the oldest nations in the world. By the study of what other book could children be so much humanized, and made to feel that each figure of that vast historical procession fills, like themselves, but a momentary space in the interval between two eternities, and earns the blessings or curses of all time, according to its efforts to do good and hate evil, even as they also are earning their payment for their work.[4]

Huxley's own mind went familiarly to biblical imagery. "Why I was christened Thomas Henry I do not know," he comments, "but it is a curious chance that my parents should have fixed for my usual denomination upon the name of that particular Apostle with whom I have felt most sympathy." [5] When he was trying to gain a foothold in the world of science,

during the four years of our absence, I sent home communication after communication to the "Linnean Society," with the same result as that obtained by Noah when he sent the raven out of his ark. Tired at last of hearing nothing about them, I determined to do or die, and in 1849 I drew up a more elaborate paper and forwarded it to the Royal society. This was my dove, if I had only known it.[6]

"I am more inconsolable than Jonah!" he wrote when a flowering clematis died.

But nothing could erase the fact that a mortal shock had been given many traditional ideas of religion. The dreadful hammers of the geologists seemed tapping at the Rock of Ages itself; the Garden of Eden was reverting to a most pestiferous jungle.

How did these things affect literature? Robert Browning cheerfully ignored the whole sorry mess. Reared in a home where he was surrounded with books—"notably old and rare Bibles"—and having been "passionately religious under the direct influence of his mother and the Bible as she read it," he had married a woman who responded to the threescore biblical allusions in his courting letters with more than twice as many in her replies.[7]

His "Paracelsus" had "sought to comprehend the works of God, and God himself, and all God's intercourse with the human mind." Then had followed *Saul,* with Israel's stricken monarch seen through the dew-fresh eyes of eager young David; "Christmas-Eve and Easter-Day," supposedly written in response to his wife's suggestion that he ought to give some expression to his own religious thinking; "An Epistle Containing the Strange Medical Experience of Karshish, the Arab Physician," wherein the puzzled medico is trying to diagnose the case of the risen Lazarus; and a series of dramas under the heading "Bells and Pomegranates," a title taken from the description of Aaron's robe in the twenty-eighth chapter of Exodus.

These came before the publication of Darwin's book; afterward Browning imperturbably published "Rabbi Ben Ezra," with its blatant optimism; "A Death in the Desert," describing the cave-hidden death of John, the last of those who knew Christ in the flesh; *The Ring and the Book,* with 568 references drawn from 28 books of the Old Testament and 25 of the New; "La Saisiaz," with its untroubled ending: "Well? Why, he at least believed in Soul, was very sure of God."

Sometimes Lord Tennyson was very sure of God, sometimes not so sure. Before *The Origin of Species* appeared Tennyson had sweated melodiously through his own Gethsemane of doubt and faith as recorded in *In Memoriam,* where his moods range from

> I falter where I firmly trod,
> And falling with my weight of cares
> Upon the great world's altar-stairs
> That slope thro' darkness up to God,
> I stretch lame hands of faith, and grope,
> And gather dust and chaff . . .

to the whistling-in-the-dark certainty of

> Strong Son of God, immortal Love,
> Whom we, that have not seen thy face,
> By faith, and faith alone, embrace,
> Believing where we cannot prove.[8]

Using biblical references in profusion—Van Dyke[9] located more than six hundred, Robinson[10] (unless her lists overlap) two thousand—Tennyson published no poem on a biblical subject, "Rizpah" being but a modern instance clothed in biblical allusion.

A curious hedging, concealed by a camouflage of forthrightness, marked his attitude. "They are right, and they are not right. They mean that and they do not. . . . I hate to be tied down to say, '*This* means *that*,'"[11] he responded when the Bishop of Ripon asked him if those were right who interpreted the three queens accompanying King Arthur upon his last voyage as being Faith, Hope, and Charity.

"The truth against the world," he laid in tiles upon the floor of his entrance hall, and then refused to state his creed lest people misunderstand. He arranged for an early copy of *The Origin of Species,* and became in the minds of both resulting camps the reconciler of science and religion, without clarifying his mind upon either. "Do you think there is any really insuperable obstacle or series of obstacles between science and religion?" Dr. Dabbs asked him, only to receive Tennyson's usual evasive reply: "I have tried to say my say about that in "In Memoriam.""[12] He helped organize the Metaphysical Society that men might try to thresh out such problems, then seldom attended and almost never took part.

"That's what I should do, if I thought there was no future life," he remarked of a suicide: yet when queried concerning his belief in a hereafter, he replied, "SIR, I have been considering your questions, but I am not a God or a disembodied spirit that I should answer them."[13]

He constantly expressed great love for the Scriptures, longing for "a translation of the *Iliad* and *Odyssey* into Biblical prose," and reading not only the Scriptures themselves but also "all notable works within his reach concerning the Bible."

For the tenth chapter of Revelation he had "boundless admiration"; for the Sermon on the Mount, "measureless admiration"; and he called the parables "perfection, beyond compare." The "It is finished" of the Christ upon the cross was to him "the most pathetic utterance in all history"; and Isaiah, "a very great artist —everything he says is complete and perfect." He learned Hebrew that he might translate (and then never did) the book of Job —"a book in which he had always rejoiced," and which he considered "one of the greatest of books." In Hebrew also he read the Song of Solomon and the book of Genesis. A week before he died he read Job and Matthew. Yet in the last three days of his life it was not the Bible but his volume of Shakespeare for which he continually called. "Where is my Shakespeare? I must have my Shakespeare"; and he died with it, not the Bible, in his hand.

Matthew Arnold, torn from the religious certainties which had nourished his great father, yearned "to make reason and the will of God prevail." In *Culture and Anarchy* he tried to evaluate the respective parts which Hebraism and Hellenism have played in life, Hebraism being the body of religious and moral thought which has emerged in Protestantism. Encouraged by the reception accorded this effort, he plunged boldly into the complex and hard-fought theological questions which had come once more into the foreground of men's thought, writing in quick succession *St. Paul and Protestantism, Literature and Dogma, God and the Bible, Last Essays on Church and Religion.*

His ideas shocked some and irritated others, as did his cocksureness. He "knows exactly what St. Paul and St. John meant to say; knows what faith is and what God is and what religion is and how it originated, and does not hesitate to tell us in emphatic language." [14] But back of the controversialist is the poet, a man of haunting sadness over the loss of the full-flowing faith of his forefathers.

> The Sea of Faith
> Was once, too, at the full, and round earth's shore
> Lay like the folds of a bright girdle furled.
> But now I only hear
> Its melancholy, long, withdrawing roar,
> Retreating, to the breath
> Of the night-wind, down the vast edges drear
> And naked shingles of the world.[15]

Arthur Hugh Clough, Dr. Thomas Arnold's pet pupil, was a chronic prize winner at school and "a holy, beautiful example," who was anxious to extend his acquaintance—"for there is a great deal of evil springing up in the school, and it is to be feared that the tares will choke much of the wheat." [16] His sensitive spirit suffered keenly under the cloudy doubts and controversies which arose, until he could lash out in pain,

Thou shalt have but one God only; who
Would be at the expense of two?

and

No graven image may be
Worship'd, except the currency.[17]

Across the Atlantic James Russell Lowell solved the whole problem of evolution in the easiest of all manners—by shutting his eyes.

I think the evolutionists will have to make a fetish of their protoplasm before long. Such a mush seems to me a poor substitute for the Rock of Ages. . . . At any rate I find a useful moral in the story of Bluebeard. We have the key put into our hands, but there is always one door it is wisest not to unlock.[18]

Again he said,

I am a conservative (warranted to wash) and keep on the safe side—with God as against Evolution.

And once more,

I continue to shut my eyes resolutely in certain speculative directions.[19]

Emerson was more philosophical. "I would rather believe," he said mildly, "that we shall rise to the state of the angels than that we have fallen from it." [20]

But in general Americans did not for some years worry overmuch about evolution; they were undergoing another kind of agony—civil war.

27. Grapes of Wrath

The ant has made himself illustrious
Through constant industry industrious.
So what?
Would you be calm and placid
If you were full of formic acid?

—OGDEN NASH[21]

IN THE 1840's the Millerites were proclaiming the imminent Judgment Day, and stores were advertising Resurrection Pills and

"Muslin for Ascension Robes." But it was a different sort of day of judgment that was brewing.

One of the shrewdest abolition moves was to organize group singing to stir antislavery enthusiasm. Special hymns were written, and antislavery songbooks—such as *Songs of the Free, The Anti-Slavery Harp,* and *Songs of Freedom*—aided the "Monthly Concerts of Prayer for Emanicipation."

Thus the technique of the religious revival and the Fourth of July rally was utilized by the abolitionists, as it was later to be used by the temperance forces and the equal suffrage advocates. "From Greenland's Icy Mountains," "My Faith Looks Up to Thee," and "America" were used as models, thus transferring their hallowed associations to the new crusade.

Even the meek grew stern. At the age of seven, John Greenleaf Whittier knew whole chapters of the Bible so well that his father would proudly invite visitors at the quarterly meeting to begin some passage in the middle of a chapter and let the lad finish. He would dream scenes from *Pilgrim's Progress*. Grown a poet, the gentle Quaker wrote biblically as naturally as he breathed. In 285 of his poems are 816 passages drawn directly or indirectly from the Bible, 284 from the Gospels alone.[22] God was "The Eternal Goodness":

> I know not where His islands lift
>   Their fronded palms in air;
> I only know I cannot drift
>   Beyond His love and care.[23]

But as the storm clouds gathered about slavery,

> He flung aside his silver flute,
>   Snatched up Isaiah's stormy lyre;
> Loosened old angers, pent and mute;
>   Startled the iron strings with fire.[24]

When Daniel Webster made his "Seventh of March" speech in 1850 in defense of the Fugitive Slave Law, Whittier's biblical, lashing "Ichabod" (the glory is departed) was born.

William Lloyd Garrison, with his antislavery *Liberator,* cried out: "I am in earnest—I will not equivocate—I will not excuse—I will not retreat a single inch—AND I WILL BE HEARD."

The source of Garrison's power was the Bible. From his earliest days he read the Bible constantly, and prayed constantly. It was with this fire that he started his conflagration. . . . To Garrison, the Bible was the many-piped organ to which he sang the song of his life, and the arsenal from which he drew the weapons of his warfare. I doubt if any man ever knew the Bible so well, or could produce a text to fit a political issue with such startling felicity as Garrison. Take, for example, the text provided by him for Wendell Phillips' speech on the Sunday morning following Lincoln's call for troops in 1861. "Therefore thus saith the Lord; ye have not hearkened unto me in proclaiming liberty everyone to his brother, and every man unto his neighbor; behold, I proclaim a liberty for you, saith the Lord, to the sword, to the pestilence, to the famine."

I doubt whether Cromwell or Milton could have rivalled Garrison in this field of quotation; and the power of quotation is as dreadful a weapon as any which the human intellect can forge. From his boyhood upward, Garrison's mind was soaked in the Bible and in no other book. His "causes" all are drawn from the Bible, and most of them may be traced to the phrases, and thoughts of Christ, as for instance Peace (Peace I give unto you), Perfectionism (Be ye therefore perfect), Non-resistance (Resist not evil), Anti-sabbatarianism (The Lord is Lord of the Sabbath). . . . He even arrived at distrusting the Bible itself, perceiving that the Bible itself is often a tyrant. . . . All this part of Garrison's mental activity is his true vocation. Here he rages like a lion of Judah.[25]

"Take away the Bible," he said, "and our warfare with oppression, and infidelity, and intemperance, and impurity is removed—we have no authority to speak and no courage to act." [26]

Julia Ward Howe took life seriously. In addition to helping edit an antislavery paper, she penned "The Battle Hymn of the Republic," with its

Mine eyes have seen the glory of the coming of the Lord:
He is trampling out the vintage where the grapes of wrath are stored,

which later gave John Steinbeck the title for his *Grapes of Wrath.* She advised:

If you have at your command three hours *per diem,* you may study art, literature, and philosophy . . .

If you have but one hour a day, read philosophy, or learn foreign languages, living or dead.

If you can command only fifteen or twenty minutes a day, read the

Bible with the best commentaries, and daily a verse or two of the best poetry.[27]

Harriet Beecher Stowe tried to estimate the effect of that same Book upon her own life and that of New England:

> I am certain that the constant contact of the Bible with my childish mind was a great mental stimulant as it certainly was the cause of a singular and vague pleasure. The wild, poetic parts of the prophecies, with their bold figures, vivid exclamations, and strange oriental names and images, filled me with a quaint and solemn delight.
>
> Just as a child, brought up under the shadow of the great cathedrals of the Old World, wandering into them daily, at morning or eventide, beholding the many-colored windows flamboyant with strange legends of saints and angels, and neither understanding the legends nor comprehending the architecture, is yet stilled and impressed, till the old minster grows into his growth and fashions his nature, so this wonderful old cathedral book insensibly wrought a sort of mystical poetry into the otherwise hard and sterile life of New England.
>
> Its passionate oriental phrases, its quaint pathetic stories, its wild, transcendent bursts of imagery, fixed an indelible mark in my imagination. . . . I think no New Englander brought up under the regime established by the Puritans could really estimate how much of himself had actually been formed by this constant face-to-face intimacy with Hebrew Literature.[28]

It wrought upon her own mind to such an extent that she wrote *Uncle Tom's Cabin* and thus helped touch off the war.

When the conflict came, there was in the White House a man who, when asked his creed, quoted Micah 6:8: "He hath showed thee, O Man, what is good; and what doth the Lord require of thee, but to do justly, and to love mercy, and to walk humbly with thy God?"—words later selected by President Eliot of Harvard as the most fitting in all literature to stand on the walls of the nation's library.

Lincoln was no churchman, but he knew the Bible intimately, having in his youth "mastered it absolutely; mastered it as later he mastered only one or two other books, notably Shakespeare; mastered it so that he became almost 'a man of one book.' "[29] At ten he had read it thrice. According to Lord Charnwood he had also stored in his memory a large number of hymns. In the White House "he was an early riser; when I came on duty, at eight in the morning, he was often already drest and reading in the library. ... And the book? It was the Bible which I saw him reading while most of the household slept." [30] "I am profitably engaged in reading the Bible," he wrote to Speed the year before his death; "take all of this book that you can upon reason and the balance upon faith, and you will live and die a better man." [31]

In November, 1863, his secretary, John Hay, wrote in his diary:

> In the morning of the 19th, I got a beast and rode out with the President and suite to the Cemetery in procession. The procession formed itself in an orphanly sort of way, and moved out with very little help from anybody; and after a little delay Mr. Everett took his place on the stand—and Mr. Stockton made a prayer which thought it was an oration—and Mr. Everett spoke as he always does, perfectly; and the President, in a firm free way, with more grace than is his wont, said a half-dozen lines of consecration—and the music wailed, and we went home through crowded and cheering streets.[32]

Those "half-dozen lines of consecration" so casually dismissed by Lincoln's secretary were the Gettysburg speech, which

> for all time will be among the memorable utterances of men. . . . Yet in large measure it is thus great, because through it there vibrate the deep organ notes of Bible words.
>
> Take away the words of Bible memory and the phrases born of Bible reading and Bible inspiration—"fourscore," "conceived," "brought forth," "dedicated," "consecrated," "gave their lives that that nation might live," "hallow," "resting-place," "increased devotion," "the last full measure," "unfinished work," "long endure," "resolve," "new birth," "perish from the earth"—and much of the solemn music has died out forever from this inspiring Battle Hymn of consecration to the Republic.[33]

While Lincoln was in the White House there was in a federal military prison a young Southerner, from a town in the Deep South where "the only burning issues were sprinkling versus immersion, freewill versus predestination," and the South against the damyankees. After the war Sidney Lanier went forth to a life of ruined health, music, poverty, and to an early death. To him two books—the Bible and Shakespeare—were indispensable. Of certain poets he said:

And if any one should say there is not time to read these poets, I reply with vehemence that in any wise distribution of your moments, after you have read the Bible and Shakespeare, you have no time to read anything until you have read these.[34]

Out of "The Marshes of Glynn" rings his magnificent cry of faith:

As the marsh-hen secretly builds on the watery sod,
Behold I will build me a nest on the greatness of God:
I will fly in the greatness of God as the marsh-hen flies
In the freedom that fills all the space 'twixt the marsh and the
  skies:
By so many roots as the marsh-grass sends in the sod
I will heartily lay me a-hold on the greatness of God:
Oh, like to the greatness of God is the greatness within
The range of the marshes, the liberal marshes of Glynn.[35]

About this time Christmas cards were invented, and Emily Dickinson watched her masculine acquaintances going off to war, thinking perhaps of the valentines she had sent them in happier days. One had ended,

I am Judith, the heroine of Apocrypha, and you the orator of Ephesus. . . . Alpha shall kiss Omega—we will ride up the hill of glory—Hallelujah, all hail.[36]

And another read,

Put down the apple, Adam,
And come along with me.[37]

Dowered with a father who wished his children to read nothing but the Bible, she had attended Mount Holyoke Seminary, which supplied wives to so many missionaries that it was nicknamed "Miss Lyon's Missionary Rib Factory." Here she dutifully agonized over her soul at intervals, until she finally made gay, almost flippant, peace with God. "Papa above," she twinklingly addressed Deity, as she impishly suggested a heavenly mansion for the rat, where, safe in seraphic cupboards, it could nibble as time's cycles wheel pompously away.

"I don't like Paradise," she pouted, "because it's Sunday all the time." [38] Again, "God is rather stern with his 'little ones,'" she commented; "'a cup of cold water in my name' is a shivering legacy February mornings." But she gently forgave him, for he is "our old neighbor, God," who good-naturedly "permits industrious angels afternoons to play." Like Blake, she found God and his patriarchs very real.

If God had been here this summer, and seen the things *I* have seen—I guess he would think His Paradise superfluous. Don't tell Him for the world, though, for after all He's said about it, I should like to see what He *was* building for us, with no hammer, and no stone, and no journeyman either.[39]

Her mother caught a burdock on her shawl, "So we know that the snow has perished from the earth. Noah would have liked mother." Snow blows through the window; "I think God must be dusting." Shall we "see God"? "Think of Abraham strolling with him in genial promenade." God's table is too high for us, "Unless we dine on tiptoe."

I have found friends in the wilderness. You know Elijah did, and to see the "ravens" mending my stockings would break a heart long hard,[40]

she commented gratefully; and,

Bravo, Lou, the cape is a beauty, and what shall I render unto Fanny, for all her benefits? I will take my books and go into a corner and give thanks.[41]

I am in a hurry—this pen is too slow for me—"It hath done what it could." [42]

She did not feel at home among her contemporaries: "They talk of hallowed things aloud, and embarrass my dog." Of her family she said, impishly, "They are religious, except me, and address an eclipse, every morning, whom they call their 'Father.' "

Had she caught cold? Her letter

will tell you some queer stories about me,—how I sneezed so loud one night that the rest of the family thought the last trump was sounding, and climbed into the currant-bushes to get out of the way; how the rest of the people, arrayed in long night-gowns folded their arms, and were waiting; but this is a wicked story. . . .[43]

Out in New Mexico after the war, General Lew Wallace—mortified by his abysmal ignorance of religion, and gripped since childhood by the majestic beauty of "Now when Jesus was born in Bethlehem of Judea"—was writing *Ben Hur,* while somewhere in the night lurked Billy the Kid, boasting, "I mean to ride into the plaza at Santa Fe, hitch my horse in front of the palace, and put a bullet through Lew Wallace." Billy the Kid failed, and *Ben Hur* reaped a double victory. "Long before I was through with my book," confessed the author, "I became a believer in God and the Christ." [44] In the thirty-third year after the book was published a new issue of a million copies was called for and distributed.[45]

Not the shattering of long-held theological beliefs, not the "baboon jargon" of new science, not a great and bitter war—not any of these things, nor all of them, could wrench the Bible from men's tongues.

28. These Restless Heads

During the nineteenth century a Quaker was forty times as likely as a non-Quaker to be elected to the Royal Society.

—J. B. S. HALDANE[46]

Some people are just naturally Pollyanna,
While others call for sugar and cream and strawberries on
their manna.[47]

THE novelists of nineteenth-century England were not naturally Pollyanna, nor were they overfond of fictional cream, sugar, and strawberries, but they did consume a striking amount of biblical manna.

For *Vanity Fair,* William Makepeace Thackeray took a title from *Pilgrim's Progress,* added a motto from the Scriptures, and wrote to his Bible-drilling mother: "What I want is to make a set of people living without God in the world (only that is a cant phrase)." [48] Four of the greatest scenes in his books are: Pendennis praying beside his dying mother; Amelia reading the story of Samuel to her boy before his departure; returned Esmond standing with Lady Castlewood where "are woven the lofty harmonies of the one hundred and twenty-sixth psalm"; and the final *"Adsum"* of Colonel Newcome.

"She was nourished on the Bible," exclaimed M. Héger of his English student Charlotte Brontë.

Of the few months which intervened between his marriage to George Eliot and her death, J. W. Cross wrote:

> We generally began our reading at Whitley with some chapters of the Bible, which was a very precious and sacred Book to her, not only from early associations, but also from the profound conviction of its importance in the development of the religious life of man. She particularly enjoyed reading aloud some of the finest chapters of Isaiah, Jeremiah, and St. Paul's epistles.[49]

"One hardly knows whether to call them novels or sermons," wrote John Kelman of the books of this woman who had broken away from her father's faith. And of her works another critic asserted:

> Her characters are always quoting the Bible. They preach a great deal. She tells us that she herself wrote Dinah Morriss's sermon on the Green with tears in her eyes. . . . George Eliot has no principal story which has not in it a church, and a priest or a preacher, with all that they involve.[50]

So robust was the religion of Charles Kingsley that it was called "muscular Christianity," somewhat to his annoyance. He liked especially the Seventy-sixth Psalm, from which John Endicott's party had taken the name "Salem" for their first settlement in America.

George Meredith disliked the clergy, thought Darwin had ruined Genesis, doubted the value of the Old Testament as juvenile reading, had Sir Austin Feverel (remembering woman's part in the Fall) call the instinct of sex the Apple Disease, yet noted:

> The Bible is outspoken about facts, and rightly. It is because the world is pruriently and stupidly shamefaced that it cannot come into contact with the Bible without convulsions.[51]

Charles Reade, upon suggestion of Sir Edwin Arnold, took up the Old Testament and read it as if it were a book new to him. It was his judgment that

> Jonah is the most beautiful story ever written in so small a compass. It contains 48 verses and 1328 English words. One does not go far in an English novel in 1328 words. There is growth of character, a distinct plot worked out without haste or crudity. Only a great artist could have hit on a perfect proportion between dialog and narrative.[52]

"If a man is not his own neighbor, who is?" inquires one of Charles Dickens' characters, thus illustrating Dickens' use of the Bible. Of 845 quotations traced in his work, 365 are from the Bible, nearly half being from Genesis, Matthew, and Luke.

"Never abandon the wholesome practice of saying your own private prayers, night and morning," he advised his son. "I have never abandoned it myself and I know the comfort of it"; [53] and again,

> I put the New Testament among your books for the very same reason and with the very same hopes that made me write an easy account of it for you when you were a little child—because it is the best book that ever was or ever will be known in the world.[54]

This veneration was constantly creeping into his work:

> Harriet complied and read—read the eternal book for all the weary and the heavy laden; for all the wretched, fallen, and neglected of this earth—read the blessed history, in which the blind, lame, palsied beggar, the criminal, the woman stained with shame, the shunned of all our dainty clay, has such a portion, that no human pride, indifference, or sophistry, through all the ages that this world shall last, can take away, or by the thousandth atom of a grain reduce—read the ministry of Him who, through the round of human life, with all its hopes and griefs, from birth to death, from infancy to age, had sweet compassion for, and interest in, its every scene and stage, its every suffering and sorrow.[55]

In another book, Little Jo is dying:

> "I'll say anything as you say, sir, for I know it's good."
> "OUR FATHER."
> "Our Father!—yes, that's wery good, sir."
> "WHICH ART IN HEAVEN."
> "Art in Heaven—is the light a comin', sir?"
> "It is close at hand. HALLOWED BE THY NAME!"
> "Hallowed be—thy—"
> The light is come upon the dark benighted way. Dead!
> Dead, your Majesty. Dead, my lords and gentlemen. Dead, Right Reverends and Wrong Reverends of every order. Dead, men and women, born with heavenly compassion in your hearts. And dying thus around us, every day.[56]

And now the French guillotine thirsts for the blood of Sidney Carton and the poor little seamstress.

"Is the moment come?"
"Yes."
She kisses his lips; he kisses hers; they solemnly bless each other. The spare hand does not tremble as he releases it; nothing worse than a sweet, bright constancy is in the patient face. She goes next before him—is gone; the knitting-women count Twenty-Two.
"I am the Resurrection and the Life, saith the Lord: he that believeth in me, though he were dead, yet shall he live: and whosoever liveth and believeth in me shall never die." [57]

But it is not only in heart-wrenching scenes that Dickens draws upon the Bible. "The still small voice . . . is a-singing comic songs within me," reports Simon Brass in *The Old Curiosity Shop*. On the Peggoty walls David Copperfield saw colored pictures—"Abraham in red going to sacrifice Isaac in blue, and Daniel in yellow cast into a den of green lions."

Dickens' pen name, "Boz," was a shortening of Boses, a mispronunciation of Moses, his nickname for a younger brother in honor of the *Vicar of Wakefield*.

The *Christmas Carol* sold six thousand copies the first day, and has maintained its supremacy for nearly a century, having been translated into a multitude of languages, "including the Chinese."

As for Thomas Hardy, a current critic rules:

It was on the heath, not in the church, that Hardy was at home. Earth-mother, not sky-father, cared for his humble people on their way through "life's little ironies," and received them kindly again when they were tired of walking . . . as a novelist, Hardy was not conscious of the divine.[58]

But his people walked in a Bible-freighted atmosphere. Their very names—Jacob Smallbury, Joseph Poorgrass, who felt "like a man out of the Bible," Reuben Dewy, Elias Spinks, Cain Ball (whose mother, "not being a Scripture-read woman, made a mistake at his christening, thinking 'twas Abel killed Cain"), Benjamin Pennyways, Laban Tall, Mark Clark, John Coggan, Matthew Moon, Andrew Randle, Gabriel Oak, Bathsheba Everdene, Susanna Bridehead—betray that fact.

"And what had I better do about it, sir?" inquired Tess of

D'Urbervilles' father, when he learns that he is descended from an anciently honorable family.

"O—nothing, nothing; except chasten yourself with the thought of 'how are the mighty fallen!' "

In the ancient rite of club walking there were a few older women "to whom the years were drawing nigh when each should say, 'I have no pleasure in them.' " Tess's brother, Abraham, viewing the stars, asked "how far away those twinklers were, and whether God was on the other side of them."

"Is he gone to heaven?" he sobbed over the grave of the horse. Bringing the chickens to the blind woman reminded Tess of a confirmation, in which Mrs. D'Urberville was the bishop, the fowls the young people presented, and herself and the maidservant the parson and curate of the parish bringing them up. When Tess was raped, the novelist cried out:

> But where was Tess's guardian angel? Where was the Providence of her simple faith? Perhaps like that other god of whom the ironical Tishbite spoke, he was talking, or he was pursuing, or he was in a journey, or peradventure he was sleeping and was not to be awaked. . . . But though to visit the sins of the fathers upon the children may be a morality good enough for divinities, it is scorned by average human nature.[59]

THY, DAMNATION, SLUMBERETH, NOT
2 Pet. ii. 3

painted the evangelistic sign painter, and

THOU, SHALT, NOT, COMMIT——

Tess loved the chanting at the church, and the Psalms, and the Morning Hymn. "Like all village girls, she was well grounded in the Holy Scriptures, and had dutifully studied the histories of Aholah and Aholibah, and knew the inferences to be drawn therefrom."

As her baby lay dying she

> thought of the child consigned to the nethermost corner of hell, as its double doom for lack of baptism and lack of legitimacy; saw the archfiend tossing it with his three-pronged fork, like the one they used for heating the oven on baking days,

and, daring the wrath of God, she woke her brothers and sisters to help her baptize it.

"SORROW, I baptize thee in the name of the Father, and of the Son, and of the Holy Ghost."

She sprinkled the water, and there was silence.

"Say 'Amen,' children."

The tiny voices piped in obedient response: "Amen!"

Tess went on:

"We receive this child"—and so forth—"and do sign him with the sign of the Cross." [60]

And so the sad tale rolls on to its destined end, bathed in the Bible continually. In four of Hardy's novels 132 passages (and that reckoning is not claimed as complete) have been found influenced by it.

The splendour of much of its language appears to fascinate him, and on occasions he can quote famous passages with great effect. Most noteworthy perhaps is the tragic horror of the scene, when Jude lies dying in his room at Christminster, and he whispers passage after passage from the book of Job, expressive of the thought of the poet, that it had been better had he never been born, and these solemn utterances are punctuated by the sounds of cheering from the crowds watching the sports, and by the echoes of the concert in the theatre near by.

Another classical example is to be found in *The Mayor of Casterbridge,* when Henchard, maddened by jealousy, demands that the choir shall sing the terrible comminatory verses of the 109th Psalm. A similar passage is to be found in the short story entitled "What the Shepherd Saw," when the lad is made to swear a terrible oath not to reveal what he has seen. The passage is obviously based on the curses contained in Deuteronomy 29. It is magnificent in its fierce splendour: "May all the host above, angels and archangels and principalities and powers—punish me; may I be tormented wherever I am—in the house or in the garden, in the fields or in the roads, in church or in chapel, at home or abroad, on land or on sea; may I be afflicted in eating or in drinking, in growing up and in growing old, in living and dying, inwardly and outwardly, and for always, if I ever speak of my life as a shepherd boy, or of what I have seen done on this Marlbury down. So be it, and so let it be. Amen and Amen." [61]

At the close of *The Woodlanders,* as Marty South stands by Giles Winterbourne's grave:

"Now, my own, own love," she whispered, "you are mine, and on'y mine; for she has forgot 'ee at last, although for her you died. But I—whenever I get up I'll think of 'ee, and whenever I lie down, I'll think of 'ee. Whenever I plant the young larches I'll think that none can plant as you planted; and whenever I split a gad, and whenever I turn the cider-wring, I'll say none could do it like you. If I ever forget your name, let me forget home and Heaven!—But no, no, my love, I never can forget 'ee; for you was a *good* man, and did good things." [62]

"Does she speak from the Psalms, or the Canticles, or the sixth chapter of Deuteronomy, or the parables, or Job, or Ecclesiastes? It is hard to say. But in her speech is the beauty and melody of all their most beautiful passages." [63]

Even when Hardy rages in his own person at the pruderies of his time, he turns to the Bible for his imprecations.

The crash of broken commandments is as necessary an accompaniment to the catastrophe of a tragedy as the noise of drum and cymbals to a triumphal march. But the crash of broken commandments shall not be heard; or, if at all, but gently, like the roaring of Bottom—gently as any sucking dove, or as 'twere any nightingale, lest we should frighten the ladies out of their wits. More precisely, an arbitrary proclamation has gone forth that certain picked commandments of the ten shall be preserved intact—to wit, the first, third, and seventh; that the ninth shall be infringed but gingerly; the sixth only as much as necessary; and the remainder alone as much as you please, in a genteel manner.[64]

The restless, questioning heads of the nineteenth-century novelists teemed with the imagery of the Book.

29. Lame Hands of Faith

If I were a cassowary
On the plains of Timbuctoo,
I would eat a missionary,
Prayer-book, Bible, and hymn-book too.

—ANONYMOUS[66]

LATE in the nineteenth century the so-called fleshly school of poetry arose, and it was berated as the Satanic school had been.

There is no limit to the fleshliness, and Mr. Rossetti finds in it its own religious justification. . . . Whether he is writing of the holy Damozel, or the Virgin herself, or of Lilith, or of Helen, or of Dante, or of Jenny the street-walker, he is fleshly all over, from the roots of his hair to the tips of his toes,

raged one critic, complaining bitterly that Mr. Rossetti was always attitudinizing, posturing, and describing his own exquisite emotions.

> Mr. Rossetti . . . is the Blessed Damozel leaning over the "gold bar of heaven"; . . . he is Lilith the first wife of Adam; he is the rosy Virgin of the poem called "Ave."[66]

The charge was not that the fleshly school failed to use biblical and related subjects, but that it used them in unconventional ways, particularly in the "amorous-religious" tone characteristic of A. C. Swinburne, who utilized biblical imagery to give new and sensuous delights.

"That book," said Swinburne, picking up a copy of Lamb's *Specimens of the English Dramatic Poets,* "taught me more than any other book in the world," and then he added, "—that and the Bible." And it was of Swinburne that Edmund Gosse said:

> It is noticeable that there is a distinct strain of the religious controversersialist running through his poems. It is true that it expresses itself in antagonism, but it is violently there; the poet is not a lotus-eater who has never known the Gospel, but an evangelist turned inside out.[67]

Another poet, James Thomson, "B. V."—self-styled "Ishmael in the desert"—was also an evangelist turned inside out, this time from an overdose of harsh religion in his childhood. But the Bible was not long absent from his thoughts, irreverent as they frequently were:

> God helpeth him who helps himself,
> . . . .
> Which seems to mean—You do the work,
>   Have all the trouble and the pains,
> While God, that Indolent Grand Old Turk,
>   Gets credit for the gains.[68]

Wilfrid Scawen Blunt confessed to his diary that he would rather have written the Song of Songs than all the rest of literature.

Alongside these were the Christian mystics. Christina Rossetti told Katharine Tynan that she never stepped upon any scrap of torn paper, but stooped and lifted it from the mud, since it might have the Holy Name written or printed upon it.[69]

Then there were the varied chants of

> the Roman Catholic poets—Gerard Manley Hopkins, with his harsh, tortured, Donne-like measures; Coventry Patmore, with his philosophy of devout eroticism; Francis Thompson, tempestuous as a river; Alice Meynell, aloof and restrained; and, beating his drum strangely among these, the young man Kipling with his Lord God of Sabaoth.[70]

To take but one from all this group, and that the bedraggled author of the majestic *Hound of Heaven:*

> The Bible as an influence from the literary standpoint has a late but important date in my life. As a child I read it, but for its historical interest. Nevertheless, even then I was greatly, though vaguely, impressed by the mysterious imagery, the cloudy grandeurs, of the Apocalypse. Deeply uncomprehended, it was, of course, the pageantry of an appalling dream; insurgent in darkness, with wild light flashing through it, terrible phantasms, insupportably revealed against profound light, and in a moment no more; on the earth hurryings to and fro, like insects of the earth at a sudden candle; unknown voices uttering out of darkness darkened and disastrous speech; and all this in motion and turmoil, like the sands of a fretted pool. Such is the Apocalypse as it inscribes itself on the verges of my childish memories. In early youth it again drew me to itself, giving to my mind a permanent and shaping direction. In maturer years Ecclesiastes (casually opened during a week in the Fens) masterfully affected a temperament in key with its basic melancholy. But not till quite later years did the Bible as a whole become an influence. Then, however, it came with decisive power. But not as it had influenced most writers. My style, being already formed, could receive no evident impress from it; its vocabulary had come to me through the great writers of our language. In the first place its influence was mystical; it revealed to me a whole scheme of existence, and lit up life like a lantern.[71]

And then the erstwhile leader of the decadents, Oscar Wilde, fallen like a meteor from the zenith of aestheticism to the horror of a prison cell, came from jail doors to write one more poem, the terrible, Bible-haunted *Ballad of Reading Gaol,* and to hand to a friend his prison-written prose *"De Profundis,"* with its poignant meditations concerning the character of Jesus.

If ever I write again, in the sense of producing artistic work, there are just two subjects on which and through which I desire to express myself: one is "Christ as the precursor of the romantic movement in life": the other is "The artistic life considered in its relation to conduct." [72]

Meanwhile, his play *Salomé,* barred from England, was being brilliantly presented abroad.

Sickly, indomitable Robert Louis Stevenson's first literary laurels were gained at the age of four when (not being yet able to write) he, in contest with his cousins, dictated his winning *History of Moses.* "My parents and Cummy" (his nurse), he notes, "brought me up on the Shorter Catechism, porridge, and the Covenanters." His earliest memories were "of nursery rhymes, the Bible, and Mr. McCheyne." *Pilgrim's Progress* grins impudently from the signature to one of his letters:

I am yours,
Mr. Muddler,
Mr. Addlehead
Mr. Wandering Butterwits
Mr. Shiftless Inconsistency
Sir Indecision Contentment.[73]

In "Books Which Have Influenced Me," he recorded:

The next book, in order of time, to influence me, was the New Testament, and in particular the Gospel according to St. Matthew. I believe it would startle and move any one if they could make a certain effort of imagination and read it freshly like a book, not droningly or dully like a portion of the Bible. Any one would then be able to see in it those truths which we are all courteously supposed to know and all modestly refrain from applying. But upon this subject it is perhaps better to be silent.[74]

But where the Bible was concerned Stevenson found it hard to be silent.

Written in the East, those characters live forever in the West; written in one province, they pervade the world; penned in rude times, they are prized more and more as civilization advances.[75]

The master of Ballantrae's way was a good way not to read it:

> He tasted the merits of the work like the connoisseur he was; and would sometimes take it from my hand, turn the leaves over like a man that knew his way. . . . But it was singular how little he applied his reading to himself; it passed high above his head like summer thunder: . . . the tales of David's generosity, the psalms of his penitence, the solemn questions of the Book of Job, the touching poetry of Isaiah—they were to him a source of entertainment only, like the scraping of a fiddle in a change-house.[76]

To Edmund Gosse, Stevenson raged at the Revised Version:

> Since the new Version, I do not know the proper form of words. The swollen, childish, and pedantic vanity that moved the said revisers to put "bring" for "lead" is a sort of literary fault that calls for an eternal hell; it may be quite a small place, a star of the least magnitude, and shabbily furnished; there shall ________, ________, the revisers of the Bible and other absolutely loathsome literary lepers, dwell among broken pens, bad, *groundy* ink and ruled blotting paper made in France—all eagerly burning to write, and all inflicted with incurable aphasia. I should not have thought upon that torture had I not suffered it in moderation myself, but it is too horrid even for a hell; let's let 'em off with an eternal toothache.[77]

That strange, far-wandering star of literature, Lafcadio Hearn, felt the same way about the revision: "Have you seen the revised Old Testament? How many of our favorite and beautiful texts have been marred! I almost prefer the oddity of Wickliffe." [78] His pronouncements are curious, and essentially these: The English Bible is, next to Shakespeare, the greatest English classic, and it will have much more influence upon the language of the English race than Shakespeare. For the advanced student of literature some knowledge of the finest books of the Bible is simply indispensable. One should read at least Genesis, Exodus, Ruth, Esther, The Song of Songs, Proverbs, and—above all—Job, since one can scarcely read any English masterpiece in which there is not reference to them. Ecclesiastes is admirable world poetry of philosophical importance. There is very little in the New Testament equal to the Old Testament in literary value.

> Indeed, I should recommend the reading only of the closing book—the book called the Revelation. . . . Whether one understands the

meaning of this mysterious text makes very little difference; the sonority and beauty of its sentences, together with the tremendous character of its imagery, cannot but powerfully influence mind and ear, and thus stimulate literary taste.[79]

And then Hearn makes a startling suggestion, which he thinks "is not altogether true, but it is partly true":

> Some persons have ventured to say that it is only since Englishmen ceased to believe in the Bible that they began to discover how beautiful it was.

Hall Caine had made repeated trips to the Bible for themes for his novels:

> I think that I know my Bible as few literary men know it. There is no book in the world like it, and the finest novels ever written fall far short in interest to any one of the stories it tells. Whatever strong situations I have in my books are not my creation, but are taken from the Bible. *The Deemster* is the story of the Prodigal Son. *The Bondman* is the story of Esau and Jacob. *The Scapegoat* is the story of Eli and his sons, but with Samuel as a little girl; and the *Manxman* is the story of David and Uriah.[80]

Now, as if to confute Hearn's idea, he plunged into the forty years of work which was to result in his thirteen hundred pages of the *Life of Christ* and add one more to the 3,152 books on that topic already upon the shelves of the British Museum.

In 1893 Alexandre Dumas, *fils,* and English Canon F. W. Farrar locked horns. "I do not see why the dramatic poet should not present sacred legends as well as historical facts," wrote Dumas.

"Any attempt to bring Biblical personages upon the boards would most deeply wound the feelings of millions of serious Englishmen," retorted Farrar.

Dramatist Henry Arthur Jones took up the fight and made a few pointed comments.

> Those who deny its lawfulness must either prove that the Bible has no relation whatever to men's lives and conduct, in which case it lies outside the dramatists' concern; or they must show reasons why this great storehouse of human experience, of man's joys and sorrows, loves and hates, hopes, fears and aspirations should be locked to the dramatist and freely opened to the painter, poet and musician. . . .

Throughout that great perpetual comedy which the Spirit of the Universe provides for the infinite delectation of His elect, in the present condition of religion and religious affairs and professors in England; throughout that most constant succession of varied scenes, here a bishop of Lincoln judgment, and there an epileptic dance to General Booth's pipes and tabors; here a churchyard riot over a dead dissenter, and there low comedian Spurgeon railing at the stage; at one moment a Church congress fixing its barometer at rain or fine, and piously imagining that it regulates the weather; at another, Mr. Gladstone and Professor Wace swallowing the whole herd of Gadarene swine with the ease of a conjuror swallowing a poker.—Oh, my brother Englishmen, do step out of the ranks for a moment and look at this medley, motley rout of your own notions and whims that you have deified and called by the name of religion! Do look at yourselves! See what tricks and antics you are playing before high heaven!—throughout all this whirling march of fantasy, and humour, and comic incident, beyond all conception of playwright's brain, no group gives a keener relish to the cosy observer than the group of British art and literature blessed and anointed by the dew of British gospel grace and the oil of British godly zeal!

It never could be to the advantage of the English drama to make one of that group and get itself blessed and anointed along with the religious magazines and religious etchings and engravings. . . . I am considering the danger to art, not the danger to religion. . . . What has our modern drama to do with the stale, withered husks that our two hundred sects fodder themselves on?

But I see no reason why the great human stories of the Bible should not be utilized on our stage. I am speaking here with the utmost reverence for a Book, or rather Books, which I have dearly loved and constantly studied from my childhood, which have been my classics, and which will, I hope, when our nation has purged its eyesight so as to be able to understand them, continue to be "a master light to all our seeing." It is with the greatest love for these Books that I hold it to be quite lawful to treat certain of their stories upon our modern stage. . . . The English theatre could not possibly make a worse use of the Bible than the sects have done, or misunderstand it so completely.[81]

It was a very pretty quarrel while it lasted.

In America, Whitman's friend John Burroughs, at the age of forty-seven, had been examining his own Bible reading with interest:

How different the feeling and purpose with which I sit down to read the Bible from that which Father and Grandfather sat down to read it! I sit down to read it as a book, a curious and instructive legend, and to suck the literary value out of it; they sat down to read it as the autocratic word of God; to learn God's will toward them; and to feed their souls upon the spiritual riches it contains. It was a solemn and devout exercise with them; with me it is simply a search after truth and beauty, in a mood more critical than devout. Yet I cannot help it. I cannot read it otherwise. I cannot believe the Bible in the way that Father and his father believed it. It would be hypocrisy to pretend I could. This reading of it was the best for them, and is not my reading of it the best for me? There is perhaps more religion in the eye with which I read Nature, than there was in the eye with which they read it; and there was more religion in the eye with which they read the Bible than in mine. . . . When you begin honestly to reason about the Bible, and to exclude all feeling, experience, sentiment, you cannot believe it other than a great primitive book—the greatest, perhaps, because the most human. The word of God, truly, as all good and wise books are the word of God, as every wise word ever spoken by man is the word of God. The Bible is naked, as it were; faces entirely toward God and eternity; whereas, other books face toward the world, or toward man. Its burden is God, righteousness, etc. There is no pride of letters here, no pride, only fear and awe and worship. It transcends all other books so much in this respect that we have come to look upon it as a record of God's word—an exceptionally inspired book. It is full of error, of course, full of human infirmities, but it is flooded with the sentiment of God, and the aspiration of the soul toward the infinite; and this is the main matter.[82]

His fellow naturalist John Muir should have hated the Bible:

The learning of a certain number of Bible verses every day was a task which his father superimposed upon the school lessons, and exacted with military precision. "By the time I was eleven years old," wrote the victim of this method, "I had about three-fourths of the Old Testament and all of the New by heart and by sore flesh. I could recite the New Testament from the beginning of Matthew to the end of Revelation without a single stop." [83]

Not even this harsh regimentation could ruin it for him.

I remember as a great and sudden discovery that the poetry of the Bible, Shakespeare and Milton was a source of inspiring, exhilarating, uplifting pleasure, and I became anxious to know all the poets, and saved up small sums to buy as many of their books as possible.[84]

The nineteenth century went out resoundingly escorted by Kipling's "Recessional" and Markham's "The Man with the Hoe." The latter caused such an uproar as was never, before or since, roused by any other single poem from an unknown author. Turned into more than forty languages, it has been reprinted twelve thousand times and parodied four thousand. Within a year of its appearance five thousand answers to it had been penned. San Francisco newspapers ran daily columns of comment for a year, after which one ran a daily page for six months more.[85]

Charles M. Sheldon's *In His Steps* sold eight million copies.

30. Playing Hob With Holy Things

God said, Let there be light, and there was light. O thank you, Sir, said the Owl and the Bat; then we're off.

—DEAN INGE[86]

IT WAS now evident that the nineteenth century had made drastic changes in the Bible's influence. Out of the new science and out of the Civil War had come a defensive surge of religious emotion. This showed itself in a marked stimulation to hymn writing. "The fifteen years following the publication of Darwin's *Origin of Species* produced more ringing lyrics of religion than has any period of the same length in English history." [87]

It soon became evident that the ancient wall between sacred and secular, which had been built up since medieval times, had been breached at many points. The rise of the fleshly school of poetry had not been an isolated phenomenon. The unabashed use of the Bible was creeping into new and strange places. The nineteenth century had experimented, too, with that secularization of hymns which was to spread far in the twentieth century, until men might lustily sing:

May the Great Kiwanian
Fill your heart and mine
With enduring courage,
Faith and peace divine.[88]

Another symptom was a new flood of humor, much of which was based upon the Bible. In the Middle Ages men had jested scandalously at the most sacred things. Shakespeare's time might still take liberties with the holy text. "I have received my proportion like the prodigious son." The Puritans, however, had tried to repress such unseemliness. Only slowly did biblical jesting regain some measure of respectability in England. Even then it was rather sedate. At Cambridge the dozen lowest ranking graduates—"passed by a miracle"—became "the twelve apostles." Because the heads of houses sat in the gallery at the university church, it was "Golgotha," "the place of skulls." Someone pointed to the Master of St. John's riding by on horseback—"St. John's head on a charger." The Thirty-nine Articles were "forty stripes save one." At Parliament's closing, withdrawal of bills not passed for lack of time was "the massacre of the Innocents." Thin William Pitt was "the bottomless Pit." But the jests were few and stately. In literature a scattered few authors—notably Sterne, and Barham in his *Ingoldsby Legends*—had allowed themselves wide latitude of laughing. But it is in nineteenth-century America that the Bible becomes the jesters' handbook.

As soon as the Widow Bedott succeeds in marrying the Reverend Shadrack Sniffles she yearns for art in the parsonage.

Them Scripter pieces that Sister Myers has got hangin' in her front parlor—them she painted afore she was married, strikes me as wonderful interestin', especially the one that represents Pharoh's daughter a findin' Moses in the bulrushes. Her parasol and the artificials in her bunnit is jest as natral as life. And Moses, he looks so cunnin' a lyin' there asleep, with his little coral necklace and bracelets on. O it's a sweet picter. And I like that other one, tew, that represents Pharoh a drivin' full tilt into the Red Sea after the Isrelites. How natral his coat-tails flies out.[89]

Mrs. Partington's late husband is a lineal descendant of one "Seek-the-Kingdom-Continually Partyngetonne," who had come from the old country, "by water probably," in the early days, largely to escape bill collectors.

Here the voice of the dunner was done, and Seek, under his own vine and pine-tree, worshipped God and cheated the Indians according to the dictates of his own conscience and the custom of the times.[90]

Mrs. Partington is never backward in saying what she thinks she means:

I am not so young as I was once, and I don't believe I ever shall be, if I live to the age of Samson, which, heaven knows as well as I do, I don't want to, for I wouldn't be a centurion or an octagon and survive my factories and become idiomatic by any means.[91]

Rascally Simon Suggs, seeking whom he may devour financially, attends a camp meeting, where sinners are being dragged to the mourner's bench, and hears a perspiring worker lead forward another candidate:

He tried to argy wi' me—but bless the Lord!—he couldn't do that nother! Ha! Lord! I tuk him, fust in the Old Testament—bless the Lord!—and I argyed him all thro' Kings—and I throwed him into Proverbs—and from that, here we had it up and down, Kleer down to the New Testament, and then I begun to see it work him!—then we got into Matthy, and from Matthy right straight along to Acts; and *thar* I throwed him! Y-e-s L-o-r-d! [92]

Simon fakes conversion, takes up a collection for building a church in his own neighborhood, and fades away with the funds.

"All I've got to say," remarks William Tappan Thompson's matter-of-fact Hoosier—when assured by the minister that a traveler fresh from Palestine had seen Lot's wife still standing in an open field as a pillar of "real genewine good salt"—"is, *If she'd drap'd in Indiany, the cattle would lick'd her up long ago!*" [93]

"And he played on a harp uv a *thou*-sand strings—sperits of just men made perfeck"—such is the singsong text for the utterly disjointed sermon of Henry Taliaferro Lewis' liquor-trading, flatboat-captaining, Hard-Shell Baptist preacher, found "somewhar 'tween the fust chapter of the book of Generation, and the last chapter of the book of Revolutions." [94]

Petroleum Volcano Nasby—"Lait Paster uv the Church uv the Noo Dispensashun"—enlivens Civil War and Reconstruction days with his mordant wit.

The South is the Prodigal Son. We went out from our father's house on an expedition wich hezn't proved altogether a success. We spent our share uv of the estate, and a little more. . . . We hev got to the husk stage uv our woe, and wood be tendin' hogs, ef the armies, wich past through these countries, hed left us any. We hev come back. In rags and dirt we hev wended our way to Washington, and ask to be taken back, Now, don't our father, the Government, fulfill the Skripter? Why don't it see us afar off, and run out to meet us? Why don't it put onto us a purple robe? Where's the ring for our finger, and the shoes for our feet? And where's the fatted calf we ought to kill? My brethren, them Ablishnists is worse than infiddles—while they preach the gospel they won't practise it.[95]

Artemus Ward, traveling showman beloved of Lincoln, is a worthy successor to Thomas Chandler Haliburton's mythical Yankee peddler who sold the gullible farmers "Polyglot Bibles *(all in English)*." With superb democracy Ward invites the visiting Prince of Wales to

be just & be Jenerus, espeshully to showmen, who hav allers bin aboosed sins the daze of Noah, who was the fust man to go into the Menagery bizniss, & ef the daily papers of his time air to be beleeved Noah's colleckshun of livin wild beests beet annything ever seen sins, tho I make bold to dowt ef his snaiks was ahead of mine.[96]

And again:

"Wiltist thou not tarry hear in the Promist Land?" sed several of the miserabil critters [the Mormon women].

"Ile see you all essenshally cussed be4 I wiltist!" roared I, as mad as I cood be at thare infernu noncents. I girdid up my Lions & fled the seen. I packt up my duds & left Salt Lake, which is a 2nd Soddum & Gemorrer.[97]

"You confounded ignoramus, did you ever hear of Adam?" snarls a traveling seatmate at Charles Farrar Browne, Ward's creator, who had pretended ignorance of every topic of conversation suggested.

"What was his other name?" inquires Browne, innocently.[98]

"I would rather be damned to John Bunyan's heaven than read that," roars Mark Twain of a certain book. He is equally harsh with God.

If I were going to construct a God I would furnish him with some ways and qualities and characteristics which the present [Bible] lacks.

He would not stoop to *ask* for any man's compliments, praises, flatteries; and he would be above *exacting* them. I would have him as self-respecting as the better sort of man in these regards. . . .

He would not be a jealous God—a trait so small that even men despise it in each other.

He would not boast. . . .

There would not be any hell—except the one we live in from the cradle to the grave.

There would not be any heaven—of the kind described in the world's Bibles.

He would spend some of His eternities in trying to forgive Himself for making man unhappy when He could have made him happy with the same effort and He would spend the rest of them in studying Astronomy.[99]

Nevertheless, Twain is constantly being drawn to the Bible as to a magnet. From it he gets "Eve Speaks," with the primal parents' puzzlement over the strange death-sleep of stricken Abel, and "Satan's Diary," with its epigrammatic "The Family think ill of death—they will change their minds." From it he gets "Noah's Ark," in which a German ship inspector tries to apply modern shipping regulations to the craft. Few parts of *Innocents Abroad* are more devastating in their attack upon sentimentalism than his eloquent tearfulness over his ancestor Adam's tomb—though, as he admits, he never met Adam personally.

In the "Wit Inspirations of the Two-Year-Olds," Clemens tells how he acquired the name Samuel. As his father and mother discussed Abraham, Isaac, and Jacob he approved, but when they came to Samuel he balked:

"Father, I have an invincible antipathy to that name."

"My son, this is unreasonable. Many great and good men have been named Samuel."

"Sir, I have yet to hear of the first instance."

"What! There was Samuel the prophet. Was not he great and good?"

"Not so very."

"My son! With His own voice the Lord called him."

"Yes, sir, and he had to call him a couple of times before he would come."

And then I sallied forth, and that stern old man sallied forth after me. He overtook me at noon the following day, and when the interview was over I had acquired the name of Samuel, and a thrashing, and other useful information.[100]

All this occurred, Clemens claims, when he lacked one hour and twenty-five minutes of being two weeks old.

So it goes; he is at one time writing stinging satires—"Letters to

Satan," "To the Person Sitting in Darkness," "A Humane Word from Satan," or "The War Prayer." At another time he is writing, with "the calm confidence of a Christian with four aces," concerning a consensus:

> Then there was a Consensus about it. It was the very first one. It sat six days and nights. It was then delivered of the verdict that a world could not be made out of nothing; that such small things as sun and moon and stars might, maybe, but it would take years and years, if there was a considerable many of them. Then the Consensus got up and looked out of the window, and there was the whole outfit spinning and sparkling in space. You never saw such a disappointed lot.
>
> his
> Adam + .
> mark [101]

In his notebook Twain wrote: "The ravens could hardly make their own living, let alone board Elijah."

Alongside this new jesting by authors, there flowed the slang of the streets and the argot of the underworld—both rich in ironic biblical allusion, and both to wax fat in the twentieth century. Most people could translate "Adam and Eve on a raft" as two fried eggs on toast and "Adam's ale" as water. "Eve with the lid on" might suggest apple pie. More difficult would probably be "Noah's boy" (ham), "forbidden fruit" as pork, "angels on horseback" as fricasseed oysters, "yesterday, today, and forever" as hash, the "Lord's supper" as bread and water. A "Nebuchadnezzar," according to the slang dictionary, is a vegetarian, "minister's face" is a boiled pig's head, "pope's nose" is a fowl's rear extremity, "balm of Gilead" is bootleg whisky, "oh be joyful" is superlatively good liquor, "heaven dust" is cocaine, and "pie in the sky" is a reward after death. A rest room for women is "Ruth"; a chamber pot is "Jerry" (Jeremiah); and a toilet seat is an "altar."

From the underworld leer "abbess" as a brothel keeper, "abbot" as her male consort, "nuns" and "sisters of charity" as members of the staff, "missionary" as procurer. It was an ill-timed jest from this source which not long since threatened to bar one of our leading humorists from future radio broadcasts: "Adam and Eve were the first bookkeepers; they invented the loose-leaf system."

Among denominations a "dipper" is a Baptist, a "blueskin" a Presbyterian, a "yea and nay man" a Quaker, a "fisheater," "chest pounder," or "craw thumper" a Catholic. A church is a "preaching shop," and Catholicism is "dolly worship." An "amen bawler" is the parish clerk. A judge, a pawnbroker, or an army sergeant is "Pontius Pilate."

To beg is to do the "missionary act." To stamp fake marks of quality on cheap jewelry is "to christen." A hideout for removing identifying marks from stolen jewelry is "a church." "Celestial poultry" are angels. "Angels" are sex perverts, financial backers, or beautiful maidens. Theological seminaries are "angel factories." Mission hall preaching is "angel food." Babies' boardinghouse keepers are "angel makers." Army bugle calls are "angels' whispers."

An "anno domini" is an elderly person. To swear is "to chant." Playing cards are the "devil's picture books." To "go to Sunday school" is to play poker. A child is a "God-forbid." A gloomy look is a "Friday face." To pray is "to grumble." A boil is a "Job's comforter." Knees are "prayer handles." A curse is a "sailor's blessing." One's wife is his "rib." A beauty is a "Sheba." "Coins are "shekels."

A "resurrection man" used to dig up corpses and sell them to medical schools. A "Jesus stiff" is a tramp addicted to scrawling Bible verses on roadside rocks and bridges. To go into voluntary bankruptcy is to "take the debtor's veil." To berate a man is to "read the Scriptures" to him.

Ministers have from time immemorial been favorite butts for jesting. They are, to name but a few designations out of many: "amen snorters," "Bible pounders," "black flies," "devil teasers," "finger posts," "fire escapes," "gluepots" (who join people in matrimony), "gospel sharks," "hallelujah peddlers," "holy Joes," "mess Johns," "mission squawkers," "pulpit cacklers," "puzzle texts," and "sky pilots."

The extent to which religion has permeated the thinking of all classes—from the literate and highly respectable to the illiterate and those of the underworld—is seen from the amount and range of this mocking or irreverently affectionate jesting and slang.

There once was a pious young priest,
Who lived almost wholly on yeast;
  "For," he said, "it is plain
  We must all rise again,
And I want to get started, at least." [102]

THE BIBLE WIDENS ITS BORDERS

31. Robins and Redbuds

Old Joe had a yellow cat,
She would not sing or pray,
Stuck her head in a buttermilk jar
And washed her sins away.

—ANONYMOUS[1]

How Job ever got an American turkey is a mystery equal to that of the Deep South's familiarity with "Adam's off ox," but—according to our nineteenth-century humorists—Job's turkey was so poor that it had but one feather in its tail, and it was so weak that it had to lean against a fence to gobble. That is but one of many birds, beasts, bugs, fishes, and bushes which once showed God's grace to men, and which now begin to come into renewed prominence. From many lands and times flock these stories.

Among the ten animals which Mohammedans allowed in their heaven were Jonah's whale, Solomon's ant, Abraham's ram, Balaam's ass, Noah's dove, and Moses' ox. Eden's snake spoke Arabic, the most suasive language in the world; Adam and Eve, Persian, the most poetic; and the angel Gabriel, Turkish, the most menacing.

Since there is no elephant in the Bible, artists are without authority in showing him coming from the ark last—"because he stopped to pack his trunk"—but medieval writers loved to allegorize him. He cannot rise unaided, the bestiaries said, so he leans against trees to rest. These the wily hunter saws half through. Down, the elephant trumpets for aid. Old ones try vainly to help. Then comes a young elephant, who with "his snout" lifts him. "So Adam fell through a tree; Moses and the prophets vainly sought to raise him. They all cried to Heaven. Christ came down as a man, and by death went under Adam and raised him and all mankind that were fallen into 'dim hell.' " [2]

The lion pursued by hunters, they said, effaces his track with his tail, as the "lion of Judah" concealed his Godhead from those who did not seek him aright. He sleeps open-eyed, typifying Christ's wakefulness spiritually while his body lay in the grave. Newborn cubs remain dead three days, when he breathes life into them, symbol of Christ's and our resurrection. The panther lies three days in his lair after feeding; then his sweet breath heals all creatures save the dragon, which it makes deathly ill. So Christ after three days in the grave, healed men and delivered them from the power of the dragon. When the stag's sweet breath draws serpents from their holes he stamps them to death, as Christ destroyed sin.

As mirrors placed in tigers' paths hold them spellbound in self-admiration while hunters capture their cubs, so Satan snatches souls when eyes are caught by worldly vanity. He tricks souls, as a fox snares fowls by pretending to be dead; and carries them off as a hedgehog does knocked-off grapes, impaled on his spines.

The whale puts sand on his back; birds drop seeds; trees grow; sailors land on the supposed island and build a fire; the whale dives. The whale is the devil, the sea the world, and the ship ourselves.

The ass received special veneration, for the cross mark on his shoulders was granted him for bearing the Christ as he entered Jerusalem. Roisterers at the Feast of Fools honored him by substituting brayings for the amens in the mock church service. The first printed collection of English riddles asks:

Demand: Who bore the best burden that ever was borne?
Reply: The ass which Our Lady rode upon when she fled with Our Lord into Egypt.
D: What became of that ass?
R: Adam's mother did eat her.
D: Who is Adam's mother?
R: The Earth.[3]

The carrion-loving hyena would not have been tolerated in the ark. Offspring of a cat and dog, it originated after the Deluge and typified in the bestiaries the Jews, who preferred the dry bones of the Law to the living Gospel.

Constantly augmented folklore adds its bits. No goat is ever seen throughout twenty-four hours, because once daily every goat visits the devil to have its beard combed. The praying mantis and the dragonfly are the devil's darning needles. Parsley is so slow in coming up because the seeds have to make seven trips to the devil before sprouting.

Doves and pigeons have no gall, for the dove sent out by Noah burst hers from grief. When a robin picked a thorn from the Saviour's brow on his way to the cross, the spurting blood dyed its breast red, and red it has been ever since. Another version is that it scorched its breast when it pityingly bore water to the thirsty souls in hell. The wren was anciently mistaken for the robin's wife, hence

> The robin red-breast and the wren
> Are God Almighty's cock and hen;
> The martin and the swallow
> Are the next two birds that follow,[4]

the swallow being in Scandinavian tradition the bird which hovered over the cross crying, "Console, console" (*svala, svala*). The stork likewise got its name from flying about the cross, calling, "Strengthen, strengthen" (*styrka, styrka*). But the yellow bunting is the devil's bird, say the Scots, with its cry of "Deil! Deil!" and its blood-marked eggs, because it flew about the cross unsympathetically.

The weathercock on church steeples reminded medieval men of Peter's sin, and the cockatrice (hatched by a toad from a cock's egg) killed all it saw, unless faced with a crystal vase—symbol of the immaculate conception.

The holly is "holy." But mandrakes are the devil's apples, stinkhorn fungi his candlesticks, puffballs his snuffbox, and starfish his fingers.

Adam, naming Eden's plants, overlooked one—the forget-me-not. The yucca—one variety of which was to Spanish Californians "the Candle of the Lord" and another variety to the early Mormons the "Joshua tree" leading them to the Promised Land—was to him, fashioning earth's first sartorial ensemble, "Adam's needle." The first apple core, sticking in Adam's throat, gave all men their "Adam's apples"; and a fruit traditionally scarred by the first bite became "Apples of Paradise."

Eve, weeping her way out of Paradise, had her tears turned into lily bulbs, which gave Gabriel flowers to bear to Mary at the Annunciation. Job's tears, Aaron's beard, Joseph's coat, and Solomon's seal all are now plants. Elijah's mantle is the larkspur, and roses began

> for as much as a fair maiden was blamed with wrong, and slandered that she had done fornication, for which cause she was demned to death, and to be burnt in that place, to the which she was led. And, as the fire began to burn about her, she made her prayers to our Lord, that as wisely as she was not guilty of that sin, that he would help her and make it known to all men, of his merciful grace. And when she had thus said, she entered into the fire, and anon was the fire quenched and out; and the brands that were burning became red rose trees, and the brands that were not kindled became white rose trees, full of roses. And these were the first rose-trees and roses, both red and white, that ever any man saw.[5]

For things to be known only between one and God, roses have become symbols of silence, carved on confessionals.

To rue means to repent, so that plant became "herb of grace," and the pansy, "herb trinity." Then there is the tiny "star of Bethlehem." Crusaders brought back from the Holy Land the "hol (l) yhock." The "passionflower" bears the emblems of the Crucifixion, and the aspen ever quakes from shame that it was the wood of the cross.

Salvia formed the pattern for the seven-branched candlestick in the Temple, and rosemary was the plant on which the Virgin Mary hung the tiny shirts of the infant Jesus to dry.

Nor were bugs or worms overlooked. Bugs were named from those bogies which fearsomely flew by night, and the ladybug was "Bishop Burnaby's beetle" and "God Almighty's cow," and since it was under Our Lady's especial protection anybody harming one might expect a broken leg or the like within a year. Palmers bore palm branches in sign that they had visited the tomb of Christ, so certain caterpillars were "called Palmer-worms by reason of their wandering life (for they never stay in one place, but are ever wandering) ."

As for the sea, many are the kinds of fishes which bear the marks of Peter's thumb and finger as he took the coin from their mouths; and the pike, since he rose and gazed when the rest dived at the Crucifixion, bears on his head the cross, nails, and sword. The stormy petrel walks the waves like Peter, and the parrot—Pierrot—is as talkative as Peter was. Davy Jones's locker is Jonah's locker. Mother Carey's chickens, the petrels, are Mater Cara's (the Virgin's) chickens, and Gabriel's hounds are wild geese, the souls of unbaptized children wandering through the air until judgment day.

These things got into literature. A favorite medieval conceit was the Mass chanted by the birds.

> The robyn redbreast,
> He shall be the preest;
>
> . . . .
>
> The owle, that is so foule,
> Must help us to howle;
>
> . . . .
>
> The kestrell in all this warke
> Shall be holy water clarke.[6]

Skelton but followed patterns made by others, as in

> The salmon sang the high mass, the herring was the clerk,
> On the organ played the porpoise, that was a merry work![7]

Puritanism poured scorn upon all such "lying legends":

> How fish in conventicles met,
> And *mackerel* were by *bait of doctrine* caught,
> How cattle have judicious hearers been!—
> How *consecrated hives* with bells were hung
> And *bees* kept mass and holy *anthems* sung
> How *pigs* to th' rosary kneel'd, and *sheep* were taught
> To bleat *Te Deum* and *Magnfiicat*.[8]

Richard Crashaw wondered why the ass upon which Christ rode did not speak, as Balaam's had—

> That he should find a tongue and vocal thunder,
> Was a great wonder;
> But O, methinks, 'tis a far greater one
> That thou find'st none.[9]

Dryden used the medieval hind and the panther as symbols in his apology for his faith. But in general the lesser creatures languished. In the nineteenth and twentieth centuries they regained prominence. Emily Dickinson remembered them.

It was a short procession,—
The bobolink was there,
The aged bee addressed us,
And then we knelt in prayer,

. . . .

In the name of the bee
And of the butterfly
And the breeze, amen! [10]

Francis Thompson wrote his multicadenced *The Hound of Heaven.* Then Chesterton's "The Donkey" voiced his poignant reply to Crashaw, and Vachel Lindsay listed the callers on King Darius:

Old man Ahab leaves his card.
Elisha and the bears are a-waiting in the yard.
Here comes Pharaoh and his snakes a-calling.
Here comes Cain and his wife a-calling.
Shadrach, Meshach and Abednego for tea.
Here comes Jonah and the whale,
And the Sea! [11]

In the far northwest H. L. Davis' Pulitzer prize novel, *Honey in the Horn,* identified the hounds:

The dog who was baying was old Reverend Spurgeon, he said, and he rather believed that Henry Ward Beecher and Dwight Moody were helping out.[12]

From the Eastern mountain section:

"Them two are good. That's Paul and Agrippa, and they're by Danger out of Yeary's old Jezebel." . . . And the stranger wanted to know why he called the pups Paul and Agrippa.

"It's easy to see you don't know your Scriptures, young man, no matter how many things you know," Gill told him. "These was second and third-born in the litter, and Paul came before Agrippa, didn't he? Leastways, that's what it says in the Bible."

"You haven't got Jesus and Pontius Pilate, then, somewhere 'around?" the stranger wanted to know. "Because I seem to have read that Jesus came before Pilate, too."

But the family was plumb scandalized at that, and they shushed him up properly.[13]

In the Southern mountains God and the sparrow argue:

"Jaybird pulling a two-mule plow;
Sparrow, why not you?"
"My laigs so long and slimber, Lord,
I's skeered they'll break in two!" [14]

In a dairy barn farther north rose a chant while milk squirted rhythmically into the pail:

Pater noster qui es in coelis, sanctificatur nomen tuum—So-o, put your foot back!—*agnus dei, qui tollis peccata mundi misere nobis!*—*Hagii Ichthyos quelque chose.*—*Arma virumque cano, senatus Populusque Romanus, amo, amas, amat, amamus, amatis, Aa-mant!*—Stand still!—*Gloria in excelsis Deo!*—There you are; all over—*Ite, missa est*—*Ite, missa est.*[15]

Out in California, John Steinbeck's reformed hell-raising sow performed a miracle.

On the morning in question, while hymns of joy and thanksgiving sounded from a hundred pious mouths, Katy rose from her seat, strode to the altar, and, with a look of seraphic transport on her face, spun like a top on the tip of her tail for one hour and three quarters. The assembled Brothers looked on with astonishment and admiration. This was a wonderful example of what a saintly life could accomplish.[16]

In Oklahoma, Governor Marland signed the bill making the redbud the state tree after the forestry officials had convinced the women's clubs that it was not the tree on which Judas hanged himself.

Whether or not the animals still kneel on Christmas Eve, they are again in fashion and safely in the Christian fold, if names are an indication—"Polly" (from "Molly," "Mary") Parrot, "Jack" Rabbit, "Tom" Turkey, "Biddy" ("St. Bridget") Hen, "Thomas and "Tabitha" Cat, "Peter" Rabbit (who has recovered from the centuries of ill fame heaped upon him when the people thought the Bible ruled him unclean because they saw him wiggling his nose and thought he was chewing his cud), "Molly" Cottontail, "Christopher" and "Jenny" Wren, "Sammy" Jay, "Jerry" Muskrat, "Benjamin" Bunny, and "Mickey" Mouse—to say nothing of "My Nanny Goat," whose name slipped from Mine "Annie" Coat.

Some of the animals even feel sorry for man:

Man that is born of a woman,
Man, her un-web-footed drake,
Featherless, beakless, and human,
Is what he is by mistake.
For they say that a sleep fell on Nature,
In midst of the making of things;
And she left him a two-legged creature,
But wanting in wings.[17]

32. The Reverend Cream Cheese

Don't you know, as the French say, there are three sexes—men, women, and clergymen? —SYDNEY SMITH[18]

Call me *Brother,* if you will;
Call me *Parson*—better still.
Or if, perchance, the Catholic frill
Doth your heart with longing fill—
Though plain *Mister* fills the bill,
Then even *Father* brings no chill
Of hurt or rancor or ill-will.

To no D.D. do I pretend,
Though *Doctor* doth some honor lend,
Preacher, Pastor, Rector, Friend,
Titles almost without end
Never grate and ne'er offend;
A loving ear to all I bend,
But how the man my heart doth rend,
Who blithely calls me *Reverend!* [19]

THE nineteenth century discovered that clergymen were human beings and not merely "Nimrods, ramrods, and fishing rods." The position of the clergy in English and American literature has been a peculiar one. They and their immediate offspring have written much more of our literature than their numbers in the total population would seem to justify. They have furnished in their profession a frequently used literary type-figure.

The minister's social standing has varied widely. Once he was the master of the community, whose sermons shaped its life and literature.[20] So exclusively his was learning that all who could read and write were automatically considered "clergy"—a fact neatly embalmed in the terms "clerical error," and "clerk." The time came when he was but an inferior member of the lordly household, permitted to eat at the master's table but required to withdraw before dessert was served, as his rank failed to warrant that delicacy. Sydney Smith likened the lower clergy to Lazarus, "doctored by dogs, and comforted with crumbs." Then came a certain sneering tolerance. "People who don't fish regard fishermen as crazy, or at least as if they belonged to another race: like monkeys or clergymen." [21] Finally, in the nineteenth and twentieth centuries, in novels and plays, came an appreciative understanding of some of their personal and professional problems. In his depiction of life in the fourteenth century Chaucer had drawn a wide and varied gallery of men and women of the church, from those of the most devoted piety and culture to those who were the veriest scoundrels. Most of his contemporaries were less tolerant. Satiric harshness was rife:

> The friars surpass all other religious in devotion, for they apply themselves to chivalry, riot and ribaldry, to great standing, and to long prayers. Who keeps their rule shall have heaven's bliss. Their appearance shows their great penances and simple sustenance; in my forty years I never saw men fatter about the ears; they are so meagre that each is a horse load. . . . They declare that they destroy sin; but they foster it, for if a man has slain his kin, they will shrive him for a pair of shoes. . . . There isn't room in hell, it is so full of friars. [One wonders if this last is a medieval pun] . . . They preach wisely, but do not practise. I was long a friar, and I know. When I saw they did not as they taught, I cast off the garb and went my way, commending prior and convent to the Devil. I am no apostate, for I lacked a month and nine or ten odd days of my twelve months. Lord God, who with bitter pain redeemed men, let never a man desire to become a friar.[22]

Later, John Skelton, poet laureate, and Rector of Diss in the time of Henry VIII, slashed at the clergy of his day. They take the cure of souls, he said, and know nothing of what they read in Paternoster, Ave, and Creed. They

> Construe not worth a whystle
> Nether Gospell nor Pystle;
> Theyr mattyns madly sayde,
> Nothynge deuoutly prayde;
> Theyr lernynge is so small,
> Thyr prymes and houres fall

And lepe out of theyr lyppes
Lyke sawdust or dry chyppes.[23]

That Skelton's condemnation was not altogether groundless is indicated by the development of the word "patter" from the lackadaisical manner in which the priests ran through the recitation of the Paternoster, and the existence of the medieval devil, Tutivillus, whose duty it was to collect and carry to hell all the words skipped over and mutilated by priests in performance of the services.

In "Ware the Hauke," Skelton raged against a fellow priest who persisted in hunting and hawking within the very church itself; he clambered upon the altar, threw down the altar cloths,

And sware horrible othes
Before the face of God,

while blood dripped down upon the desecrated altar as his hawks gorged on slain pigeons.

Jonson, in *Bartholomew Fair* and *The Alchemist,* mocked the whining nasal tones of the Puritan preachers. So did many other writers, including Swift, who wrote in the *Tale of a Tub* that his Calvinist brother had a tongue so muscular and flexible that he could twist it up his nose and deliver thence a strange kind of speech. "He was also the first in these kingdoms who began to improve the Spanish accomplishment of braying."

Milton's *Lycidas* flays unworthy churchmen. Prior's "A Dialogue Between the Vicar of Bray and Sir Thomas Moor" pictures mercilessly that unsavory vicar who traditionally managed to keep his place and perquisites by adroit and unscrupulous juggling of his conscience—so called—through fifty-seven years of the religion-changing reigns of Henry VIII, Edward VI, Mary, and Elizabeth, ever remaining true to the cardinal point of his religion, which was to keep himself Vicar of Bray. Pope, in "Dr. Swift, the Happy Life of a Country Parson," pictured one who knew well how to live at ease in Zion.

He that has these, may pass his life,
Drink with the 'Squire, and kiss his wife;
On Sundays preach, and eat his fill;
And fast on Fridays—if he will;
Toast Church and Queen, explain the News,

Talk with Church-Wardens about Pews,
Pray heartily for some new Gift,
And shake his head at Doctor S—— T.[24]

As the eighteenth century developed, the figure of the parson began to change, to acquire dignity and substance. Fielding, intent on writing in *Joseph Andrews* a burlesque of Richardson's *Pamela,* found gentle, learned, high-minded Parson Adams growing under his pen into one of the great characters of fiction, unworldly, clever at repartee, and physically quite able to meet an emergency.

Then came lovable Dr. Primrose, in Goldsmith's *Vicar of Wakefield,* with his troubles and trust; and in "The Deserted Village," that man of God, worthy to stand beside Chaucer's parson, to whose door came the needy, and were fed physically and spiritually, until even the fools who came to scoff remained to pray.

Gradually, as the controversies of the nineteenth century took shape, the preacher ceased to be a type and became an individual, beset with doubts he must resolve, fears he must face, and problems he must master. He ceased to be Sydney Smith's "average, ordinary, uninteresting Minister . . . in one of those Shem-Ham-and Japhet buggies—made on Mount Ararat soon after the subsidence of the waters, driving in the High Street of Edmonton—among all his pecuniary, saponaceous, oleaginous parishioners."[25] He ceased to be that mythical, pedantic Dr. Jonas Dryasdust whom the then anonymous author of the Waverley Novels brought forward frequently as consultant, friend, and fellow antiquarian.

He became, instead, the flesh-and-blood clergyman of the body of Scott's novels, acting upon—and acted upon by—the turmoil of his times. He became the clearly etched churchman of Browning's poems, that bishop, instinct with all the virtues and vices of the Renaissance, who ordered his tomb at St. Praxed's; that other bishop, Blougram, who shrewdly philosophized on the virtue of following the line of least resistance; the monsignor of *Pippa Passes,* tempted, yet rallying to his better self; high-minded Caponsacchi in *The Ring and the Book,* trying to rescue Pompilia from her venomous husband; the cynical pope and his fish net; in "Christmas Eve and Easter Day," the stupid preacher at the nonconformist chapel.

He became the tragic, suffering, hounded figure of the Reverend

Arthur Dimmesdale in Hawthorne's *Scarlet Letter;* and that of the bland, hypocritical "vessel," the Reverend Mr. Chadband, in Dickens' *Bleak House.*

He became, in George William Curtis' *Potiphar Papers,* the Reverend Cream Cheese, the superaesthetic object of Polly Potiphar's silly prittle-prattle.

> You know that aristocratic-looking young man, in white cravat and black pantaloons and waistcoat whom we saw at Saratoga a year ago, and who always had such a beautiful sanctimonious look, and such small, white hands. Well, he is a minister, as we supposed,—"an unworthy candidate, an unprofitable husbandman," he calls himself in that delicious voice of his.[26]

He affects hemstitched cambric handkerchiefs, parts his hair beautifully behind, and has wavy gestures. When asked what color Mrs. Potiphar should bind her prayer book, he talks for twenty minutes, concluding, as she reports it:

> Therefore, dear Mrs. Potiphar, as your faith is so pure and childlike, and as I observe that the light from the yellow panes usually falls across your pew, I would advise you to cymbalize your faith (wouldn't that be noisy in church?) by binding your prayer-book in pale blue, the color of skim-milk, dear Mrs. Potiphar, which is full of pastoral associations.[27]

So fond of the Reverend Cream Cheese does Mrs. Potiphar become that

> I ordered from Martelle the sweetest sprig of *immortelle* he had in his shop and sent it anonymously on St. Valentine's Day. Of course I didn't wish to do anything secret from my husband, that might make people talk; so I wrote, "Reverend Cream Cheese; from his grateful *skim-milk.*" I marked the last words, and hope he understood that I meant to express my thanks for his advice about the pale-blue cover. You don't think I was too romantic, do you dear?[28]

Now appeared Anthony Trollope's *Chronicles of Barsetshire,* wherein the squabblings, jealousies, heartburnings, antagonisms, and schemes for advancement of the clergymen whose lives are centered about the episcopal palace of Barchester are mercilessly uncovered. It is not a pretty picture, but one feels that it is a true one, of a community where ecclesiastical claws are not always sheathed. Yet there are sincerities and high devotions, also. Not all Trollope's ministers are Bishop Proudies, with arrogant wives, or bullying, mean-minded Dr. Slopes. Some are high-minded scholars and generous souls laboring serenely under difficulties.

George Eliot's *Scenes from Clerical Life,* which announced to the world that a new author of ability had arisen, was followed by *Adam Bede,* with its telling delineations of Dinah Morriss, the woman preacher, and Mr. Irwine, the easygoing, old-fashioned parson.

Mrs. Oliphant's *Salem Chapel* presented a clerical Boanerges, who anathematizes all not of his own elect and then "sits down pleasantly to his tea and makes himself comfortable."

"If I can put one touch of rosy sunset into the life of any man or woman in my cure, I shall feel that I have worked with God," mutters the eager young curate in George MacDonald's *Annals of a Quiet Neighborhood,* as he hears a lad wish to be a painter so he could help God paint the sky.

Harriet Beecher Stowe's *Old Town Folks* introduces Parson Lothrop, whose Addisonian English awes the village ne'er-do-well:

> He was gret on texts, the doctor was. When he had a p'int to prove, he'd jest go thro' the Bible, and drive all the texts ahead o' him like a flock o' sheep, and then, if there was a text that seemed agin him, why he'd come out with his Greek and Hebrew, and kind o' chase it around a spell. . . . I tell you, there wa'n't no text in the Bible that could stand agin the doctor when his blood was up.[29]

Far from this is Blackmore's giant Parson Stoyne Chowne, in *The Maid of Sker,* with his villainy and doom of hydrophobia.

Readers of new books in 1888 could choose Mrs. Humphrey Ward's *Robert Elsmere,* with a liberal-minded minister married to a religiously narrow wife, or Margaret Deland's *John Ward, Preacher,* which reversed the problem. They might meet the fervid young minister in Howell's *Annie Kilburn,* or read Barrie's *Auld Licht Idylls.* His *Little Minister* would not appear for three years; but Mary G. Tuttiett's *The Silence of Dean Maitland* had been out two years.

The Gay Nineties brought Crockett's *The Stickit Minister,* with its unappreciated, consumptive, ministerial student and its heart-broken, libeled minister; George Bernard Shaw's *Candida,* with its strong, successful minister, weak in his strength; Elizabeth

Stuart Phelps' *A Singular Life,* with its murder of the young minister of "unsound" tenets; and Henry Arthur Jones's *Michael and His Lost Angel,* wherein the ascetic Reverend Michael Faversham forgets his vow of celibacy and wrecks his career.

In 1903 Samuel Butler's *The Way of All Flesh* attacked "the religion of the Scribes and Pharisees in the Anglican church and its clergy"; and in 1907 came Charles Rann Kennedy's *The Servant in the House,* with Manson (Son of Man) the butler, and its vicar whose church is poisoned by the rotting traditions under its altar, its pious Bishop of Benares, and worldly Bishop of London.

After the stir caused by Churchill's *The Inside of the Cup,* in 1913, the subject lagged in the war decade, then in the twenties leaped into prominence with the unlovely missionary in John Colton and Clemence Randolph's *Rain,* the clerical intrigue in Walpole's *The Cathedral,* the itinerant street-preacher parents in Dreiser's *An American Tragedy.*

Then came the self-loathing cowardice of the parson in Galsworthy's *Escape,* the kaleidoscopic religion-shiftings of the Reverend Aubrey Garden in Rose Macaulay's *Told by an Idiot,* the unsavory Elmer Gentry of Sinclair Lewis, the mother-dominated missionary son in Louis Bromfield's *A Good Woman,* and—to break the depressing monotony—the solid missionary labors in Willa Cather's *Death Comes for the Archbishop,* the puzzled striving of the ex-evangelist in Steinbeck's *Grapes of Wrath,* and A. S. M. Hutchinson's *He Looked for a City.*

The minister is no longer merely "the duck that runs the Gospel mill"; he is a human being, with weaknesses and strengths, striving manfully to accomplish earth's most magnificent task.

33. Thus Saith . . .

Even Balaam's ass acquired speech when he had something definite to say. —MAX S. NORDAU[30]

THE Bible "has outsold and outcirculated every other book every year since printing began." [31] In addition, more than sixty thousand books about it have been written.[32] Daily about three new books of a religious nature come from English and American presses, keeping books of this type steadily in first place in annual production except for fiction (and occasionally juveniles, or some other field of unusual temporary interest).

But men talk more than they write. Literally billions of speeches have been generated by the Bible. The United States now has approximately a quarter of a million houses of worship. If there is but one sermon a week in each, and no other religious address of any sort there or elsewhere, Americans will hear during a year about thirteen million Bible-born speeches.

Back of these runs a long muster roll of magnetic pulpit personalities—Aldhelm, Ælfric, Wycliffe, the Mathers, Jonathan Edwards, the Wesleys, Whitefield, Newman, Beecher, Spurgeon, Moody, Sunday. For centuries Englishmen and Americans have listened to an amount of pulpit oratory stupefying to contemplate.

The Bible's part in political oratory is less well known.

Edmund Burke's forensic fame was so great that even his distant relatives basked in its warmth, as is seen from an epitaph:

Here lies Lady O'Looney,
Great-niece of Burke, commonly called "The Sublime."
She was bland, passionate, and deeply religious;
Also she painted in water-colors,
And sent several pictures to the Exhibition.
She was first cousin of Lady Jones,
And of such is the Kingdom of Heaven.[33]

Before delivering one of his vigorous orations it was Burke's custom to read a chapter of Isaiah. "Isaiah," he said, "possesses both the blaze of eloquence and the light of truth." Burke,

indeed, consciously modelled his majestic periods on the prose of the authorized version and thereby wove for his thought a garment as richly broidered as the curtains of the sanctuary.[34]

Beginning his indictment of Warren Hastings, he said:

I hope your lordships . . . will say to this unfaithful servant of the Company, what was said to another unfaithful person, upon a far less occasion, by a far greater authority, "Out of thy own mouth will I judge thee, thou wicked servant." [35]

In closing he pleaded for justice in the name of

that religion which says that their God is love, that the very vital spirit of their institution is charity; a religion which so much hates oppression, that when the God whom we adore appeared in human form, he did not appear in a form of greatness and majesty, but in sympathy with the lowest of the people—and thereby made it a firm and ruling principle, that their welfare was the object of all government; since the person, who was the Master of Nature, chose to appear himself in a subordinate position . . . he who is called first among them, and first among us all, both of the flock that is fed and of those who feed it, made himself "the servant of all." [36]

William Wilberforce, fighting the British slave trade, faced Parliament with insistent words.

There is a principle above everything that is political; and when I reflect on the command which says: "Thou shalt do no murder," believing the authority to be Divine, how can I dare to set up any reasonings of my own against it? . . . What is there in this life that should make any man contradict the dictates of his conscience, the principles of justice, the laws of religion, and of God? Sir, the nature and all the circumstances of this trade are now laid open to us; we can no longer plead ignorance, we cannot evade it.[37]

Evade it Parliament could not, with Wilberforce hammering insistently away; and the slave trade was at length abolished. "Through all my perplexities and distresses, I seldom read any other book," he said of the Bible, "and I as rarely have felt the want of any other. It has been my hourly study."

William E. Gladstone's diary reveals how constantly he sought courage in the pages of the Book. "On most occasions of very sharp pressure or trial, some word of Scripture has come home to me as if borne on angel's wings. Many could I recollect. The Psalms are a great storehouse." [38] In the harrowing Oxford contest of 1847 it was, "O Lord God, Thou strength of my health, Thou hast covered my head in the day of battle." At the time of his first budget speech he leaned upon the verse "Turn thee then unto me, and have mercy upon me: give thy strength unto thy servant, and help the son of thine handmaid." "It is supremacy, not precedence, that we ask for the Bible," he said, bluntly.

John Bright, "the Moses of English liberalism," was the ablest orator of his day. "His mind was steeped in the Bible; in his loftier flights, he seemed to be breathing the atmosphere of the Old Testanent; the thoughts and cadences of Milton were ever on his lips." [39] In the Crimean War he thrilled men mightily with his plea for peace. "The Angel of Death is abroad in the land; you may almost hear the very beating of his wings. There is no one to sprinkle with blood the lintel and the side-posts of our doors that he may spare and pass on." [40]

Upon one memorable occasion, however, his fondness for biblical symbolism left him open to withering counterattack. He remarked of an opponent of the Reform Bill of 1866, "The right honorable gentleman is the first of the new party who has retired into what may be called his political cave of Adullam." A new political term, "Adullamite," had been born. But the opponents also knew their Bible. One arose and dryly retorted that the band in the cave was hourly increasing, and would in time enable David (I Samuel 22:1, 2) to deliver the House from Saul (Gladstone) and his armor-bearer (Bright).

In America, James Otis, in opposing the nefarious Writs of Assistance, had lashed out against the unrestricted right of search: "What is this but to have the curse of Canaan with a witness on us; to be the servant of servants, the most despicable of God's creation?" [41] Thereby he started the country toward revolution.

Out of the Bible, Patrick Henry wove the strands of his "Give me liberty or give me death" speech:

> Are we disposed to be of the number of those, who, having eyes, see not, and having ears, hear not, the things which so nearly concern their temporal salvation? . . . I have but one lamp by which my feet are guided, and that is the lamp of experience. . . . Suffer not yourselves to be betrayed with a kiss. . . . An appeal to arms and the God of Hosts is all that is left us! . . . The battle, sir, is not to the strong alone. . . . Gentlemen may cry, Peace, peace—but there is no peace. . . . Why stand we here idle? . . . I know not what course others may take; but as for me . . .[42]

Daniel Webster's first Bible was his mother's gift. One Saturday his schoolmaster offered a pocket knife to the student who would memorize the most Bible verses over the week end. Daniel won, but complained. The teacher had stopped him after a mere sixty or seventy verses. He yearned to recite several chapters more.

Webster's father

had a sonorous voice, an untaught but correct ear, and a keen perception of all that was beautiful or sublime in thought. How often after the labors of the day, before twilight had deepened into obscurity, would he read to me his favorite portions of the Bible, the Book of Job, the Prayer of Habakkuk, and extracts from Isaiah! It was doubtless his impressive manner on such occasions, his suffused eye, his broken voice, and reverential intonation, that gave me a taste for the inspired authors, and preserved me from that danger of neglect into which our early familiarity with these books—a familiarity in the meantime rather with the sounds of the words than with their sense and beauties—too often threaten to precipitate us.[43]

The son soon followed in his Bible-reading father's footsteps:

Something about him made an impression on strangers. He often entertained guests at the tavern by reading aloud from the Bible; and teamsters as they pulled up at the door, would say, "Come, let's go in and hear a psalm from Dan Webster." [44]

Webster's own testimony is explicit:

From the time that, at my mother's feet or on my father's knee, I first learned to lisp verses from the sacred writings, they have been my daily study and vigilant contemplation. If there be anything in my style or thoughts to be commended, the credit is due to my kind parents in instilling into my mind an early love of the scriptures.[45]

He is said not to have felt qualified to speak in the Senate "until he had taken as a tonic the eighth Psalm and the fortieth chapter of Isaiah." The people of the North are against slavery, he explained in his crucial "Seventh of March" speech, because they say,

It is not according to the meek spirit of the Gospel. It is not "kindly affectioned"; it does not "seek another's and not its own"; it does not "let the oppressed go free." [46]

When James A. Garfield heard of Lincoln's death, he spoke from a balcony of the New York customhouse to a frenzied mob:

Fellow citizens: Clouds and darkness are around Him; His pavilion is dark waters and thick clouds; justice and judgment are the establishment of His throne; mercy and truth shall go before His face! Fellow citizens! God reigns, and the government at Washington still lives.[47]

Not always is oratory so stately. Fiery Thomas F. Marshall of Kentucky was speaking at Buffalo when a heckler interrupted. Marshall turned to the chairman and blazed forth:

Mr. President, on the last day, when the angel Gabriel shall have descended from the heavens, and, placing one foot upon the sea and the other upon the land, shall lift to his lips the golden trumpet and proclaim to the living and the resurrected dead that time shall be no more, I have no doubt, sir, that some infernal fool from Buffalo will start up and cry out, "Louder, please, sir, louder!" [48]

Henry W. Grady, speaking to a Northern audience, began his famous laudation of the New South:

There was an old preacher once who told some boys of the Bible lesson he was going to read in the morning. The boys, finding the place, glued together the connecting pages. The next morning he read on the bottom of one page: "When Noah was one hundred and twenty years old he took unto himself a wife, who was"—and then turning the page—"one hundred and forty cubits long, forty cubits wide, built of gopher wood, and covered with pitch inside and out." He was naturally puzzled at this. He read it again, verified it, and then said: "My friends, this is the first time I ever met this in the Bible, but I accept it as an evidence of the assertion that we are fearfully and wonderfully made." If I could get you to hold such faith tonight I could proceed cheerfully to the task I otherwise approach with a sense of consternation.[49]

Robert G. Ingersoll attacked vigorously things biblical. Then his brother died. No cadences more haunting, save Lincoln's, can be found than Ingersoll's at his brother's grave:

Life is a narrow vale between the cold and barren peaks of two eternities. We strive in vain to look beyond the heights. We cry aloud, and the only answer is the echo of our wailing cry. From the voiceless lips of the unreplying dead there comes no word; but in the night of death hope sees a star, and listening love can hear the rustle of a wing.[50]

Young William Jennings Bryan approached his prospective father-in-law: "Mr. Baird, I have been reading Proverbs a good lately, and find that Solomon says, 'Whoso findeth a wife, findeth a good thing and obtaineth favor of the Lord.'" The reply was seemingly grave: "I believe Solomon did say that, but Paul suggests that while he that marrieth doeth well, he that marrieth not doeth better." The Boy Orator of the Platte thought a moment, then triumphed: "Solomon would be the best authority upon this point, because Paul never was married, while Solomon had a number of wives." [51]

In his first important speech before Congress, "he quoted the Bible to them, which had already become his favorite oratorical practice." At the tense Chicago convention of 1896 the full armor of righteousness clanked softly in his opening remarks: "The humblest citizen in all the land, when clad in the armor of a righteous cause . . . " Saul's jealousy of David peeped from his central onslaught: "If protection has slain its thousands, the gold standard has slain its tens of thousands." Then came the impassioned climax: "You shall not press down upon the brow of labor this crown of thorns, you shall not crucify mankind upon a cross of gold." [52] With twenty-four Bible-borrowed words he had focused upon himself the attention of the world.

On July 25, 1912, the *Nation* noted that "one trait of contemporary public oratory and political eloquence is the rediscovery of the Bible as a treasure house of argument and invective." That very month Theodore Roosevelt, who loved to coin terms from the Bible and *Pilgrims Progress*—"Ananias club," "incense swingers," "muckrakers"—and was once described by John Morley as "half St. Paul, half St. Vitus," trumpeted forth the Bull Moose call. Hiram Johnson and his Californians brought a hymn-tune banner:

I want to be a Bull Moose,
And with the Bull Moose stand,
With Antlers on my forehead,
And a Big Stick in my hand.[53]

The Michigan delegation stampeded the convention into a parade with its camp-meeting song:

Follow! Follow!
We will follow Roosevelt
Anywhere! Everywhere!
We will follow on!

A famous Jewish philanthropist led the New York delegation down the aisle, lustily roaring a Christian hymn:

Onward, Christian soldiers!
Marching as to war.

Albert J. Beveridge sounded the keynote:

For the call that comes to us is the call that came to our fathers. As they responded, so shall we.

"He has sounded forth a trumpet that shall never call retreat,
He is sifting out the hearts of men before His judgment seat,
Oh, be swift our souls to answer Him, be jubilant our feet,
Our God is marching on." [54]

The Bull Moose lifted his voice and challenged: "We stand at Armageddon and battle for the Lord!" The *Nation* was right. The Bible and the hymnbook had been rediscovered in American politics—if they had ever been lost.

34. News, the Manna of a Day

"Dar's gwine to be a' obberflow," said Noah, looking solemn—
Fur Noah tuk the Herald, *an' he read de ribber colmn.*

—IRWIN RUSSELL[55]

THE first publishers were suspected of selling their souls to Satan, and the idea occasionally lingers. In 1490, Aldus Manutius, inventor of italic type, eager to clear himself of the suspected satanic qualities of his Negro slave boy, advertised:

I, Aldo Manuzio, printer to the Doge, have this day made public exposure of the printer's devil. All who think he is not flesh and blood, may come and pinch him.[56]

But the "printer's devil" is still a part of every well-regulated print shop, and the "hellbox"—to receive discarded type—is also occasionally found.

The first English press was in abbey grounds; naturally, English typographical terms smell of the church. *Pica* type was once the great black letter beginning some new order in the liturgy. *Brevier* was for printing breviaries. *Long primer* formed the font for the small prayer book called primers. The *dagger* now used to mark footnotes once showed the priest where to make the sign of the cross. The Greek cross indicated something wrong with the text. Dim sheets were *friars;* overinked ones, *monks.* Since certain paper of large size was at one time stamped IHS it became *Jesus paper.* In some newspaper offices the *Balaam's box* supplies the asinine jokes and news of three-headed calves used for filler.

America's first newspaper, *Public Occurrences,* began on September 25, 1690, to keep memorable occurrences of divine providence from being neglected or forgotten, to spread understanding of public affairs, and "That something may be done toward the Curing, or at least the Charming of that Spirit of Lying, which prevails among us." [57] It ended on the same day, as the authorities promptly suppressed so pernicious an undertaking.

Early in the nineteenth century journalism discovered the value of sensationalism. The first three numbers of *Blackwood's Magazine* having been apathetically received, the editors—Lockhart, Wilson, and Hogg—determined upon an audacious bid for notoriety. In the next issue appeared a "Chaldee MS," in which, in language and typographical form parodied from Scripture, leading citizens were satirized and ridiculed. The trick worked. The magazine became the talk of Edinburgh, then of Scotland, and then of England. There brewed a storm of criticisms, threats, duels, and libel suits. But no one appeared to know who was responsible. The "Chaldee MS" seemed to have slipped in without sponsor, according to official explanations, and the article was deleted (after many copies were sold).

That journalism became hard-hitting in the nineteenth century is indicated by Swinburne's attack on the *Quarterly Review:*

> We know that from the earlier days of Shelley onwards to the later day of Tennyson, "whatsover things are true, whatsoever things are honest, whatsoever things are just, whatsoever things are pure, whatsoever things are lovely, whatsoever things are of good report," become untrue, dishonest, unjust, impure, unlovely and ill-famed when passed through the critical crucible of the *Quarterly Review.*[58]

But the Bible had other values for journalism than sensation and vituperation, according to Charles A. Dana, of the New York *Sun.* Addressing a class of prospective journalists, he urged:

> There are some books that are absolutely indispensable to the kind of education that we are contemplating and to the profession that we

are considering; and of all these the most indispensable, the most useful, the one whose knowledge is most effective, is the Bible. There is no book from which more valuable lessons can be learned.

Then he continued:

I am considering it now, not as a religious book, but as a manual of utility, of professional preparation and professional use for a journalist. There is, perhaps, no book whose style is more suggestive and more instructive, from which you learn more directly that sublime simplicity which never exaggerates, which recounts the greatest event with solemnity, of course, but without sentimentality or affectation—none which you open with such confidence and lay down with such reverence: there is no book like the Bible.[59]

To a reporter assigned a thousand words for an article but insisting on fifteen hundred he wired: "1000. MOSES COVERED THE CREATION IN 864."

Sir Edwin Arnold, editor of the powerful London *Daily Telegraph,* when asked what he owed the Bible, replied:

My short reply would be *everything;* my long reply, to be sufficiently serious and comprehensive, would run to reams of paper. But, if I am addressed as a man of letters, I would simply say that I owe my education as a writer more to the Bible than to any other hundred books that could be named.[60]

The crusading editor of the *Pall Mall Gazette* and *Review of Reviews,* William T. Stead, was more specific:

After I left school, Proverbs influenced me most; and I remember when I was first offered an editorship, reading all the Proverbs relating to kings as affording the best advice I was likely to get anywhere as to the right discharge of editorial duties.

As his tasks varied, so did his reading.

When I was busy with active, direct work among the ignorant and poor, the story of Moses' troubles with the Jews in the wilderness was most helpful. Later, when from 1876 to 1878, no one knew when he went to bed but that by morning Lord Beaconsfield would have plunged the Empire into war, the Hebrew prophets formed my Bible. In 1885 it was the story of the evangelists.

Looking back, he summed it all up:

> If I had to single out any one chapter which I am conscious of having influenced me most, I should say the first of Joshua, with its oft-repeated exhortation to be strong and to be very courageous; and if I had to single out any particular verses, it would be those which were taught me when a boy, and which I long afterwards saw on the wall of General Gordon's room at Southampton: "Trust in the Lord with all thy heart; lean not unto thine own understanding. In all thy ways acknowledge Him, and He shall direct thy paths." [61]

Thomas L. Masson, once literary and managing editor of the then humorous magazine *Life,* discovered Samson, David, Goliath, Delilah, *Robinson Crusoe,* and dime novels when he was fourteen. As a young editor he read that no one could become a good writer unless he became a student of the Bible. So he started in.

> I found I had an occupation that created more new values for me than anything I had ever tried. . . . It is the bedrock foundation of all our literature and, therefore, if you want to know anything, the Bible is where you must go to find it. It contains all the latest news. No newspaper man, no sage or scientist, no philosopher or statesman has ever been able to get up early enough in the morning to get ahead of the Bible.[62]

Seven years later he was saying:

> I read the Bible two hours every day. . . . I read the Psalms through every month. . . . There is nothing like the Psalms as a spiritual gyroscope.[63]

William Allen White, famed editor of the Emporia *Gazette,* felt likewise:

> Every time I pick up the Bible, and I pick it up frequently in the course of a busy life, I find some new quotation which I can use until I pick it up again. The Bible is to me an eternal spring of wisdom and joy.[64]

For a commencement address in 1936 his theme was, "Your young men shall see visions."

Maurice Hindus, one time Russian-Jewish immigrant boy, has added his word:

I have travelled far and wide over this earth, and I have never been without a King James version of the Bible. Like thousands of men in my profession I have found its lucid and majestic prose an inestimable help in my work.[65]

But final proof of a newspaper's pudding is in its pages. On January 1, 1920, the Press-Radio Bible Service was initiated. It flourished to such an extent that

in the year 1933 . . . the Press-Radio Bible Service served newspapers having a daily circulation of more than fourteen million copies, or during the year four billion, three hundred and eighty-two million copies of papers were printed, each of which carried a helpful verse from the Bible.[66]

In 1923 twenty newspaper syndicates sold biblical features regularly to more than eight hundred newspapers in the United States and Canada.[67]

Journalistic use is varied. When the Revised Version of the New Testament was released in America on May 20, 1881, both the Chicago *Tribune* and the Chicago *Times* reprinted the entire book two days later. "No such reception was ever accorded any other book in the history of the world." [68]

T. K. Whipple once sarcastically threw together:

Were "Job" Just Published
(Review in almost any metropolitan daily)

The story deals with the troubles of a big ranch owner, a Western cattle king and sheep raiser. . . . the extreme modernism of the work is evident in all its aspects. . . .

To put the whole matter in a nutshell, "The Book of Job" may be described as out of T. S. Eliot by Carl Sandburg. . . . In short, "The Book of Job" is simply one more piece of evidence which would tend to show a failure of nerve in the younger generation.[69]

The New York *Times* on November 21, 1936, blossomed forth with:

Fig Leaf Held First Invention

The fig leaf was recognized officially today as man's first invention. Apologizing for being tardy in getting around to Adam, Patent officials listed "the fig leaf apron" as the forerunner of a long line of costume design patents.

In 1933 the *Sun* ran daily for almost eight months a series of rare biblical etchings, with condensed text.

The San Francisco *Chronicle* for Saturday, August 27, 1938, contained:

WANDERING TEACHER CONTROLS STORM
By D. C. Williams
Staff Writer, The Judean Herald

Tiberius, Galilee, A. U. C. 766 (A. D. 28)—Two of the strangest feats yet accredited to Jesus were reported this afternoon immediately after he landed a short distance north of here as he returned from a hurried trip across the lake to the decapolis. . . .

The April 8, 1939, Alhambra (California) *Post Advocate* had front-page banner heads of the Crucifixion, Resurrection, etc., with Jerusalem dates and a Jerusalem weather report.

The July 6, 1940, *Saturday Evening Post* described an entire baseball game in biblical quotations, citing always chapter and verse.

That these are not isolated instances of biblical journalistic use is indicated by two test studies. In the first, all the materials (except the advertising) in twenty-four issues of the *Atlantic Monthly* (twelve just before the outbreak of World War I, twelve soon after the Great Depression descended) were searched. Of 2,693 allusions to literature, 607 were to the Bible.[70]

A check of six issues of ten popular magazines of 1938 and 1939[71] revealed the following number of biblical references, quotations, and allusions:

Cosmopolitan	393
Country Gentleman	231
American Magazine	178
Collier's	141
Ladies' Home Journal	93
Saturday Evening Post	65
Good Housekeeping	59
Life	58
Time	53
McCall's	39
Total	1,310

Of the biblical books, Luke proved to be drawn upon most frequently, Matthew next, with Romans, Genesis, Ephesians, and Revelation following in order. Of people, Jesus was mentioned most frequently and, curiously enough, Balaam next. Of places, Eden led and Egypt followed. Of stories, the birth and death of Christ and the Garden of Eden were the principal subjects, by a large margin.

The investigators need not have shunned the advertising columns, for there, too, they would have found rich treasure:

> If it hadn't been for an apple, where would the clothing business be?

In the personals, one finds offered for fifty cents a typed list of his ancestors for five generations, "if you have that many. We have some that go back to Adam."

A famous oil company runs a display series under such headings as:

> METHUSALEH LIVED 969 YEARS—BUT WHAT FOR?
>
> WHEN THE PRODIGAL REACHED HOME
>
> JONAH IS ABOUT THE ONLY MAN WHO—WHEN HE NEEDED A WHALE—FOUND ONE WITHOUT LOOKING

A fishing-net maker uses, "They that go down to the sea in ships, that do business in great waters"; and a cutie-nudie show offers "SEVEN OF THE SWEETEST ANGELS THIS SIDE OF HEAVEN."

On the motion-picture page a bow-tied, silk-hatted, bemonocled serpent watches a bitten-apple-framed kiss and blurbs, "OH BOY! *The Lady Eve* certainly knows her apples!"

One newspaper runs a full-page advertisement for newspapers, "Give Us This Day Our Daily Truth," and another runs a "Bible Game," in which it gives five thousand dollars in prizes.

It was at a cracker makers' convention that a sales manager for a typewriter company said:

> The Bible is the background of the language of all the great advertising experts in the world, and all the great salesmen have read the Old Testament through and through. . . . The Bible is the paragon of all books for vitalizing your language.[72]

In 1923 Bruce Barton, speaking to the Public Relations section of the National Electric Light Association, took as text: "And Joseph died, and . . . there arose up a new king, . . . which knew not Joseph."

I submit, gentlemen, that this is one of the most staggering lines that has ever been written in a business biography. Here was a man so famous that everybody knew him and presto, a few people die, a few new ones are born, and *nobody* knows him . . . all the advertising that the name "Joseph" had enjoyed in one generation is futile and of no avail, because that generation is gone. . . . If advertising is worth doing at all, it is worth doing all the time. For every day, gentlemen, the "king" dies, and there arises a new "king" who knows not Joseph.[73]

In 1925, under the title "Give Moses a Chance," there appeared in *Collier's:*

Many advertising men are finding in the Bible a gorgeous chance to break tradition; to get away from selling talk which has a tendency to become phrase-ridden and flabby.

Observe this recent advertisement of a large manufacturer of electrical equipment. Its headline reads, "When there shall be no more Marthas." And in two terse paragraphs we are told again of the two sisters of Lazarus . . . and how household burdens are being lifted by means of electrical motors.

Here is an advertisement whose author evidently knew the second Book of Kings.

WHEN YOU ASK AN EXPERT WHY NOT FOLLOW HIS ADVICE?

When Naaman asked Elisha what would cure his leprosy, Elisha told him to go bathe in Jordan.

But Naaman got mad. He wouldn't follow the advice. Why Jordan? Abana and Pharphar were far more fashionable watering places. Elisha hadn't studied his case. . . .

Then one of Naaman's servants (probably his advertising agent) suggested that he try Elisha's way. . . .

So Naaman washed in the Jordan, and was immediately cured.

There doesn't seem to be anything more to be said.[74]

THE BIBLE MEETS THE TWENTIETH CENTURY

35. Sex O'clock

Stay me with Hitchens, comfort me with Beerbohm; for I am sick of Shaw. —LOUIS MCQUILLAND[1]

WHEN the Bible met the twentieth century, what happened? The influence of the Bible then ended, according to many watchers by the way. "Modern writers are leading the younger generation on a merry downhill race to perdition"; "The Bible, as a force to be reckoned with in writing, is dead"; "The old conception that the King James translation of the Bible is the best monument to prose style is hopelessly out of date"—these are the remarks which an observer in 1934 says "have become commonplace today." [2]

Only five years earlier another watcher reports just the opposite:

> It cannot be said of our age that it reads the Bible alone. Yet it can be said that it cannot leave the Bible alone. . . . It has translated it, epitomized it, abbreviated it, modernized it, dramatized it, and fictionized it.[3]

Which point of view is the more nearly accurate? Let us look first at those authors who came from out the preceding century and then glance at our current writers. Stephen Crane died in 1900.

> He passed his childhood in an atmosphere of Methodism, intellectually anaesthetic, emotionally stimulative. His father . . . doctor of divinity and preacher of note . . . was a Methodist with misgivings. Stephen's mother, Mary, the daughter and sister of ministers, took her Methodism straight. She was a fundamentalist of the old Ocean Grove order. . . . His intellect early rebelled against Methodism, but for his emotions it was a permanent enrichment.[4]

"You must not be offended by Mr. Hueffer's manner," he wrote to a friend concerning Joseph Conrad's literary helper. "He patronizes Mr. James. He patronizes Mr. Conrad. Of course he patronizes me and he will patronize Almighty God when they meet, but God will get used to it, for Hueffer is all right." [5]

Among Joel Chandler Harris' favorites were Sir Thomas Browne, Addison, Steele, Goldsmith, "and later the Bible and Shakespeare."

Said the dean of American letters, William Dean Howells:

I have read somewhat of the theology of the Swedenborgian faith I was brought up in, but I have not read other theological works; and I do not apologize for not liking any. The Bible itself was not much known to me at an age when most children have been obliged to read it several times over; the gospels were indeed familiar, and they have always been to me the supreme human story; but the rest of the New Testament I had not read when a man grown, and only passages from the Old Testament, like the story of the creation, the story of Joseph, and the poems of Job and Ecclesiastes, with occasional Psalms. I therefore came to the Scriptures with a sense at once fresh and mature, and I can never be too glad that I learned to see them under the vaster horizon and in the truer perspective of experience.[6]

It is 1922, in the room of a man just dead. On the table is a prayer book, inscribed by him that very morning:

Teach me thy way, O Lord, and I will walk in thy truth; O knit my heart unto thee that I may fear thy Name. Psalm 86:11. Thomas Nelson Page.

Hamlin Garland, the later dean of American letters, confessed that he had read the Bible

"from kivver to kivver," as the old people used to say. The old King James version was our Bible and both my grandsires were students of it. They knew it almost by heart. . . . As I grew toward manhood I heard much talk of its noble simplicity. I doubt if it influenced me directly, but indirectly it undoubtedly served as a corrective to the vernacular of my neighbors and the slovenly English of the press.[8]

Next comes Rupert Hughes.

Since childhood I have been a constant student of the Bible in all its versions. As I lost my belief in the inspiration or even the truthfulness of the texts as revealed religion, I have perhaps come to admire all the more the ingenuity and fervor of the authors as authors.[9]

Since Winston Churchill created sensations with *The Inside of the Cup* and other biblically titled books, one expects to find him feeling, as he does, that the purity and beauty of the English language is best expressed by the King James Bible.

Among women writers Zona Gale read the Bible "virtually daily" from the age of fourteen to sixteen, and "frequently" for twenty years thereafter, getting from it titles and suggestions for stories and articles. Willa Cather's *Death Comes for the Archbishop* and *Shadows on the Rock* were climaxed by her turning to the Roman Catholic faith. Dorothy Canfield Fisher's *The Bent Twig* shows in its title the origin of its theme. Bess Streeter Aldrich has movingly told her own story:

> Born of a pioneer mother who was deeply religious, I have no earlier recollection than her deep-throated voice intoning the majestic lines of the Psalms. I can hear it yet: "Oh, Lord, how manifold are thy works. In wisdom hast thou made them all. The earth is full of thy riches." The lilting words meant more to me as poetry than as any statement of religious fervor.
>
> She seemed to half sing the verses,—they accompanied my whole childhood as a deep-toned organ accompanies a service. This—more than a study of the Bible on my own part—has had its influence upon my writing. Sometimes as I work, if perchance there comes a musically turned sentence, it seems in some queer way to be connected with that long silenced intonation of the Psalms. . . . Does this early influence help me write? I do not know. All I know is that when I have agonized over a clumsy sentence and have finally turned it into something satisfying, for the brief fraction of a moment I have a feeling of oneness with that deep-throated singing of the Psalms.[10]

Pulitzer prize winner Julia B. Peterkin's Scarlet Sister Mary was scarlet against the religious life of the Negro. Margaret Mitchell titled *Gone with the Wind* from Dowson's "Cynara," and Dowson got the idea from the Bible.

Nobel prize winner Pearl Buck's "narrative method is the method of the Old Testament, unmistakable in its rhythm and balance," despite her bitter repudiation of her missionary-parented childhood:

Therefore, I say to the unborn novelist, whatever your group may be, let them not be merely *good* people—let them be humorous and wayward and gay and intelligent and feeling and sensitive and let them not care to save either their own souls or the souls of others. Let them be those who remember what Jesus Christ said, "He that saveth his soul shall *lose* it!" Be born anywhere, little embryo novelist, but do not be born under the shadow of a great creed, not under the burden of original sin, not under the doom of salvation. Go out and be born among gypsies or thieves or among happy workaday people who live in the sun and do not think about their souls.[11]

Ellen Glasgow said in 1938:

As a very small child, I was a believing animal. . . . I believed in Santa Claus and in Original Sin; I believed in souls. . . . I believed that, by some miraculous performance, all this countless multitude of souls would be taken care of, through a sabbath day without ending, in an infinite heaven. But in one thing, I cannot recall that I ever believed; and that was the kind of God who had once savored the smoke of burnt offerings, and to whose ghost, in churches everywhere, good people were still chanting hymns of immelodious praise. . . . I could not trust an Everlasting Mercy, whether stern or mild, which was omnipotent, but permitted pain to exist, and the Prince of Darkness to roam the earth in search of whom he might devour. . . . It is true that the ineffable dim figures of the Christ and the Buddha affected me deeply. . . . I believe that the greatest need of the modern world is not for a multitude of machines but for a new and a higher conception of God.[12]

Rebecca West's words were clear:

The spectacle of the rise of Fascism, and some contact with the Eastern Church . . . have made it clear to me that the life of Christ should have been an incomparable blessing to man and a revelation of the way he must follow if he is not to be a beast, and a failure at that. Christ was an incarnate denunciation of cruelty. He was sinless, he was full of love, he was ingenious in devising prescriptions of mercy; he was what the world needed. . . ." [13]

At about the same time a critic said of Marjorie Rawlings' Pulitzer-prize-winning presentation of Penny in *The Yearling:*

It is as though the author had said, "Come unto me all ye that are weary and heavy laden with Jeeter Lester and Studs Lonigan and Hemingway's tough guys and I will give you Penny Baxter." [14]

In best seller *Rawleigh's Eden,* Inglis Fletcher paralleled her American plot with the ancient story of Sarah and Hagar.

And now for the men again.

The sex-soaked novels of James Branch Cabell are also Bible-saturated. Jurgen praises the devil for delivering man.

> How insufferable would be our case if you and I, and all our fellow parishioners, were today hobnobbing with other beasts in the Garden which we pretend to desiderate on Sundays! To arise with swine and lie down with the hyena?—oh intolerable!

He suspects that his wife has been "carried off by a devil, poor fellow." Lovers all passed in couples, "as though they came from the Ark." A certain story is old, "and old it was when Methuselah was teething." One should "render the law what is due the law." A man rode toward him, "full armed in black, and having a red serpent with an apple in its mouth painted upon his shield." The failure of a demon to impersonate his wife well "raises the staggering supposition that the majority of married women must go to Heaven." Says Jurgen to himself:

> Why, then, this monarch reminds me in all things of David of Israel, who was so splendid and famous, and so greedy, in the ancient ages. For to these forests and islands and necks and other possessions, this Arthur Pendragon must be adding my one ewe lamb; and I lack a Nathan to convert him to repentance.[15]

Guenevere is the "loveliest thing God ever made, with joy in the new skill that had come to His fingers," so Jurgen "talked like an angel, without confining himself exclusively to celestial topics." " 'Well, my pet,' says Jurgen, 'the Jews got into Jericho by trying.' " The vampire's "clothes were orange-colored, for a reason sufficiently well known in Hell, and were embroidered everywhere with green fig-leaves."

"The religion of Hell is patriotism, and the government is an enlightened democracy," troubled by "pro-Celestial propaganda." Hell's aim is to make the world safe for democracy, "because Heaven clung to a tyrannical form of autocratic government" and was "ruled by an autocrat Who was not duly elected to His position."

Whatsoever a generation soweth that shall it also reap; and a generation that soweth to the flesh shall of the flesh also reap the neurotic alcoholics who stagger through the novels of Ernest Hemingway and Theodore Dreiser,[16]

remarks a critic, biblically. Dreiser said of his father:

I never knew a narrower, more hide-bound religionist, nor one more tender and loving in his narrow way. He was a crank, a tenth rate Saint Simon or Francis of Assisi, and yet a charming person if it had been possible to get his mind off the subject of religion for more than three seconds at a time. He worked, ate, prayed, slept and dreamed religion. With no other thought than the sanctity and glory and joy of the Catholic Church, he was constantly attempting to drive a decidedly recalcitrant family into a similar point of view.

Dreiser's mother was

a pagan mother taken over into the Catholic Church at marriage, because she loved a Catholic and would follow her love anywhere. A great poet mother, because she loved fables and fairies and half believed in them, and once saw the Virgin Mary standing in our garden, blue robes, crown and all, and was sure it was she.[17]

Reading Huxley, Tyndall, and Spencer caused Dreiser to give up, he says, the "lingering filaments of Catholicism" which were "trailing about" him.

His account of his "conversion" is undoubtedly sincere. Yet there are depths in his subconsciousness into which he has not dived—depths where "lingering filaments of Catholicism" still trail. He has written scarcely a short story or novel in which he does not at one place or another indicate his leanings toward the mystic.[18]

In the same spirit another critic reports of Hemingway:

Mr. Hemingway, who, if he ever sees this comment will probably be annoyed, has the hard lapidary verbiage of the book of Joshua.[19]

Sinclair Lewis once stood in a Kansas City pulpit and dared God to strike him dead—a publicity-grabbing stunt probably not altogether divorced from the sales report on his caricature of the clergy, *Elmer Gantry*, which, "more of a cartoon strip than a study of religion," is nevertheless crammed with biblical things.

In *Main Street* Fern Mullins flares out:

> My dear, Mrs. Bogart's God may be—Main Street's God, but all the courageous, intelligent people are fighting him—though he slay us.[20]

In *Arrowsmith* plague-dying Sondelius babbles:

> Gottlieb is right about these jests of God. Yey! His best one is the tropics. God planned them so beautiful, flowers and sea and mountains. He made the fruit to grow so well that man need not work—and then He laughed, and stuck in volcanoes and snakes and damp heat and early senility and the plague and malaria. But the nastiest trick he ever played on man was inventing the flea.[21]

In the same book Arrowsmith prays the prayer of the scientist:

> God give me unclouded eyes and freedom from haste. God give me a quiet and relentless anger against all pretense and all pretentious work and all work left slack and unfinished. God give me a restlessness whereby I may neither sleep nor accept praise till my observed results equal my calculated results or in pious glee I discover and assault my error. God give me strength not to trust to God! [22]

One does not easily forget Sherwood Anderson's description of his father:

> There were tales to be told and he was the teller of tales. "It is sufficient. Can a man live by bread alone? There is food on the table now. Eat! . . . I am a man of faith. I tell you a sparrow shall not fall to the ground without my notice. I will make a tale of it—tell why and how it fell. The most marvellous tale in the world might be made from the fall of a sparrow. Is not the workman worthy of his hire? What about the lilies of the field, eh? They toil not and neither do they spin—do they?"
>
> And yet, was Solomon, in all his glory,
> arrayed like one of these? [23]

In *Adam and Eve* John Erskine describes Adam's "social life" before he met Lilith, his first wife, or Eve, his second. Observing certain animals switching away at flies, Adam "suspected cows."

Then came Thornton Wilder, probing into God's ways in *The Bridge of San Luis Rey* and in *Heaven's My Destination* letting George Brush try, "with big muscles, a tenor voice, and not an atom of common sense, what every one else is sure will never work—the gospel."

The question in the nineteen thirties and forties was not whether Lloyd Douglas would be on the best seller list, but which and how many of his fictional pulpits would be on that magic Ark at any given time. As the thirties went out, Robert Munson Grey published *I, Yahweh,* "a novel in the form of an autobiography" of God. William Saroyan explained the Trouble with Tigers: he had, he said, written two million false words to find one word—God.

> I have two more words, but each is only partly achieved.
> What is the second word? said the young Jew.
> *Is,* I said.
> *Is?*
> Yes.
> And what is the third?
> *Love,* I said.
> The last two words are not yet completely achieved, I said.
> Your translation is a little trite, isn't it? said the young Jew.
> On the contrary, I said.[24]

Ben Hecht issued his *Book of Miracles,* in which

> the screen's greatest lover . . . is snatched away to heaven during Hollywood's filming of the Life of Christ, and endowed by God with a dose of divinity so that he may play the main role more accurately.[25]

This, making him invisible to cameras, ruins his career. He insists that he has seen God. Hollywood thinks he has taken to dope.

In England, meanwhile, George Moore had long since created a rumpus with his unorthodox fictionizing of the life of Christ, in *The Brook Kerith,* and H. G. Wells had written *God the Invisible King.* In *The Undying Fire* he had gone to the Book of Job, and in *Mr. Britling Sees It Through* he had said that man should be patient with God; He was doing the best He could.

Arnold Bennett had told a dancing partner that he never went to church.

Did I believe in a supreme being? Yes. Did I believe in the divinity of Christ? No. Did I believe in the Bible? Parts of it.[26]

Galsworthy had written:

Hitherto God, if it means anything, has been accepted as the highest, remotest, most infinite and final—not idea or conception but—emotional speculation of which man is capable. . . . We shall never know, never find out, and this it is which constitutes "the glory and poetry of God." [27]

For Easter, 1938, James Hilton wrote with sad prescience:

What shall we do to be saved? . . . We see the Gadarene pace of events with wide-open eyes; we are alive at our own funeral. . . .

There is no clear answer except one we can give to ourselves, and it is not a new or, today, a fashionable answer. We must watch—perhaps we must even pray.[28]

The war, which Hilton foreboded, came. Fiction took on a deeper note, with overtones of religion more frequent.

36. The Demnition Bowwows

The age of Amen has given way to the age of Oh, yeah?
—GAIUS GLENN ATKINS[29]

AUBREY DE VERE's idea of eternal punishment was quaint—it would be listening to Huxley and Tyndall disputing eternally on the nonexistence of God. In these later days it would be listening to a symposium upon the decay of the Bible.

Since it is always easier to assume than to ascertain, and since a substantial part of each generation invariably assumes that its contemporaries are going to the demnition bowwows by the swiftest possible route, the list of wailings is long and the voices loud. Says one:

One cannot very well deny that the battle has gone against the Bible. . . . The evidence is too strong, and comes from too many quarters, that the old saturation with Biblical phraseology and imagery and illustration is a thing of the past. . . . Take the orations, the essays, the poems, especially the novels, of the last twenty-five years, and . . .

you will find in them not one Biblical illustration to a hundred that you would have found a century ago in similar writings.[30]

Interesting if true. Another bewails:

Those who talk of the Bible as a "monument of English prose" are merely admiring it as a monument over the grave of Christianity. . . . The Bible has had a *literary* influence upon English literature *not* because it has been considered as literature, but because it has been considered as the report of the Word of God, and the fact that men of letters now discuss it as "literature" probably indicates the *end* of its literary influence.[31]

A third asserts:

The English Bible is dying. I do not mean its theology nor its historical or spiritual content. . . . It . . . is losing, or has already lost, a power over the imagination almost unexampled in history. . . . To urge a youth entering any department of modern life to form his style upon the Bible is as foolish as to advise tilting, camel-riding and the study of medicinal herbs as a preparation for engineering and the law.[32]

To a fourth,

it is the prose, indeed, of the long face, the knitted brow, and the patriarchal gesture.[33]

A fifth cynically says:

It is still the book of which the greatest number of copies are sold, and perhaps the smallest proportion of copies read, in relation to sales.[34]

Two more hit with heavy hand:

Was the new freedom in sex morality and speech a turn toward the courtly-chivalrous code as it stood before the Reformation darkened chivalry with the Hebraic shadow? If so we might read much of the hullaballoo of casting the old taboos overboard as the effort to shake off habits formed by five hundred years of Bible reading ending with the death of Victoria, which either by effect or by coincidence marks the time when we decided that the Bible was a bore.[35]

There is but one accurate reply to such diatribes. It is to say as gently as possible, "Gentlemen, your words are vigorous, but—the facts are against you." We have just seen that the Bible has not departed from twentieth-century fiction. Let us look at nonfictional prose.

In 1909 John Kendrick Bangs had a hilarious time with *The Autobiography of Methuselah* and the patriarch's reactions to Noah's ark (Noah's Folly, the neighbors called it) and Noah's "International Marine and Zoo Flotation Company."

Two years later Ambrose Bierce concocted the *Devil's Dictionary,* from which the following definitions are selected:

DELUGE, *n.* A notable first experiment in baptism which washed away the sins (and sinners) of the world.

. . . *House of God,* a building with a steeple and a mortgage on it.

INFIDEL, *n.* In New York, one who does not believe in the Christian religion; in Constantinople, one who does.

OBSESSED, *pp.* Vexed by an evil spirit, like the Gadarene swine and other critics.[36]

While Bierce denied being a Christian, his determining test of right was:

"What in the circumstances would Jesus have done?"—the Jesus of the New Testament, and not the Jesus of the commentators, theologians, priests and parsons.[37]

A few years earlier Helen Keller had exulted:

But how shall I speak of the glories I have since discovered in the Bible? For years I have read it with an ever-broadening sense of joy and inspiration, and I love it as I love no other book.[38]

In 1913 Arthur Christopher Benson confessed:

I used as a child to pore over the Apocalypse, which I thought by far the most beautiful and absorbing of all the books of the Bible; it seemed full of rich and dim pictures, things which I could not interpret and did not wish to interpret, the shining of clear gem-like walls, lonely riders, amazing monsters, sealed books, all of which took perfectly definite shape in the childish imagination. The consequence is that I can no more criticize it than I could criticize old tapestries, or pictures familiar from infancy. They are there, just so, and any difference of form is inconceivable.

In one point, however, the strange visions have come to hold for me an increased grandeur; I used to think of much of it as a sort of dramatic performance, self-consciously enacted for the benefit of the spectator; but now I think of it as an awful and spontaneous energy of spiritual life going on, of which the prophet was enabled to catch a glimpse. Those "voices crying day and night" "the new song that was sung before the throne," the cry of "Come and see"—these were but part of a vast and urgent business, which the prophet was allowed to overhear. It is not a silent place, that highest heaven, of indolence and placid peace, but a scene of fierce activity and the clamour of mighty voices.[39]

In 1917 G. Stanley Hall wrote significantly:

Finally, from all the data sketched in this chapter the psychologist draws his inevitable conclusions. . . . The first is that no theme, save, perhaps, the perennial theme of love, has ever made so strong an appeal to literary imagination as the story of Jesus. . . . The recent productions show that the tide is now setting against the conceptions of the Antichrist or the Superman as the consummation of human ideals, and from disparagement to ardent affirmations of the essentials of Christianity.[40]

In 1920 Clayton Hamilton suggested that no man had ever become a master of English prose whose ear had not in early childhood been habitually trained upon the King James Version, "the slow dark march of measured and majestic syllables that were applauded in the high and far-off times of that curious and futile king who patronized the arts and wrote a treatise on tobacco."

The Book of Job . . . was written with a grandeur of great prose that must remain forever unforgettable so long as men have ears for hearkening.[41]

The same idea was expressed by Davida McCaslin later in the decade.

I sometimes think that those who have attended a ritualistic church regularly for a lifetime ought to write better prose than others. . . . I am not sure how much theological good it does to learn the catechism, but I am confident it is a help to style. Rhythm is a matter of nerves, not of brain.[42]

Meanwhile, Irvin S. Cobb had announced:

When the last trump sounds and the quick and the dead come trooping to be weighed in the balance for their deeds done in the flesh I expect to be there along with the rest of the tribe of fictionists. . . . In conclusion, I would state that I wear a seven and three-eighths halo and I figure that I shall require an oversized set of wings, with a spread of at least fourteen feet from tip to tip. Where do I get my harp? [43]

H. L. Mencken joyously hurled his murderous vocabulary at William Jennings Bryan:

Wherever the flambeaux of Chautauqua smoked and guttered, and the bilge of Idealism ran in the veins and Baptist pastors dammed the brooks with the sanctified, and men gathered who were weary and heavy laden, and their wives who were full of Peruna and as fecund as the shad (Alosa Sapidissima)—there the indefatigable Jennings set up his traps and spread his bait. . . . And when he rose at the end of the day to discharge his Message there would be such breathless attention, such a rapt and enchanted ecstasy, such a sweet rustle of amens as the world had not known since Johann fell to Herod's ax. . . . When he died he was the peer of Abraham.[44]

In more solemn mood Sir James G. Frazer, of *The Golden Bough,* bore witness:

The Bible . . . unrolls a vast panorama in which the ages of the world move before us in a long trail of solemn imagery. . . . Against this gorgeous background, this ever shifting scenery, now bright with the hues of heaven, now lurid with the glare of hell, we see mankind strutting and playing their little part on the stage of history . . . and then, last scene of all, we see the great white throne. . . . The love of the Bible is not confined to those who accept its dogmas. Though many of us can no longer, like our fathers, find in its pages the solution of the dark, the inscrutable riddle of human existence, yet the volume must still be held sacred by all who reverence the high aspirations to which it gives utterance, and the pathetic associations with which the faith and piety of so many generations have invested the familiar words. The reading of it breaks into the dull round of common life like a shaft of sunlight on a cloudy day, or a strain of solemn music heard in a mean street.[45]

Bruce Barton wrote *The Man Nobody Knows* and *The Book Nobody Knows.*

Gamaliel Bradford's experience was illuminating. When he was fifty-eight he scorned the Bible as "a mass of picturesque and chaotic legends, which would be infinitely diverting if it were not awe-inspiring from having worked such enormous havoc with the destiny of mankind."

The Bible itself has become utterly remote from me in these latter years. I cannot read it, never read a word of it. It partly bores me, and partly afflicts me with a strange uneasiness, as if, after all, hell were waiting for me round the corner.[46]

Four years later he found it necessary to read the Gospels in preparation for a chapter of his autobiography. When his book appeared it minced no words:

Among the varied agencies for disciplining the mutinous, rebellious, all-engrossing I, none probably has been more notable or more efficient than the life and teaching of Jesus. Therefore it seems fitting, as typical of those agencies, to make the figure of Jesus and what he represents a central element and as it were the keystone, in the structure of this book.[47]

The great biographer had found the Great Biography.

The 1930's multiplied materials. When at the beginning of the decade the London *Morning Post* asked Sir Arthur Quiller-Couch to name the finest literary passage in the Bible, he replied:

If one required perfection of historical narrative, there is David questioning the messengers for news of Absalom, or the walk to Emmaus; if romantic mystery, Jacob's wrestling at the ford; if pellucid parable, the Prodigal Son; if the fibre of an exquisite short story, that of Ruth or of St. Paul's letter to Philemon; if dramatic solemnity, Solomon's prayer or a chapter from Job; if thankfulness for comfort, or lament and hope in exile, Psalms 23 and 137; and if for an epithalamium, Psalm 45; for passion the Song of Songs; for sad wisdom, Ecclesiastes; for odic magnificence passage after passage in Isaiah; for the eloquence of faith, as many in St. Paul's Epistles to the Romans, Corinthians, and Hebrews.

I cite a passage which, being put into the mouth of the Almighty, has to dare sublimity, and to my mind achieves it.[48] Then he cited II Esdras 6:1-6.

"Dean Stiff" prefaced his handbook for hoboes, *The Milk and Honey Route,* with a hoboes' hymn:

Nobody knows where the hobo goes,
Nobody knows where he gets his clothes;
Nobody knows but Jesus.
Nobody knows, nobody heeds,
How he gets his beer or bums his feeds;
Nobody knows but Jesus.[49]

About this time muckraker Lincoln Steffens decided to read the New Testament.

What did the Christians believe, exactly? I decided then and there to read the New Testament the next time I was at home and had time, not myself to believe, but to see what the good church-going Christians believed.

The experience was an adventure so startling that I wanted everybody else to have it; I still recommend people to read the New Testament as I read it, without reverence, with feet up on a desk and a pipe in the mouth, as news. It is news. It made the stuff I was writing in the magazine, old stuff. All my stories of all the cities and states were one story . . . and these were all in that old story of Christ in the New Testament. . . . I never heard Christianity, as Jesus taught it in the New Testament, preached to the Christians. But I did see it practised in Politics.[50]

Upton Sinclair was shouting at Catholics, Presbyterians, Methodists, Episcopalians, Baptists, and Unitarians—

You serpents, you generation of vipers, how can you escape the damnation of hell? [51]

"The Bible had a great influence upon me," he said, as he paused to get his breath.

I read it continually when I was young. . . . In my student days, I read both the Old and New Testaments through in English, and I read the New Testament half a dozen times in Latin, once in Greek, and once in German, as a part of my study of those languages.[52]

In 1935 Bliss Perry's *And Gladly Teach* appeared. Of books, Perry said:

Job and *Don Quixote* and *Faust* are more timeless pages still. . . . If I were to make a choice . . . I should certainly begin with the most fascinating book, or rather library of books, ever put between covers: the Bible.[53]

To keep things from getting too serious, Reginald Arkell reported that

the Hundred Years' War was brought to an end by Joan of Arc, a French descendant of Noah of Ark, who became inspired, thus unfairly defeating the English in several more decisive battles.[54]

In 1936 a survey at the University of Iowa, on the search for "cultural literature," ignoring entirely religious values, found the Bible placed first.

Henry C. Link wrote *The Return to Religion.*

In 1937 Kipling's autobiography appeared, with the glint of Scripture rich in its ore. His housemaster at school had been "cumbered about with many cares." "C— broke his precious ointments" over his head. When General William Booth offered to walk on his head and play the tambourine with his toes if he could thereby win one more soul, Kipling thought, "He had the right of it ('if by any means I can save some')." When offspring appeared imminent at the Kipling home,

the Committee on Ways and Means "considered a field and bought it"—as much as ten whole acres. . . . (I here earnestly commend to the attention of the ambitious young a text in the thirty-third chapter of Ecclesiastes which runs: *"So long as thou livest and hast breath in thee, give not thyself over to any."*)[55]

In the same year Aldous Huxley turned to an earnest consideration of human problems.

From Isaiah to Karl Marx the prophets have spoken with one voice. In the golden age to which they look forward there will be liberty, peace, justice, and brotherly love. "Nation shall no more lift sword against nation, . . . the world shall be full of the knowledge of the Lord, as the waters cover the sea."[56]

In 1937, too, Albert J. Nock wrote *Free Speech and Plain Language*—a book which does not belie its name, furnishing such tidbits as:

The fifteenth chapter of the First Epistle to the Corinthians is one of the few passages of the Scripture that remain at all generally well known; we hear it read at funerals. . . .

Bill McN plucked my sleeve and whispered, "Harry won't be in heaven half an hour before you'll hear him say, 'Dammit, this gold hurts my feet.' "[57]

Yet in "Isaiah's Job" he makes an eloquent plea for someone to do today what Isaiah did in his day—minister to the intelligent minority.

In the year of Uzziah's death, the Lord commissioned the prophet to go out and warn the people of the wrath to come. "Tell them what a worthless lot they are," he said. "Tell them what is wrong, and why, and what is going to happen unless they have a change of heart and straighten up. Don't mince matters. . . . I suppose I ought to tell you," he added, "that it won't do any good . . . and you will probably be lucky if you get out with your life."

This causes Isaiah to raise the obvious question of the good sense of starting something foredoomed to failure.

"Ah," the Lord said, "you do not get the point. There is a Remnant there that you know nothing about. They are obscure, unorganized, inarticulate, . . . they are the ones who will come back and build up a new society. . . . Your job is to take care of the Remnant, so be off now and set about it."

Then says Nock:

If I were young and had the notion of embarking in the prophetical line, I would certainly take up this branch of the business.[58]

In 1937, also, Earl Cranston ended his *Swords or Plowshares?* with:

A certain man went down a road to Jericho—it might have been not merely a man, but a people, and the road might have been not only in Palestine, but in Eastern Asia, Northern Africa, Central Europe, or anywhere else. He fell among thieves, who stripped him and left him half dead. There passed by on the other side a priest and a Levite—it might have been a legalist, a profiteer, or an isolationist. Then there came a Samaritan, a foreigner, with no material interest to further; he sympathized, bound up the wounds, cared immediately for the victim, and arranged for his permanent future. Who was the good neighbor? The one who showed mercy and imagination. Across the expanse of space and time there may still be heard a voice, now with the sanction of eternity, saying even to favored America, "Go thou and do likewise." [59]

And in 1937, too, the *Publishers' Weekly* was moved to comment:

Three of the most discussed publishing projects of last year were . . . the great Oxford Lectern Bible . . . of which almost the entire limited edition at two hundred and sixty-five dollars had been sold out . . . the spectacular printing of five hundred thousand complete Bibles which retailed at twenty-five cents and sold at a profit at that price . . . And finally there was the best seller . . . "The Bible Designed to be Read as Living Literature," of which about half a million dollars' worth were sold in a year's time with every buyer seemingly delighted with his purchase.[60]

The end of the 1930's went busily. Logan P. Smith was remarking quizzically:

That God should spend His eternity—which might be so much better employed—in spinning countless Solar Systems, and skylarking, like a great child, with tops and teetotums—is not this a serious scandal? I wonder what all our circumgyrating Monotheists really do think of it.[61]

E. M. Forster was saying:

My lawgivers are Erasmus and Montaigne, not Moses and St. Paul. My temple stands not upon Mount Moriah but in that Elysian Field where even the immoral are admitted. My motto is "Lord, I disbelieve—help thou my unbelief." [62]

Lusty Hendrik Willem Van Loon was trumpeting:

I am all for truth. But the Truth, in the Pauline sense of the word, is as little to my liking as cyanide of potassium. . . . Now I have long since given up any desire to pinch-hit for the great Jehovah. . . . This leads me to still another question which no man of this Western world has been able to escape these last two thousand years: "What think you of Christ?"

Fortunately, I can give you a completely straightforward answer. I think everything of him. I unqualifiedly accept him as one of the greatest of my gay philosophers. But I have always experienced great difficulties in getting at him because his figure was completely obscured by the dark shadow of that Paul of Tarsus. . . . The simple, lovable carpenter of Nazareth, so beautifully and sublimely unconscious of the practical world around him, so bravely fighting his lonely battle against those forces of malice and evil and greed which turn our lovely planet into a perpetual vale of tears—yes, he is a teacher whom I would most happily follow unto the ends of the earth. But not if Paul the tentmaker was to be one of our companions.[63]

Newspaper columnist Oscar Odd McIntire is reported as always having kept on his work table two favorite books—a dictionary and a Bible.

In 1939 a Gallup poll revealed that the people of America rated the Bible as "the most interesting" book they had ever read.

Nearly one person in five, of those having opinions, name the *Bible.* It was ranked first by men, by persons over thirty, and by Southerners, Mid-Westerners and Westerners.[64]

As the 1940's entered, the *United States Catalog* revealed that book titles drawn from the Bible were increasing. The three most commonly used words in motion-picture titles were "heart," "devil," and "hell," the first having been used in 88 movie titles, the second in 70, and the third in 41.

Halford E. Luccock was getting irritated by candid cameras:

Whither may I flee from thy presence? If I go abroad in the street, thou art there, and if I hide at home, thou art there. And if I take the wings of the morning and fly to the uttermost part of the earth, thou art in the midst of me.[65]

Modern religion was being challenged, but the Bible was not being abandoned.

37. Back to Methuselah

The worst three weeks
In the show business credo:
Holy Week, Christmas Week,
And a week in Toledo.

—ANONYMOUS[66]

IT IS easy to misunderstand America and to find religious meanings where there are none. A newly arrived Irishman, told to wait for the green light before crossing the street, and noting the brief period the orange light shone, is said to have remarked, "They don't give the Protestants much time to get across, do they?" There is also the Polish refugee professor who reported (with a twinkle in his eye) that he had found in America a new saint, the patron saint of torn-up streets. Wherever he had found repair gangs, they had been working under the advertised protection of "St. Closed."

It is easy to misunderstand America, but it is not easy to misinterpret the significance of the fact that the New York Public Library in 1931 issued a list of 1,948 plays based upon the Bible, the work of 1,387 English-writing and 75 foreign authors and editors.[67] This is in spite of the fact that drama in England was long kept from the Bible.

Hannah More, who lived well into the nineteenth century, put the matter succinctly:

> Light and darkness are not more opposed to each other than the Bible and the play book. If the one be good the other must be evil. The only way to justify the stage, as it is, as it has ever been, as it is ever likely to be, is to condemn the Bible—the same individual cannot defend both.[68]

Not everybody was so antagonistic to the stage, but English censorship barred new biblical plays from the professional stage until within the twentieth century. In 1907 seventy-one people, including the leading authors of England, joined in a public letter of protest against this censorship. By 1909 it was definitely on the defensive.

> The new censor, Mr. G. Redford, came under examination. . . . He had to acknowledge that he issued his edicts without any principle to guide him: asked why he had banned Laurence Housman's *Bethlehem* he asserted that plays on sacred subjects were not allowed, yet he acknowledged he had passed Miss Buckton's *Eager Heart* which introduces the same sacred characters.[69]

So things went, without rhyme or reason. Old plays upon biblical subjects were allowed; new plays upon the same subject were barred. Wilde's *Salomé,* forbidden as a play, was permitted as an opera. The ban was lifted from a play on David when ten characters had been renamed. Joseph and Potiphar's wife were taboo, but the same tale in modern dress was approved. *Green Pastures* was forbidden on the stage, allowed in the cinemas. Plays barred from the professional stage might be given in churches or before subscriber audiences.

Finally, in 1913, Louis Parker's *Joseph and His Brethren* was licensed and ran for nearly two hundred performances.

> *It was the first Biblical play licensed since the old Mysteries.* And this was all the more remarkable as whole slabs were verbal transcriptions from Genesis. I dare say the censor did not recognize the source. Of course, the restrictions having been broken through, a lot of quasi-Biblical plays have been done; but none has had anything like the success of *Joseph.*[70]

One of the archfoes of English censorship has been George Bernard Shaw, who asserts that it makes the theater "that last sanctuary of unreality." In *You Never Can Tell* Mrs. Clandon is told that there is only one place where her opinions would still pass as advanced.

> "The Church? perhaps?"
> "No: the theatre."

The church, however, takes many drubbings at his hands. A revival of religion is occurring, he says, touching "even clergymen," and so strong that "not the church of England itself can keep it out." The average clergyman's life is a routine which "does not necessarily touch Christianity at any point except the point of the tongue." Men say, "We are not talking about God: we are talking about practical affairs"; and in *Man and Superman* "We are told that when Jehovah created the world he saw that it was good. What would he say now?" Yet in play after play—*The Devil's Disciple, Saint Joan, Androcles and the Lion, Candida, Back to Methusaleh,* etc.—he discusses matters emanating from the Bible, and in one preface he said, "After contemplating the world and human nature for nearly sixty years, I see no way out of the world's misery but the way which would have been found by Christ's will." [71]

Then in his old age he turned away from drama to write *The Adventures of a Black Girl in Her Search for God.* The inquiring maiden met successively the God of Noah, with his fondness for the perfume of fresh blood; the God of Job, who proved to be an incorrigible and usually-off-the-track arguer; the nonexistent God of Ecclesiastes; the justice-loving God of Micah; the discarded-hypothesis God of science; the father God of Jesus, and she formed her personal conclusion regarding each.

In 1938 Shaw protested against an article of Laurence Housman's because it did not express preference for the verse style of the King James Version over the paragraph style of later translations. Said Shaw:

> I noticed that when the popular newspapers went back to the old Bible style, which demands that every sentence shall be more or less an epigram or a statement of real importance and impressiveness, the effect upon the style of our journalists was altogether to the good.

To this, Housman replied in mock-biblical form:

To the Editor of THE LONDON [a]MERCURY AND BOOKMAN

DEAR SIR,—

1. [b]Concerning tastes there can be plenty of disputation; but we stick to our own [c]conclusions.

2. G.B.S. likes paragraphs that [d]catch the eye. I like paragraphs that [e]catch the sense.

3. I have no use for paragraphs which [f]end in commas, [g]or semi-colons, [h]or colons which ought not to be colons.

4. If I find myself preferring these things I conclude that my education was bad, and that I have not [i]put away childish things.

5. [j]When I have to differ from G.B.S. I do so with regret;

6. But as he is my elder and my better [k]I do not rebuke him.

7. All the same, if he thinks that this [l]letter is improved by its Biblical and Jacobean construction, I don't.

Yours [m]faithfully,
LAURENCE HOUSMAN[72]

Longmeadow Street, Somerset.

[a] Acts XIV. 12.
[b] Ps. XXXIV. 8.
[c] Eccles. XII. 12, 13.
[d] Luke 11: 34.
[e] Ps. XXXII. 9.
[f] I Kings IX. 10, 17, 18, and X. 4, 14.
[g] I Kings VII. 41, 42, 46, 47.
[h] I Kings VIII. 22, 28.
[i] I Cor. XIII. 11.
[j] Prov. IX. 12.
[k] I Tim. V.1.
[l] Gal. VI. 11.
[m] Rev. II. 10.

In America there was no general censorship, but neither was there much native drama. The extreme recency of the profession may be seen in the fact that the first American dramatist to make his living by writing for the stage—Bronson Howard—died in 1908.

There were, of course, forerunners, such as George Washington Park Custis' *Pocahontas* (1830), whose dusky heroine paused to declaim melodramatically,

For know that I have abjured thy senseless gods and now worship the Supreme Being, the true Manitou, and the father of the universe; 'tis his Almighty hand that sustains me, 'tis his divine spirit that breathes in my soul and prompts Pocahontas to a deed which future ages will admire,[73]

before—with one eye turned toward God and the other cocked at the headlines of posterity—this simple child of nature hurled her lissome form athwart the endangered body of John Smith.

When native American drama finally got under way, pagan-puritan William Vaughn Moody followed his poetic trilogy, *The Firebringer, The Masque of Judgment,* and the unfinished *Death of Eve,* by two prose stage plays, *The Great Divide* and *The Faith Healer,* based upon conflicts set up by religious backgrounds.

Augustus Thomas looked back through the years to the influences which had been important in his own life:

The books, after the nursery jumble was past, were, in order of discovery, the Bible, Shakespeare, some other poets already named, Washington Irving, Holmes, Hawthorne, Ingersoll, Plutarch, Emerson, Dr. Thomas Jay Hudson, William James, Thomas Jefferson, Hugo, Voltaire, Montaigne. I think the Bible, Shakespeare, Holmes, and Emerson influenced my vocabulary as far as it was permeable under the callous of the railroad yard.

I didn't select the reading by any superior resolve or instinct. The New Testament I learned by rote to recite in Sunday-school for tickets exchangeable for prizes. I have a recollection of reciting on one Sunday one hundred and forty-four verses, beginning with, "In those days came John the Baptist," and so on. This was not a religious exercise with us boys. It was a business proposition. I have since gone to the New Testament with various motives; once to study out and as far as possible deduce from the speech and story the personal appearance of the Man of Nazareth when there was a project to produce a passion play. The Old Testament I read for its entertaining stories, skipping, boy fashion, the begats.[74]

After the war Maxwell Anderson and Laurence Stallings' *What Price Glory?* was greeted with anguished charges of blasphemy, by those who forgot that war itself might be blasphemous.

That was as perfect an example of straining at a gnat and swallowing a camel as can be conceived.[75]

Their play was outspoken:

Captain Flagg: Damn headquarters! It's some more of that world-safe-for-democracy slush. Every time they come around here I've got to ask myself is this an army or is it a stinking theosophical society for ethical culture and the Bible-backing uplift! I don't want that band of Gideons from headquarters! . . .

Kiper: The chaplain said my folks was all praying for me to come through, and for God to spare me after hearing their prayers. God, I ain't that dirty a coward! That's a case of saying, Oh God, don't kill our child. Kill every kid in the neighborhood, but bring the one marked Kiper safe back home. . . . No. I don't want none of that for mine. And you can take all your New Testaments with the khaki backs and throw them in the incinerator so far as I want anything out of 'em. I'd rather have a book of cigarette papers any time.[76]

Already a few alert observers were noting that, the world over, a renaissance of biblical plays was beginning to appear.

One interesting feature of twentieth century drama has been the notable increase in the use of the Bible as dramatic material. This is a curious recrudescence of the Mystery Play—a return to the origins of the modern theatre. . . . Whether the large number—and they are surprisingly numerous—of modern "passion plays" has had anything to do with the growing use of the Bible as quarry for the dramatist, I do not know; possibly just the contrary is a stronger factor, I mean the secularization of the Sacred Books. Whatever the cause, the fact is that Mystery Plays have come to life again, and many modern playwrights simply take a story from the Bible, add or subtract as they please, and a new play is born. . . . There is no doubt that we are to behold an increasing number of Biblical plays.[77]

Such was William Lyon Phelps's conclusion; then he mentioned Oscar Wilde's *Salomé,* Stephen Phillips' *Herod,* Louis Parker's

Joseph and His Brethren, Richard Burton's *Rahab,* Josephine Preston Peabody's *The Piper,* John Masefield's *Good Friday,* Stuart Walker's dramatization of Job, Ben Greet's revival of *Everyman,* and the preface to Shaw's *Androcles and the Lion,* as well as Jerome K. Jerome's *The Passing of the Third Floor Back* and Charles Rann Kennedy's *The Servant in the House.*

Of the 205 "modern morality plays and plays containing morality elements" which Myrta Ethel McGinnis listed in 1917 as written in various countries since 1838, three were in the twenty years begining in 1838, seven in the twenty years beginning in 1858, thirty in the twenty years beginning in 1878, and 165 in the twenty years beginning in 1898.[78] In 1918 Tudor Lanius made a similar survey of the miracle play, finding a like rapid growth; he named as the first modern miracle play William Butler Yeats's *The Countess Cathleen,* 1892.[79]

Emma Fisher Hyde's study of the mystery play, completed in 1925, discussed 150 such plays written in various countries since 1840. Of those in English, one was written in the twenty years beginning in 1840, one in the twenty years beginning in 1860, four in the twenty years beginning in 1880, and fifty-five in the twenty years beginning in 1900.

> The chronological consideration has shown an almost continuous interest since 1888, with a decided acceleration from 1900 to the present time. The indications are that this interest is continuing. . . . The indications are . . . that America is, since 1910, the country most actively interested in the modern mystery play.[80]

The 1927 Pulitzer prize went to Paul Green's *In Abraham's Bosom.* Three years later the same prize went to Marc Connelly's *Green Pastures,* with its clambake in heaven, its Negro spirituals, and the Lord smoking a ten-cent cigar. Thrice-Pulitzer-winner Eugene O'Neill turned at last from his dramas of frustration to *Lazarus Laughed* and then to *Days Without End,* with its climax of victorious prayer before the Figure on the Cross.

In 1937 Maxwell Anderson's *Star Wagon* was using hymns: "Jerusalem the Golden," and "Hark, 'Tis the Shepherd's Voice I Hear"; while John Murray and Allen Boretz's *Room Service* was closing with the first words of "Abide with Me," and Moss Hart and George Kaufmann's hilarious *You Can't Take It with You* was ending with the saying of grace before meals. Then came Brian

Doherty's *Father Malachy's Miracle,* setting things topsy-turvy. "A miracle? . . . Fancy that now! That's a type of law-breakin' I never run into before. . . . Did ye have a permit?"

In 1938 the critics were turning startled eyes to the New York stage and saying:

> It has been many a day since the New York theatre placed its money on the proscribed themes of death, miracles, and religion. . . . This season Broadway . . . plunged with the tabooed scripts and the customers liked it. . . . Nobody supposes for an instant that the producers have gone mystic or religious, but the fact that they have chosen to present a half dozen plays of this kind—with success—is dramatic evidence that they sensed the renewed interest.[81]

The metropolitan newspapers remarked upon the phenomenon, one mentioning *Susan and God,* and continuing:

> "Shadow and Substance" is another forthrightly religious play on Broadway. Also "Many Mansions." "Our Town" and "On Borrowed Time" are more oblique in their approach but they deal with righteousness.
>
> Plays are reflectors of trends. Has the long-talked-of revival of religion set in?
>
> Will the movies catch the contagion?[82]

In 1939 the Hollywood *Pilgrimage Play* reached its seven-hundredth performance.

Ever since Eve got ambitious for herself and her husband, asserts one of our essayists,

> we have all had to earn our livings by the sweat of our brows, but even if St. Michael did stand over our first parents with a flaming sword, and even if our factories do stand over us with flaming furnaces and filthy chimneys—or locked gates—even so, there was, I think, a sweet and humorous and playful angel, not in the best of favor in Heaven, who sneaked out of Eden with Adam and Eve, and afterwards, when they got tired of their hoes and accounts, led them to fishing streams and to abandoned orchards, to old pastures with mushrooms, and to blackberry patches.[83]

Nowadays he could fittingly take them to the theater occasionally, too.

38. Melody in Chaos

Mr. Bogardus said Oh all right, and speaking of lords,
he couldn't remember who was the king before
David, but Solomon was the king affidavit.
Mr. Ballatine buried Mr. Bogardus in the cellar and
went out in search of love.

—OGDEN NASH[84]

THOSE who claim that in the twentieth century the Bible has faded from modern poetry are grotesquely in error.

In Ireland and England, Yeats and Kipling continued to sing, sometimes of birds and butterflies. In Yeats's poem the moorfowl chanted devoutly:

Who holds the world between His bill and made us strong or weak
Is an undying moorfowl, and He lives beyond the sky.
The rains are from His dripping wing, the moonbeams from His
eye.[85]

And Kipling wrote, in his inimitable style, of "The Butterfly That Stamped," [86] wherein it appears that the Queen of Sheba, that lovely tourist who came avidly sightseeing through Solomon's realm, and the great king who was her magnificent host, had in common, according to Kipling, a most unusual accomplishment —each was a fluent linguist in the language of the butterflies, speaking, as butterflies no doubt gravely assured their majesties, without the slightest trace of accent, and flitting gracefully from topic to topic.

"Read Kipling's *Collected Verse* with the Old Testament at your elbow," [87] advised a critic.

Richard Le Gallienne paid belated homage.

So many of us grew up with what one might call a natural prejudice against the Bible.

Then some of us who cared for literature took it up casually and found its poetic beauty. We read the *Book of Job*—which, by the way, Mr. Swinburne is said to have known by heart; and as we read it even the stars themselves seemed less wonderful than this description of their marvel and mystery:

Canst thou bind the sweet influences of Pleiades
or loose the bands of Orion?

Canst thou bring forth Mazzaroth in his season?
Or canst thou guide Arcturus with his sons?

Or we read in the thirty-seventh chapter of the *Book of Ezekiel* of that weird valley that was full of bones—"And as I prophesied, there was a noise, and behold a shaking, and the bones came together bone to bone," surely one of the most wonderful visions of the imagination in all literature.

Or we read the marvellous denunciatory rhetoric of Jeremiah or Isaiah, or the music of the melodious heart-strings of King David; we read the solemn adjuration of the "King Ecclesiast" to remember our creator in the days of our youth, with its haunting picture of old age; and the loveliness of the *Song of Songs* passed into our lives forever.

To this purely literary love of the Bible there has been added within the last few years a certain renewed regard for it as the profoundest book of the soul, and for some minds not conventionally religious it has regained even some of its old authority as a spiritual guide and stay, and I will confess for myself that sometimes, as I fall asleep at night, I wonder if even Bernard Shaw has written anything to equal the Twenty-third Psalm.[88]

"Art and literature," asserted Alfred Noyes, "are confronted here by a Presence that shrivels them into insignificance; and there is no answer to its instant question—'Whom say *ye* that I am?'—but the answer of Peter, 'Thou art the Christ, the Son of the Living God.' "[89]

Masefield's *The Everlasting Mercy* has been followed by *Good Friday, The Trial of Jesus,* and *The Coming of Christ.*

T. S. Eliot came from *The Waste Land* to *Ash Wednesday.*

When C. Day Lewis wrote his "Transitional Poem," with its

Come up Methuselah,
You doddering superman!

he sectioned it "In the beginning was the Word," "And the Word was with God," "And the Word was God," "And the Word was made flesh."

In America, Markham was still reading to packed audiences "The Man with the Hoe"—written, he said, with the Bible as one part of its background.

I have read the King James version of the Bible since I was a shepherd boy on the Suisun Hills in Central California. I began by reading the Gospels of Jesus, and I soon saw that they were not merely theological documents, but were political documents with a vast social and industrial aim. These Gospels coupled with *The Man Who Laughs* by Victor Hugo were my chief inspirations when I wrote *The Man With the Hoe*. They were constantly in the background of my mind.

Yes, I have consciously studied the style of the great prophets. Undoubtedly the remarkable simplicity and directness of those masters of speech helped greatly to fashion my style in both prose and verse.[90]

Coming from a home in which there were only the Bible, the story of the Pyramids in their relation to Scripture, and an almanac, he could repeat as a child a hundred pages of the Gospels from memory—pages which he had learned while herding sheep.

In his manhood, claiming to know the contents of the twelve thousand books in his own library, Markham named the ten (which turned out to be fourteen) most precious books—ones which he would wish to have on a desert island:

I would take first of all the Gospels of Jesus. . . . Then I would take as my second treasure, *Amiel's Journal*. . . . Shakespeare's dramas would go into my bag next. . . . Then would come *The Selected Poems of Robert Browning*. . . . The *Poems* of John Milton would come next. . . . William James' *The Will to Believe* would have the next place. . . . *A Study of Religion,* by James Martineau, would go into my library. . . . Then *Evolution in Its Relation to Religious Thought,* by Joseph Le Conte. . . . *Natural Law in the Spiritual World,* by Henry Drummond would be next. . . . Then would come *Heaven and Hell,* by Emmanuel Swedenborg. . . . Next in importance on my desert-island shelf would come *The Arcana of Christianity,* by Thomas Lake Harris. . . . Victor Hugo's *Les Miserables* and *The Man Who Laughs* would find a place. *The Words of a Believer,* by Félicité Robert de Lamennais, would complete the list.[91]

This list is almost, though not quite, as Bible-centered as the volumes which Augustine and his comrades in A.D. 597 threw into their dufflebags to take to the then culturally desert island of England.

William Herbert Carruth brooded over science and religion until he wrote the hauntingly beautiful "Each in His Own Tongue." Willard Wattles read this and Sheldon's *In His Steps,* and as a result—aware of "certain tendencies toward a religious and spiritual awakening in Europe and America now patent to all observers"—published *Lanterns in Gethsemane*.

William Vaughn Moody brought religion and social ills face to face in his tenderly savage "Gloucester Moors."

Edgar Lee Masters wove into the texture of his *Spoon River Anthology* such a plentitude of biblical allusion as is found in few modern books, and he did it so deftly that it passes unnoticed.

When Vachel Lindsay was eight years old he read *Paradise Lost* and fell in love with Eve. When he was eleven he joined the Disciples' church and wrote biblical verses ("He that is weary come, refreshed," etc.). At college he started to keep six different notebooks, in each of which he wrote as dedication, "This book belongs to Christ." Christ spent the first thirty years in preparation for his lifework; so would Lindsay:

> Let it be definitely understood that every inch of my will up to thirty-one years goes to the evolution of myself, and the perfection of the mental, physical and spiritual machine. Not till then am I to choose any great scheme of suffering, and self spending. I have a world to save, and must prepare, prepare, prepare.[92]

At the Art Institute he opened a book of daily report—"the book of common prayer of N. V. Lindsay": "There is not enough of the dramatic stirring in the art world. . . . There is not enough of Isaiah, Ezekiel, Job, or the Song of Songs." [93]

When he started his westward walking tour he carried a book of his readings, on the inside front cover of which was pasted his "Gospel of Beauty" with its prologue: "I am starting a new religious idea. . . . The church of beauty has two sides: The love of beauty with the love of God." [94] Opposite this he pasted a picture of the Shepherd Christ.

When Lindsay's alma mater gave him an honorary degree he responded by writing "The Ezekiel Chant." When *Poetry* accepted "General William Booth Enters into Heaven" he commented: "Every time the General hits the drum he hits the Devil in the eye for me." [95] The man was saturated with the rhythms of religion.

> His training in music did not proceed beyond Campbellite hymnology. This he mastered unconsciously but thoroughly. Indeed, it grew into him in his childhood and became a part of him. If he were asking for a room at a hotel, the inflection of his voice might echo a phrase

from "When the Roll Is Called Up Yonder" or "What a Friend We Have in Jesus." If he were leaving the platform after reading he would probably be marching to the rhythm of "Onward Christian Soldiers." [96]

Edwin Arlington Robinson, with his restless, probing mind, early decided that "the world is a kind of spiritual kindergarten, where millions of bewildered infants are trying to spell God with the wrong blocks";[97] and he insisted that was not pessimism.

Robinson, who had freed himself from the orthodoxies of his Congregational background, leaned toward unitarianism. He went so far as to approve. . . . Robert Ingersoll, for exposing the absurdities of dogmatism, but he was convinced that a man who was destitute of the religious sentiment was no higher than an animal and that it were better for a man to swallow all the camels of orthodoxy than to have no religion at all.[98]

Robinson wrote "Matthias at the Door" at white heat during the summer of 1930. Before August was done, he had completed the poem's twenty-five hundred lines. Possessed by the theme, he returned to the third chapter of the gospel of St. John, which had been his inspiration, and, in three days, with his conscious faculties at the point of exhaustion, let "Nicodemus" write itself.[99]

Amy Lowell experimented endlessly and produced two outstanding poems, one of which ends, "Christ! What are patterns for?" and the other, "While all about us peal the loud, sweet *Te Deums* of the Canterbury bells."

Joyce Kilmer remarked—as all the world now knows—that only God can make a tree; he also wrote "The Fourth Shepherd" and many other religious poems less famous than "Trees."

Edna St. Vincent Millay, after reading *The Rime of the Ancient Mariner,* wrote *Renascence;* also *A Few Figs from Thistles,* "God's World," and "To Jesus on His Birthday."

Carl Sandburg produced such diversities as his raucous attack on Billy Sunday—"To a Contemporary Bunkshooter"—and his tender tribute in "Child" ("The young child, Christ, is straight and wise").

Lola Ridge wrote *Firehead;* Don Marquis *The Dark Hours*—both powerful presentations of biblical themes.

"God," declared Robert Frost, "is that which a man is sure cares, and will save him, no matter how many times or how completely he has failed"; and, "The *belief* in God is a relationship you enter into with Him to bring about the future"; and yet once more, "The self belief, the love belief, and the art belief, are all related to the God belief." [100]

Lew Sarett wrote "God Is at the Anvil." Analyzing his own relationship to the Bible he summarizes it thus:

> I have studied the Bible, King James version, carefully. I was interested especially in its literary beauty, in the factors that contribute to the nobility, power, and economy of its expression. I have re-read at least a hundred times "The Sermon on the Mount" for its literary and persuasive values, and Solomon's "Song of Songs" for its unparalleled beauty, its fervor, its vividness of imagery, and its sensuousness.
>
> I have consciously studied the stylistic qualities of portions of the Bible. I have never tried to use the elements of its style. But I respond so deeply to those portions, particularly the two I have mentioned, that perhaps unconsciously I have been influenced by them somewhat.[101]

The Negro poets arose; among them were Countee Cullen, with his mingled heritage of Christianity and paganism, and James Weldon Johnson, with his vivid Negro sermons, *God's Trombones.*

From a denominational college came shocking Robinson Jeffers, where he shone in such courses as Biblical Literature, and The Grounds of Christian and Theistic Belief. He wrote first the Bible—titled *Flagons and Apples,* with its flyleaf adorned with quotations from an Italian folk song, from Emerson, and from the Song of Songs:

> Stay me with flagons, comfort me with apples;
> For I am sick of love.

(This verse a flippant short story writer later revised to: "They comforted him with applesauce and presently stayed him with flagons, edged with mint.") With his own hands Jeffers laid the stones for his Hawk's Tower study, and set into the wall, from the Sixty-eighth Psalm: "Why leap ye, ye high hills? this is the hill which God desireth to dwell in." *Tamar* is the biblical name he bestowed on one of his much-discussed books, and *Dear Judas* is another.[102]

So marked was the tide of religious work coming from the pens of poets that Martha Foote Crow—her curiosity roused by Josiah Strong's phrase "the return to Christ that is now taking place"—began to investigate.

I ran through some fifty volumes of poems of about 1890. I found few or no poems about Jesus. Then I plunged in again at 1895 and found but a lonely one here and there. At 1900 there were more, distinctly more. At 1905 there was a still brighter dawn. But when I came to 1910 and thereabouts, times were changed. Something had verily happened. The fascinating theme of Jesus, the dramatic quality of his human career, the miracle of his personality, had been discovered; and the position of the poem that illuminated some incident in the life of Christ or that enthroned some quality of his character was now securely established in nearly every book of poetry.[103]

Following this clue a later investigator checked all references to the life of Jesus found in 260 books of American verse published between 1890 and 1919. The last decade showed an increase of 30 per cent over the two preceding decades. When all brief casual references were discarded and only longer references or complete poems retained, the changed appeared yet more dramatically:

The extended use of material concerning Christ has increased in comparative frequency from the decade 1890–1899 to the decade 1910–1919 by a full 88%. . . . Two things, then, are apparent: reference to Christian material is increasing; Biblical and Christian material is becoming more diffused in literature—less a thing apart.[104]

In 1939 a third investigator scanned more than twelve thousand pages of American poetry published between 1919 and 1938, for both Old Testament and New Testament references. The 1930's showed an increase of 50 per cent over the 1920's in biblical references within poems. For complete poems the increase was 100 per cent, the increase being centered chiefly in the New Testament rather than in the Old Testament.[105]

Instead of fading from literature in the twentieth century, as charged, the Bible was entering it at a rapidly accelerating pace.

The emergence of Jesus as a theme and motive is apparent not only in the so-called religious poetry but in poetry unqualified by any adjective. Since 1910 there has been a new resurrection of Jesus from the tomb of convention and tradition.[106]

Then came Pearl Harbor. The war had brought a reading boom to England; what would be its effect upon America?

39. Foxholes and Atom Bombs

Cliff Hill can't understand why we make so much fuss about the power of the atom when everyone knows the whole human race sprang from Atom and Eve.

—LEE SHIPPEY[107]

IT SOON became obvious that this was, emotionally, a very quiet war. There was not much fanfare. The bands were missing. Oratory and going-away dinners for enlistees and draftees soon dwindled. Nobody seemed very eager to sing "It's a Long Way to Tipperary" or "Pack Up Your Troubles in Your Old Kit Bag." And the new songs somehow failed to click.

The goals for the armed forces rose and continued to rise—one million men, five million, ten—and the relentless arithmetic continued inexorably to climb. It began to dawn upon America that this was not a play war.

The surplus energies that had effervesced in World War I were in this one channeled into aircraft factories, shipyards, and victory gardens. Americans realized with a shock, for the first time in their lives, that they did not have an inexhaustible, easily secured supply of everything. They were rationed. They were sobered.

They turned to religion. Even veteran booksellers were astonished by the sharp upswing in Bible sales. From all over America poured reports from bookstores. The figures were different, but the meaning was the same.

From Cleveland it was: "Our Bible and Religious Book department has outdone itself for 1942." From Louisville: "We have sold more Bibles and Testaments than we have ever sold in the history of our organization." From Portland, Oregon: "Sales of Bibles, Testaments, and Prayer Books have just doubled." One group of twenty stores, according to *Publishers' Weekly* for March 13, 1943, found that its volume of business in religious books in 1942 was 29 per cent above that of the preceding year.

Early in 1940 the great Oxford Press had imported a two years' supply from England. In 1941 it had built up large reserves of paper in this country. In July, 1943, it was forced to quit taking orders for three months, to prorate the Bibles on hand, to cancel the remaining orders, and to initiate a system of rationing. This applied only to the Bible department; all other departments were functioning as usual.[108]

In 1942 the American Bible Society sent out over the world more than 8,200,000 volumes—its highest number in history—bringing the society's record since its founding in the early nineteenth century to more than a third of a billion copies of the Scriptures or parts thereof.

This astounding distribution of the Scriptures is a new thing in history. For the first fifteen hundred years after Christ, all copies were laboriously handwritten. After the invention of printing, the editions, though many, were relatively small. It is estimated that in 1800 there were in the world four million Bibles. So great has been the growth in the nineteenth and twentieth centuries that it is now estimated that since the invention of printing 1,500,000,000 copies of the Bible or parts of it have been published. Best seller indeed, and running away with the bit in its teeth at the middle of the twentieth century.

In the accelerated buying several factors became significantly evident.

> Although ministers are buying lots of books, the real increase is among lay people who buy religious books for their personal reading.[109]

These laymen were buying with more than usual discrimination.

> There's a significant preference for "study" Bibles over "show" Bibles; purchasers insist on large type, references, and marginal notes.[110]

A Gallup poll for 1942 estimated that four million people were reading the Bible more than they did before.[111] This increase continued to climb. A second Gallup poll indicated that 64 per cent of America was reading the Bible in 1943 as compared to 59 per cent in 1942. One person in every ten reported he read it daily. While it was still true that, the older people get, the more of them read the Bible, the 1943 survey found that one notable effect of the war has been to increase reading of the Bible among the young people of America more than any other age group.[112]

Nearly 20 per cent more young people were reading the Bible than had done so the year before.

This turning to the Bible brought with it a marked increase in the reading of other books of a religious nature: books on personal religion, books of consolation, books of inspiration, books on the religious life of other peoples and races. (Lin Yutang's *The Wisdom of China and India* became a best seller.) *Strength for Service to God and Country* sold half a million copies in nine months; E. Stanley Jones's *Abundant Living* sold well, as did C. S. Lewis' *The Screwtape Letters.*

Certain religious novels held the center of the stage—*The Robe, The Song of Bernadette, The Keys of the Kingdom, The Nazarene.* H. G. Wells launched *All Aboard for Ararat;* ten distinguished novelists brought together in one volume, *The Ten Commandments,* ten new stories on those ancient themes. Thomas Mann, now an American citizen, issued the fourth and final volume of his story of Joseph.

Old books took a new lease of life.

> *Daily Strength for Daily Need,* . . . that book sells at least twice as fast now as it did in peace time. . . . We have studied . . . nine titles, all more than two years old. . . . The exact increase in one year's time was 110%.[113]

Sheldon's *In His Steps*—which in 1899 had sold eight times as many copies as *Gone with the Wind* did in its best year, and had continued to sell steadily since—took a spurt and began selling at the highest point in twelve years. Thomas à Kempis' *Imitation of Christ* came out in a noteworthy new edition.

The trend became noticed elsewhere. The National Broadcasting Company separated its religious programs from its educational office and set up a separate department of religion. A biblical comic book for juveniles was started, with the approval of leading religious groups.[114] In 1943 a seventeen-year-old silent movie film, *The King of Kings,* was shown some fifteen hundred times in the United States. In 1944

Hollywood has "got religion" according to advance schedules of leading film companies at the movie capital, and will offer a "religious cycle" to its box-office patrons this year. Every major studio has announced at least one religious picture for the new year, Metro-Goldwyn-Mayer topping the list with four. . . . The companies also have scheduled a number of revivals such as "Quo Vadis," "The Sign of the Cross," "The Miracle," "Ben Hur," "King of Kings," "The Ten Commandments," and others.[115]

While all these things were happening to civilians, the American fighting man was becoming "the best Bibled warrior in the world." [116]

If he wished a New Testament it was his for the asking. Before October, 1943, he had asked for more than seven million copies. They were not mere decorations.

During the entire time I was in Japanese prisons I never saw an idle Bible. In the daylight hours those little volumes were being being read constantly.[117]

Captain Eddie Rickenbacker's poignant recital of life aboard his raft in the South Seas dramatized the Bible mightily, and soon caused all lifeboats and rafts to be equipped with New Testaments and hymns in specially invented waterproof cases. For troops in combat zones hymn leaflets were wrapped around K-rations. Among the hymns included were "Faith of Our Fathers," "America the Beautiful," "There's a Church in the Valley," "Abide with Me," "God Bless America," "Mine Eyes Have Seen the Glory," "God Will Take Care of You," and "O God, Our Help in Ages Past." A film, "Hymns from Home," was prepared for army posts and general hospitals throughout the world.

The world's most exciting volume was once more upon the march. The many-voiced tome of a thousand tongues was still learning new languages and going into strange places. It was making printing presses strain and roar as they never had done before.

The gadabout book was roving again, speaking many languages, but one especially. In English it went forth to the ends of the earth. With Englishmen, with Americans, with Australians—with soldiers and sailors and marines and their feminine counterparts—it traveled again the pathways of the world which it knew so well. And always it was HOME to all who spoke the English tongue.

And then came the atom bomb, with its percussions in the hearts of two Japanese cities and its repercussions in the hearts of men everywhere. The war was over, and a new world era had irrevocably begun. Subdued and chastened at thought of the tremendous power at last placed in the hands of man, men everywhere prayed with biblical fervor for wisdom and strength to use this power aright. With spirits molded for centuries by the Bible, the English-speaking race, guardians of the new power, entered the Atomic Age.

It is now nearly fourteen centuries since that mighty book was catapulted by Gregory's poor puns onto English soil. And in those fourteen centuries it has become native to our souls. Its words are upon our lips; its cadences are in our ears; its thoughts are in our hearts.

It met the men of Anglo-Saxon times, enriched their language, enlarged their literature, and changed their spirit.

It sent the men of Anglo-Norman days on far crusades, from which they returned sadder but wiser men, with enriching wealth of new ideas. It taught them their stage plays and their poetry. It named for them their places and their people. It took a simple hero tale and turned it into the Round Table and the Holy Grail. It gave to some a vision of democracy and social justice.

It took the England of the teeming sixteenth century and taught Englishmen the glory of their native language—its suppleness and its sturdy strength. It made more vivid the diction and more terse the style.

It taught Englishmen, alas, to quarrel, and in the seventeenth century sent Englishmen to America. Out of those quarrelsome days came scholarship and many other gains, and grievous losses; but the gains outweighed the losses.

In the eighteenth century it carried America into political self-determination and intellectual broadening; England it helped through the drowsy decades.

It came in power upon the early nineteenth century as a potent fertilizer of literature, and as the century progressed it burst the barriers built up by puritanism and went again everywhere without let or hindrance, as it had done in medieval times.

In the twentieth century—partly from the momentum bequeathed it from the nineteenth, and partly from the power of countless copies of the Scriptures avalanching as never before from the presses—decade by decade it seeped ever more permeatingly into literature and into common everyday thought.

Not since the Middle Ages had it been so much at home. As men and women of English speech everywhere face the second half of the twentieth century, they face it fortified and deepened in spirit by fourteen centuries of contact with the Bible. Increasingly they are heeding the words spoken long ago:

> My Masters, there's an old book you should con,
> For strange adventures, applicable yet,
> 'Tis stuffed with.

REFERENCES

THE BIBLE ENTERS ENGLISH

1. *Reading the Bible* (New York: The Macmillan Co., 1919), p. 17.

2. The Venerable Bede, *Ecclesiastical History of the English Nation* (New York: E. P. Dutton & Co., 1910), p. 64.

3. J. G. K. McClure, *The Supreme Book of Mankind* (New York: Charles Scribner's Sons, 1930), p. 8.

4. L. P. Smith, *The English Language* (New York: Henry Holt & Co.. 1912), pp. 158 f.

5. F. J. Gillman, *The Evolution of the English Hymn* (New York: The Macmillan Co., 1927), p. 96.

6. A. S. Cook and C. B. Tinker, *Select Translations from Old English Poetry* (Boston: Ginn & Co., 1902), p. 76.

7. R. K. Gordon, *Anglo-Saxon Poetry* (New York: E. P. Dutton & Co.), p. 126.

8. *Ibid.*, p. 207.

9. *Ibid.*, p. 298.

10. A. S. Cook and C. B. Tinker, *Translations from Old English Prose* (Boston: Ginn and Co., 1908), p. 101.

11. A. S. Cook, *Biblical Quotations in Old English Prose Writers* (New York: The Macmillan Co., 1898), *passim.*

12. *Ibid.*

THE BIBLE DOMINATES THE MIDDLE ENGLISH PERIOD

1. E. Folting, "Something to Chew On," *This Week,* Aug. 27, 1939, p. 14. Perhaps the basis for this story is the fact that pretzels were eaten on fast days, as affording less nourishment than ordinary bread. The word "pretzel" means "little arms."

2. C. W. Bardsley, *Curiosities of Puritan Nomenclature* (London: Chatto & Windus, 1880), pp. 2 ff.

3. Smith, *op. cit.*, pp. 167 ff.

4. "Kulhwch and Olwen," *The Mabinogion,* tr. T. P. Ellis and J. Lloyd (Oxford: The Clarendon Press, 1926), I, 182 ff.

5. "Layamon's *Brut,*" in *Arthurian Chronicles,* ed. E. Mason (New York: E. P. Dutton & Co., 1912), p. 209.

6. *Ibid.*, p. 210.

7. D. Wecter, *The Saga of American Society* (New York: Charles Scribner's Sons, 1937), p. 86.

8. Modernized from W. M. Auld, *Christmas Traditions* (New York: The Macmillan Co., 1931), p. 143. *Wholdaroo* means "wonder."

9. *Henry V,* Act II, scene 3, 11. 9-11.

10. New Haven: Yale University Press, 1918, p. 88.

11. *Idylls of the King.*

12. "Song of the Exposition."

13. Quoted in M. B. Crook and others, *The Bible and Its Literary Associations* (New York: The Abingdon Press, 1937), p. 360.

14 C. F. Fiske, "The Reflection of the Bible in Early English Literature," *Poet Lore,* XXX (1919), 219.

15. K. L. Bates, *English Religious Drama* (New York: The Macmillan Co., 1893), p. 21.

16. *Ibid.,* p. 44.

17. H. C. Schweikert, *Early English Plays* (New York: Harcourt, Brace & Co., 1928), p. 125.

18. Eighty per cent of the cycle plays were from the New Testament.

19. E. D. Coleman, *The Bible in English Drama* (New York: New York Public Library, 1931), p. 8.

20. E. C. Brewer, *Dictionary of Phrase and Fable* (Philadelphia, J. B. Lippincott Co., 1926), p. 551.

21. F. E. Ward, E. H. Booth, and G. J. L. May, *Earning Our Heritage* (New York: Harcourt, Brace & Co., 1937), I, 596.

22. Bates, *op. cit.,* p. 201.

23. "A Woman's Wrongs," in *The Genteel Female,* ed. C. J. Furness (New York: Alfred A. Knopf, 1921), p. 250.

24. "A Good Orisoun of Our Ladie," in *The Chief Middle English Poets,* ed. J. L. Weston (Boston: Houghton Mifflin Co., 1914), p. 341.

25. *Ibid.,* p. 363.

26. "A Praising of Women," in M. R. Adamson, *A Treasury of Middle English Verse* (New York: E. P. Dutton & Co., 1930), p. 118.

27. See J. E. Wells, *A Manual of the Writings in Middle English* (New Haven: Yale University Press, 1926), p. 280.

28. *Ibid.,* p. 276.

29. Sir J. Mandeville, *Travels* (London: Macmillan & Co., 1900), pp. 41 f.

30. A. R. Benham, *English Literature from Widsith to the Death of Chaucer* (New Haven: Yale University Press, 1916), pp. 233 f.

31. Brewer, *op. cit.,* p. 40.

32. F. H. Loughead, *Dictionary of Given Names* (Glendale, California: Arthur H. Clark Co., 1934), p. 15.

33. Two thirds of the presidents of the United States have had one or more names popularized by the Bible, as have the wives of half of them.

34. Popular rhyme quoted in J. R. Green, *A History of the English People* (New York: National Library Co., n.d.), p. 153.

35. Brewer, *op. cit.,* p. 768.

36. A. W. Dellquest, *These Names of Ours* (New York: Thomas Y. Crowell Co., 1938), p. 153.

37. *The Babee's Book,* ed. E. Rickert (London: Chatto & Windus, 1923), p. 93.

38. M. W. Smith, *Biblical Quotations in Middle English Before 1350* (New York: Henry Holt & Co., 1911), p. lxix.

39. *Ibid.,* pp. lxix and *passim.*

40. G. Kitchin, *A Survey of Burlesque and Parody in English* (Edinburgh: Oliver & Boyd, 1931), p. 2.

41. G. A. Plimpton, *The Education of Chaucer* (New York: Oxford University Press, 1935), pp. 18 ff.

42. "British Apollo," in Brewer, *op. cit.*, p. 774.

43. Fiske, *Poet Lore,* XXX (1919), 212 ff.

44. C. Noble, "The Bible in Chaucer," *The Cue* (n.d.), p. 174; also Plimpton, *op. cit.*, pp. 153-71.

45. T. R. Lounsbury, *Studies in Chaucer* (New York: Harper & Bros., 1891), II, 468.

46. R. Macaulay, *Some Religious Elements in English Literature* (London: Hogarth Press, 1931).

47. Sister C. Sullivan, *The Latin Insertions and the Macaronic Verse in Piers Plowman* (Washington, D. C.: Catholic University of America, 1932), p. 47.

48. J. Froissart, in E. P. Cheyney, *Readings in English History* (Boston: Ginn & Co., 1922), pp. 260 f.

49. G. Herbert, "Proverbs," *Works,* (London: Bell & Daldy, 1859), I, 370.

50. H. Knighton, in Cheyney, *op. cit.*, 267.

51. *The Puritans,* ed. P. Miller and T. H. Johnson (New York: American Book Co., 1938), p. 770.

52. W. S. Walsh, *A Handy-Book of Curious Information* (Philadelphia: J. B. Lippincott Co., 1913), p. 7.

THE BIBLE HELPS THE MODERN AGE BE BORN

1. From *I'm a Stranger Here Myself* by Ogden Nash. Reprinted by permission of Little, Brown & Company.

2. E. C. Chilton and H. Agar, *The Garment of Praise* (New York: Doubleday, Doran & Co., 1929), p. 141.

3. L. A. Buckingham, *The Bible in the Middle Ages* (London: T. C. Newby, 1853), pp. 154 ff.

4. *A Mirror for Magistrates,* ed. L. B. Campbell (Cambridge, Eng.: University Press, 1938), p. 350.

5. K. E. Thomas, *Real Personages of Mother Goose* (Boston: Lothrop, Lee & Shepard Co., 1930), p. 77.

6. *Ibid.*, p. 78.

7. *Ibid.*, p. 87.

8. *Ibid.*, p. 91.

9. *Ibid.*, p. 103.

10. *Ibid.*, pp. 95 f.

11. *Ibid.*, p. 70.

12. *Ibid.*, p. 74.

13. H. Bett, *Nursery Rhymes and Tales* (New York: Henry Holt & Co., 1924), pp. 74 ff.

14. J. O. Halliwell, *The Nursery Rhymes of England* (London: Percy Society, 1841-42), pp. 2 ff.

15. Bett, *op. cit.*, pp. 49 f.

16. *Ibid.*, p. 119. See also O. D. Campbell and C. J. Sharp, *English Folk*

Songs from the Southern Appalachians (London: Oxford University Press, 1932), pp. 300 f.

17. Walsh, *op. cit.*, pp. 646 f.

18. Thomas, *op. cit.*, p. 180.

19. *Ibid.*, pp. 21 f.

20. *Hallelujah, or Britain's Second Remembrancer* (London: J. R. Smith, 1857), p. 277.

21. W. P. Ker, *The Dark Ages*, quoted in J. B. Reeves, *The Hymn as Literature* (New York: The Century Co., 1924), pp. 83 f.

22. See H. M. Studley, "Milton and His Paraphrases of the Psalms," *Philological Quarterly*, IV (1925), 365.

23. Quoted in Crook and others, *The Bible and Its Literary Associations*, p. 197. (Modernized.)

24. In C. S. Nutter and W. F. Tillett, *The Hymns and Hymn Writers of the Church* (New York: Methodist Book Concern, 1911), p. 93.

25. In R. E. Prothero, *The Psalms in Human Life* (New York: E. P. Dutton & Co., 1904), p. 149.

26. *Ibid.*, p. 172.

27. Reeves, *op. cit.*, p. 139.

28. Gillman, *The Evolution of the English Hymn*, p. 201.

29. J. F. Dobie, *The Longhorns* (Boston: Little, Brown & Co., 1941), pp. 127 f.

30. See J. C. Squire, *Books in General*, 2d series (New York: Alfred A. Knopf, 1920), p. 109.

31. From *The Grapes of Wrath*, copyright 1939 by John Steinbeck. By permission of The Viking Press, Inc., New York.

32. A. Maltz, "Season of Celebration," in E. Knight and others, *The Flying Yorkshireman* (New York: Harper & Bros., 1938), p. 137.

33. "Bible for Castaways," *Newsweek*, XXI (1943), 76.

34. Robert of Brunne, *Handlyng Synne*, in *Christmas Carols Printed in the Sixteenth Century*, ed. E. B. Reed (Cambridge: Harvard University Press, 1932), p. xv. (Modern rendering.)

35. Dame Berners, "A Carolle of Huntynge," in W. S. Walsh, *Curiosities of Popular Customs* (Philadelphia: J. B. Lippincott Co., 1897), p. 192.

36. Reed, *op. cit.*, p. xxxi. (Modern rendering.)

37. R. Herrick, *Hesperides and Noble Numbers* (New York: E. P. Dutton & Co., n.d.), p. 426.

38. Walsh, *op. cit.*, p. 232.

39. "Darky Sunday School," in *Humor in American Song*, ed. A. Loesser (New York: Howell, Soskin, 1942), p. 267.

40. G. H. McKnight, *Modern English in the Making* (New York: D. Appleton & Co., 1928), p. 114.

41. Tyndale's preface, quoted in J. P. Smyth, *How We Got Our Bible* (New York: J. Pott & Co., 1912), p. 87.

42. See Green, *op. cit.*, II, 222.

43. J. Baikie, *The Romance of the Bible* (Philedelphia: J. B. Lippincott Co., n.d.), p. 261.

44. New York: Longmans, Green & Co., 1905, p. 5.

45. J. R. Green, *A History of the English People*, III, 15 ff.

46. *Loc. cit.*

47. In W. S. Walsh, *Handy-Book of Literary Curiosities* (Philadelphia: J. B. Lippincott Co., 1925), p. 511.

48. P. Sidney, "Apology for Poetry," in *Elizabethan Critical Essays*, ed. G. G. Smith (Oxford: Clarendon Press, 1904), I, 158. (Spelling modernized.)

49. "Foure Letters," in G. G. Smith, *ibid.*, II, 234. (Spelling modernized.)

50. Lyly, *Works* (Oxford: Clarendon Press, 1902), III, 395.

51. F. Bacon, *Essays* (New York: The Macmillan Co., 1865), pp. 2 f.

52. J. E. Maltby, *Spenser's Use of the Bible in the Faerie Queene, Books I and II* (Seattle: University of Washington, 1926), p. 7.

53. G. R. Landrum, "Spenser's Use of the Bible and His Alleged Puritanism," *Publications of the Modern Language Association of America*, XLI (1926), 517 f.

54. L. B. Wright, "The Scriptures and the Elizabethan Stage," *Modern Philology*, XXVI (1928), 55.

55. Jonson, *Works* (London: T. F. Unwin, n.d.), II, 149.

56. See E. W. Work, *The Bible in Literature* (New York: Fleming H. Revell Co., 1917), p. 172.

57. See R. Noble, *Shakespeare's Biblical Knowledge* (New York: The Macmillan Co., 1935), pp. 19 f, 281 ff.

58. E. M. Robinson, *Tennyson's Use of the Bible* (Baltimore: Johns Hopkins Press, 1917), pp. 80 ff.

59. In Walsh, *Handy-Book of Literary Curiosities*, p. 615.

60. G. Puttenham, "The Arte of English Poesie," in G. G. Smith, *op. cit.*, II, 97.

61. See I. Disraeli, *Curiosities of Literature* (New York: Thomas Y. Crowell Co., 1881), I, 386.

62. Walsh, *op. cit.*, p. 272.

63. G. Herbert, "The Altar," *Works*, II, 19.

64. "Easter Wings," *ibid.*, II, 38.

65. R. Herrick, in *Hesperides and Noble Numbers*, p. 469.

66. Anonymous, in Walsh, *op. cit.*, p. 276. In the crosses are sayings of Christ and the two thieves crucified with him. These have been ingeniously woven into a unified poem beginning "My God! My God! In Rivers of my tears, I come to Thee . . ."

67. *Spectator* (London: H. G. Bohn, n.d.), No. 58, p. 84.

68. *Ibid.*

69. Anonymous, "Life Goes Calling on Alexander Woollcott," *Life*, Oct. 30, 1939, p. 87.

70. "Hymn to God My God, in My Sickness," in *Devotional Poets of the Seventeenth Century*, ed. H. Newbolt (London: T. Nelson & Son, n.d.), p. 48.

71. G. Herbert, "The Temper," *op. cit.*, II, 53.

72. "Sunday," *ibid.*, II, 77.

73. "Sion," *ibid.*, II, 115.

74. "The Bag," *ibid.*, II, 171 f.

75. "The Dawning," *ibid.*, II, 122.

76. "Psalm Twenty-three," *Poems* (London: George Routledge & Sons, Ltd., n.d.), p. 32.

77. "Saint Mary Magdalene, or The Weeper," *ibid.*, p. 126.

135.

78. *Ibid.*, p. 123.

79. "The Flaming Heart," *ibid.*, p. 138.

80. See J. W. Cousin, *Short Biographical Dictionary of English Literature* (London: E. P. Dutton & Co., 1910), p. 390.

81. Walsh, *op. cit.*, p. 931.

82. In S. C. Mathews, *Wit and Humor* (Chicago: S. C. Griggs & Co., 1888), p. 313.

83. *The Professor at the Breakfast Table* (Boston: Houghton, Mifflin Co., 1859), p. 262.

THE BIBLE BRINGS THE GOOD AND BAD RESULTS OF QUARRELING

1. In Gillman, *The Evolution of the English Hymn*, p. 218.

2. J. Lyly, "Pappe with a Hatchet," *Works*, III, 93.

3. "Sermon," in *The Cambridge History of English Literature* (New York: G. P. Putnam's Sons, 1907-17), VI, 424.

4. Stubbes, *The Anatomy of Abuses*, in S. Cheney, *The Theatre* (New York: Tudor Pub. Co., 1929), pp. 287 ff.

5. H. Crosse, in Wright, *op. cit.*, p. 49.

6. W. Crashaw, in Cheney, *op. cit.*, p. 286.

7. H. M. Paull, *Literary Ethics* (London: T. Butterworth, Ltd., 1928), p. 135.

8. F. Watson, "Scholars and Scholarship," *The Cambridge History of English Literature*, VII, 363 *n*. Used by permission of The Macmillan Company, New York, and the Cambridge University Press, London.

9. V. Starrett, "Presbyterian Hell," *Saturday Review of Literature*, II (1926), 817. Used by permission.

10. See *The New England Primer*, ed. P. L. Ford (New York: Dodd, Mead Co., 1899), p. 113.

11. *Ibid.*, p. 112.

12. G. Fox, *Journal*, I, 36, quoted in M. B. Crook, *op. cit.*, p. 327.

13. Smith, *The English Language*, p. 208.

14. Bardsley, *Curiosities of Puritan Nomenclature*, p. 37.

15. W. B. Bowman, *The Story of Surnames* (New York: Alfred A. Knopf, 1931), p. 93.

16. *Autobiography* (New York: Sheed & Ward, 1936), pp. 160 f.

17. Watson, *op. cit.*, pp. 365 ff.

18. *Works*, II, 227.

19. E. L. Masters, *This New World* (New York: D. Appleton-Century Co., 1937), p. 28.

20. Captain J. Smith, in P. M. Simms, *The Bible in America* (New York: Wilson-Erickson, Inc., 1936), pp. 16 f.

21. See G. K. Smart, "Private Libraries in Colonial Virginia," *American Literature,* X (1938-39), 33.

22. H. L. Mencken, *The American Language* (New York: Alfred A. Knopf, 1936), p. 535.

23. N. V. deG. Sanchez, *Spanish and Indian Place Names of California* (San Francisco: A. M. Robertson, 1930), p. 45.

24. See H. W. Lawrence, *The Not-Quite Puritans* (Boston: Little, Brown & Co., 1928), p. 174.

25. N. Ward, in Miller and Johnson, *The Puritans,* p. 230.

26. See Simms, *op. cit.,* pp. 189 f.

27. C. Angoff, *A Literary History of the American People* (New York: Alfred A. Knopf, 1931), I, 333.

28. "Sinners in the Hands of an Angry God," in E. C. Stedman and E. M. Hutchinson, *A Library of American Literature* (New York: C. L. Webster & Co., 1888), II, 391.

29. "The End of the Wicked Contemplated by the Righteous," *ibid.,* p. 397.

30. T. G. Wright, *Literary Culture in Early New England, 1620-1730* (New Haven: Yale University Press, 1920), p. 82.

31. I. Mather, "Presidential Address," in Miller and Johnson, *op. cit.,* p. 721.

32. See Miller and Johnson, *op. cit.,* p. 696.

33. Ford, *op. cit.,* p. 51.

34. Ady's "Candle in the Dark," in Walsh, *Handy-Book of Literary Curiosities,* pp. 822 f.

35. C. Hunt, "Howlers," *This Week,* Jan. 22, 1939.

36. J. Gairdner, "England: Tudor and Stuart," in H. S. Williams, *The Historians' History of the World* (New York: The Outlook Co., 1904), XIX, 431.

37. *Ibid.,* p. 475.

38. F. W. Faber, in J. P. Smith, "Three Centuries of the English Bible," *Review of Reviews,* XLIII (1911), 575.

39. G. Saintsbury, in A. S. Cook, *The Bible and English Prose Style* (Boston: D. C. Heath Co., 1892), p. xxxviii.

40. B. Jowett, in W. Muir, *Our Grand Old Bible* (New York: Fleming H. Revell Co., 1911), p. 230.

41. *Works* (Boston: Houghton, Mifflin & Co., 1876), I, 173.

42. *The Complete Writings of . . .* (Boston: Houghton, Mifflin Co., 1927), VII, 238.

43. *"Praeterita," Works* (Boston: Dana, Estes & Co.; n.d.), p. 35.

44. *Ibid.,* p. 37.

45. R. H. Wilenski, *John Ruskin* (New York: Frederick A. Stokes Co., 1933), p. 364.

46. "Sesame and Lilies," *Works,* p. 105.

47. J. G. Lockhart, *Memoirs of the Life of Sir Walter Scott, Bart.* (London: Frederick Warne & Co., Ltd., n.d.), II, 363.

48. W. G. Perry, "Literature's Debt to the Bible," *North American Review,* CXCVIII (1913), 237.

49. *Loc. cit.*

50. In W. J. Price, *The One Book* (Philadelphia: The John C. Winston Co., 1928), p. 216.

51. In T. Tiplady, *The Influence of the Bible* (New York: Fleming H. Revell Co., 1924), p. 83.

52. See *Something of Myself* (New York: Doubleday, Doran & Co., 1937), p. 246.

53. In Hall Caine, *A Syllabus for the Life of Christ* (New York: Doubleday, Doran & Co., 1938), p. 8.

54. *Five Plays* (Boston: Little, Brown & Co., 1914), p. viii.

55. "The English Bible," *London Mercury,* XXXVII (1937), 116.

56. "The Lost Bible," *Good Housekeeping,* CI (1935), 82.

57. *On the Art of Writing* (New York: G. P. Putnam's Sons), p. 151.

58. *Collectanea* (Bristol, Eng.: J. W. Arrowsmith, 1902–04), II, ii, 748.

59. In G. H. Gerould, *Saints' Legends* (Boston: Houghton Mifflin Co., 1916), p. 21.

60. T. B. Macaulay, *Critical and Miscellaneous Essays* (New York: D. Appleton & Co., 1856), I, 367.

61. "Satires and Epistles of Horace Imitated," *Poetical Works* (New York: Thomas Y. Crowell, 1896), II, 314.

62. E. A. Boyd, *Literary Blasphemies* (New York: Harper & Bros., 1927), pp. 10, 49, 54 f.

63. See J. M. French, "Milton's Family Bible," *PMLA,* LIII (1938), 366.

64. In J. G. Lawson, *Greatest Thoughts About the Bible* (Cincinnati: Standard, 1918), p. 30.

65. See H. F. Fletcher, *The Use of the Bible in Milton's Prose* (Urbana: University of Illinois Press, 1929), pp. 93 f.

66. *Ibid.,* p. 13.

67. H. Belloc, *Milton* (Philadelphia: J. B. Lippincott Co., 1935), p. 308.

68. Smith, *The English Language,* p. 114.

69. G. Saintsbury, "Milton," in *The Cambridge History of English Literature* (New York: G. P. Putnam's Sons, 1907-17), VII, 145.

70. C. B. McAfee, *The Greatest English Classic* (New York: Harper & Bros., 1912), p. 146.

71. M. H. Nicholson, in Crook and others, *The Bible and Its Literary Associations,* p. 301.

72. Boyd, *op. cit.,* p. 63.

73. *Diary,* Apr. 11, 1712, in Miller and Johnson, *op. cit.,* p. 515.

74. Hawthorne, "Notebooks," Aug. 5, 1842, *Complete Works* (Boston: Houghton, Mifflin & Co., 1882), II, 9 f.

75. Clemens, "Adam's Soliloquy," *Europe and Elsewhere* (New York: Harper & Bros., 1923), p. 381.

76. "Eve's Diary," *The $30,000 Bequest, etc.* (New York: P. F. Collier, 1917), p. 342.

77. "Extracts from Adam's Diary," *ibid.,* p. 342.

78. Nicholson, *op. cit.,* p. 307.

79. "The Marriage of Heaven and Hell," *Poetical Works* (London: Oxford University Press, 1914), p. 249.

80. *Table Talk* (London: George Routledge & Sons, Ltd., 1884), p. 158.

81. C. Hunt, "Howlers," *This Week,* Jan. 1, 1939, p. 13.

82. Cowper, "Tirocinium," *Poetical Works* (Edinburgh: Nicoll, 1884), I, 347.

83. T. B. Macaulay, "John Bunyan," *Encyclopedia Britannica,* 14th ed., IV, 393.

84. G. E. Woodberry, *Studies in Letters and Life,* p. 218, quoted in *Library of Literary Criticism* (Buffalo: Mailton Publishing Co., 1901-5), II, 398.

85. Bede, *Ecclesiastical History,* p. 91.

86. In Work, *The Bible in Literature,* p. 188.

87. In Moulton, *Library of Literary Criticism,* II, 388.

88. Bunyan, "A Confession of My Faith," *Works* (Philadelphia: Bradley & Co., 1866), II, 204.

89. W. J. Price, *The One Book* (Philadelphia: John C. Winston Co., 1928), p. 224.

90. *Table Talk,* p. 99.

91. T. B. Macaulay, *Essays* (New York: D. Appleton & Co., 1856), I, 358.

92. C. G. Osgood, *The Voice of England* (New York: Harper & Bros., 1935), p. 269.

93. In Tiplady, *op. cit.,* pp. 52 f.

94. "Introduction," *Pilgrim's Progress, VII,* in Moulton, *op. cit.,* II, 399.

95. "Books That Have Influenced Me," *Works* (New York: Charles Scribner's Sons, 1925), XXII, 303.

96. "Love Affairs of a Bibliomaniac," in Moulton, *op. cit.,* II, 399.

97. *Mosses from an Old Manse* (Boston: Houghton, Mifflin & Co., 1882), p. 212.

98. In W. Blair, *Native American Humor* (New York: American Book Co., 1937), pp. 449 ff.

99. In Moulton, *op. cit.,* II, 397 f.

100. In Edwards, *New Dictionary of Thoughts,* p. 472.

101. *Hudibras* (London: George Routledge & Sons, Ltd., n.d.), p. 224.

102. *Ibid.,* pp. 9, 13.

103. "Heroic Stanzas, on the Death of Oliver Cromwell," *Poems* (New York: Thomas Y. Crowell Co., n.d.), p. 28.

104. *"Astraea Redux," ibid.,* pp. 29, 31.

105. "Absalom and Achitophel," *ibid.,* p. 90.

106. "The Medal," *ibid.,* pp. 148, 150.

107. Dryden, "The Hind and the Panther," *ibid.,* p. 251.

108. Prior, "The Hind and the Panther Transvers'd, *Dialogues of the Dead and Other Works in Prose and Verse* (Cambridge, Eng.: The University Press, 1907), p. 8.

109. Swift, "The Tale of a Tub," *A Tale of a Tub, the Battle of the Books and Other Satires* (New York: E. P. Dutton & Co., 1909), p. 56.

110. "An Argument to Prove That the Abolishing of Christianity," etc., *Prose Writings* (London: Walter Scott Publishing Co., n.d.), p. 240.

111. New York: E. P. Dutton & Co., 1906, p. 230.

112. "The Dunciad," *Poetical Works,* p. 383.

113. "Moral Essays," *ibid.,* pp. 266 f.

114. *Ibid.,* p. 241.

THE BIBLE SURVIVES THE LUKEWARM YEARS

1. In Edwards, *op. cit.*, p. 82.
2. *Robinson Crusoe* (New York: E. P. Dutton & Co., 1906), p. 58.
3. *Ibid.*, p. 156.
4. *Ibid.*, p. 158.
5. *Ibid.*, p. 180.
6. *Ibid.*, pp. 317 f.
7. *Ibid.*, p. 321.
8. *Ibid.*, p. 333.
9. *Ibid.*, p. 335.
10. *Ibid.*, p. 338.
11. *Ibid.*, p. 346.
12. Adam Clarke, as quoted by R. A. Willmott, in Edwards, *op cit.*, p. 426.
13. *William Blake* (Boston: Houghton Mifflin & Co., 1924), p. 16.
14. Perry, *North American Review*, CXCVIII (1913), 233.
15. In W. P. Trent, *Daniel Defoe* (Indianapolis: Bobbs-Merrill Co., 1916), p. 318.
16. *The Spectator*, No. 405.
17. In Nutter and Tillett, *Hymns and Hymn Writers*, p. 49.
18. Pope, *op. cit.*, p. 475.
19. In L. Stephen, *Samuel Johnson* (London: Macmillan & Co., 1878), p. 101.
20. *Ibid.*, p. 112.
21. J. Hoole, in J. Boswell, *Life of Johnson* (New York: Harper & Bros., 1851), II, 526.
22. "Tenth Sermon," in R. E. Prothero, *The Psalms in Human Life*, pp. 320 f.
23. Mrs. M. Oliphant, *Sheridan* (London: Macmillan & Co., 1883), p. 74.
24. R. P. Utter and G. B. Needham, *Pamela's Daughters* (New York: The Macmillan Co., 1936), p. 277.
25. W. L. Cross, *Life and Times of Laurence Sterne* (New Haven: Yale University Press, 1925), I, 277.
26. *Tristram Shandy* (New York: E. P. Dutton & Co., 1912), p. 396.
27. *Ibid.*, p. 312.
28. *Ibid.*, p. 218.
29. *A Sentimental Journey Through France and Italy*, "Harvard Classics Shelf of Fiction" (New York: P. F. Collier & Son, 1917), p. 129.
30. In Simms, *The Bible in America*, pp. 228 f.
31. In "How Not to Write," *Atlantic Monthly*, CLIII (1934), 494 f.
32. In Knight and others, *The Flying Yorkshireman*, p. 139.
33. A. G. Kennedy, *Current English* (Boston: Ginn & Co., 1935), p. 314.
34. Bowman, *Story of Surnames* (New York: Alfred A. Knopf, 1931), p. 153.
35. In Walsh, *Handy-Book of Literary Curiosities*, p. 833.
36. "Don Juan," Canto III, stanza 71, *Works*.
37. "H.M.S. Pinafore," *A Treasury of Gilbert and Sullivan* (New York: Simon & Schuster, 1941), pp. 59-60.
38. In Walsh, *Handy-Book of Literary Curiosities*, p. 833.

39. Green, *A History of the English People,* I, 238.
40. T. B. Macaulay, in Walsh, *op. cit.,* p. 835.
41. "A Complete Collection of Genteel and Ingenious Conversation," *A Tale of a Tub, etc.,* pp. 245 ff.
42. *Tristram Shandy,* p. 387.
43. *Ibid.,* p. 131.
44. R. B. Sheridan, *The Rivals,* in P. H. Houston and R. M. Smith, *Types of World Literature* (Garden City: Doubleday, Doran & Co., 1930), pp. 469 ff.
45. McKnight, *Modern English in the Making,* p. 506.
46. B. Johnson, "The Everyday Profanity of Our Best People," *Century,* XCII (1916), 312 f.
47. W. L. Phelps, "Some Cursory Remarks on Swearing," *New Republic,* XII (1917), 300 ff.
48. S. Robertson, *Development of Modern English* (New York: Prentice-Hall), p. 444.
49. Kennedy, *op. cit.,* pp. 314 f.
50. H. L. Mencken, *The American Language* (New York: Alfred A. Knopf, 4th ed., 1936), pp. 305 f.
51. M. Duffield, "The Pulps: Day Dreams for the Masses," quoted in *Amrican Speech,* IX (1934), 276.
52. E. Ainsworth, "Along El Camino Real," Los Angeles *Times,* Mar. 8, 1939.
53. H. W. Hulbert, "Profanity," *Biblical World,* LIV (1920), 72.
54. E. M. Johnson, "On the Comfort of Cussing," *North American Review,* CCXXV (1928), 188 ff.
55. Anonymous, *Living Age, CCCLIV* (1938), 75.
56. "New England Two Centuries Ago," *Among My Books, Complete Writings* (Cambridge: Riverside Press, 1904), IV, 16.
57. H. L. Mencken, *The American Language* (New York: Alfred A. Knopf, 4th ed., 1936), pp. 248 f.
58. *S. Sewall's Diary,* ed. Mark Van Doren (New York: Macy-Masius, 1927), p. 259.
59. *Ibid.,* p. 102.
60. In Lawrence, *The Not-Quite Puritans,* pp. 18 ff.
61. *Ibid.,* p. 8.
62. In H. E. Jackson, *The Thomas Jefferson Bible* (New York: Boni Liveright, 1923), pp. 7 f.
63. *Journals of the Continental Congress,* XXXIII (1782), 572 ff.
64. *The Complete Works* (New York: G. P. Putnam's Sons, 1887), V, 373.
65. *Ibid.,* 376 ff.
66. In C. Van Doren, *Benjamin Franklin* (New York: The Viking Press, 1938), pp. 31 f.
67. *Complete Works,* VI, 287.
68. In P. L. Ford, *The Many-Sided Franklin* (New York: The Century Co., 1899), p. 251.
69. J. B. McMaster, *Benjamin Franklin as a Man of Letters* (Boston: Houghton, Mifflin & Co., 1887), pp. 87 ff.
70. In Walsh, *Handy-Book of Literary Curiosities,* p. 322.

71. Franklin, *Complete Works,* IX, 429 f.

72. In F. G. Lankard, *The Bible and the Life and Ideals of the English-Speaking People* (New York: American Bible Society, 1936), p. 7.

THE BIBLE CAPTURES SAINT AND SINNER

1. "SOS to De Lawd," pamphlet *Atlantic Contests for College Students, 1935-36,* p. 17.

2. In Nutter and Tillett, *Hymns and Hymn Writers,* p. 56.

3. "Jerusalem," *Poetical Works,* p. 390.

4. "The Everlasting Gospel," *ibid.,* pp. 146 ff.

5. "Song," *ibid.,* p. 13.

6. "Poems from Letters," *ibid.,* p. 187.

7. "Milton," *ibid.,* p. 375.

8. O. Burdett, *William Blake* (New York: The Macmillan Co., 1926), p. 4.

9. E. H. Short, *William Blake* (London: P. Allan & Co., 1925), pp. 41 f.

10. In P. Soupalt, *William Blake* (London: John Lane, 1928), p. 22.

11. Short, *op. cit.,* p. 120.

12. Blake, "The Marriage of Heaven and Hell," *op. cit.,* pp. 253 f.

13. Blake, "The Vision of the Last Judgment," in Damon, *William Blake,* p. 66.

14. Coleridge, *Biographia Literaria* (Washington: Dunne, 1901), pp. 379 f.

15. In Lawson, *Greatest Thoughts About the Bible,* p. 178.

16. In *The Cambridge History of English Literature* (New York: G. P. Putnam's Sons, 1916), XII, 313.

17. *Ibid.,* IV, 50.

18. Shelley, "Notes on Queen Mab," *Poetical Works* (New York: Thomas Y. Crowell Co., n.d.), pp. 60 f.

19. In B. Weaver, *Toward the Understanding of Shelley* (Ann Arbor: University of Michigan Press, 1932), p. 23.

20. P. B. Shelley, *A Defense of Poetry* (Boston: Ginn & Co., 1890), p. 43.

71. In Shelley, *op. cit.,* p. 224.

22. In Weaver, *op. cit.,* pp. 26 f.

23. Massingham, *The Friend of Shelley* (New York: D. Appleton & Co., 1930), p. 125.

24. Shelley, "Preface to Adonais,"*op. cit.,* p. 423.

25. Letter to George Keats, in A. Lowell, *Keats* (Boston: Houghton, Mifflin & Co., 1925), II, 196.

26. *Endymion* (New York: Thomas Y. Crowell Co., n.d.), p. 263.

27. Burns, *Complete Poems* (Boston: Houghton, Mifflin & Co., 1897), p. 30.

28. *The Complete Writings* (Boston: Houghton, Mifflin & Co., 1927), VII, 238.

29. Prothero, *The Psalms in Human Life,* p. 322.

30. Wordsworth, "It Is a Beauteous Evening Calm and Free."

31. In F. W. Boreham, *A Bunch of Everlastings* (New York: The Abingdon Press, 1920), pp. 74 ff.

32. In *The Influence of the English Bible Upon the English Language*

and Upon English and American Literature, ed. O. L. Joseph (New York: National Commemoration Committee, 1935), p. 18.

33. Lockhart, *Life of Scott,* II, 363 ff.

34. Hunt, *Autobiography* (New York: E. P. Dutton & Co., 1903), I, 68.

35. W. A. Neilson, in Crook and others, *The Bible and Its Literary Associations,* p. 364.

36. *Works* (Edinburgh: Constable & Co., n.d.), III, 198 ff.

37. *Ibid.,* II, 27 f.

38. W. Hazlitt, "On Persons One Would Wish to Have Seen," *Essays* (New York: Charles Scribner's Sons, 1924), p. 133.

39. De Quincey, "Suspiria de Profundis," *Works,* I, 173.

40. *Ibid.,* I, 241.

41. In Edwards, *New Dictionary of Thoughts,* p. 731.

42. R. Quintana, *Byron* (San Marino: Huntington Library, 1938), p. 14.

43. Southey, in *Works of Lord Byron* (New York: Bigelow, Brown, 1900), III, 239.

44. *Ibid.,* p. 247.

45. Byron, "The Vision of Judgment," *ibid.,* pp. 249 ff.

46. In McAfee, *The Greatest English Classic,* p. 157.

47. In R. Edgcombe, *Byron, the Last Phase* (London: John Murray, 1909), pp. 74 f.

48. *Ibid.,* pp. 77 f.

49. A. C. Coxe, in A. Mordell, *Notorious Literary Attacks* (New York: Boni & Liveright, 1926), pp. 123 ff.

50. In J. Hawthorne, *Nathaniel Hawthorne and His Wife* (Boston: J. R. Osgood & Co., 1884), I, 272.

51. McAfee, *op. cit.,* p. 188.

52. W. M. Forrest, *Biblical Allusions in Poe* (New York: The Macmillan Co., 1928), pp. 152 ff.

53. Poe, *ibid.,* p. 185.

54. *Ibid.,* p. 164.

55. L. Pound, "On Poe's 'The City in the Sea,'" *American Literature,* VI (1934), 22; and VIII (1936), 70.

56. G. W. Allen, "Biblical Echoes in Whitman's Works," *American Literature* VI (1934), 302.

57. *Complete Prose Works* (Philadelphia: D. Mackay, n.d.), p. 381.

58. In *Reader's Digest,* XXIV (1939), 37.

59. In S. T. Williams, *The Life of Washington Irving* (New York: Oxford University Press, 1935), I, 7.

60. *Ibid.,* II, 234.

61. In N. F. Adkins, *Fitz-Greene Halleck: An Early Knickerbocker Wit and Poet* (New Haven: Yale University Press, 1930), pp. 197 f.

62. New York: D. Appleton & Co., 1859, p. 19.

63. New York: D. Appleton & Co., 1860, p. 104.

64. *Ibid.,* p. 219.

65. H. R. Zink, *Emerson's Use of the Bible* (Lincoln: University of Nebraska, 1935), p. 60.

66. *Ibid.,* pp. 59, 61 ff.

67. In A. H. Strong, *American Poets and Their Theology* (Philadelphia: Griffith & Rowland, 1916), p. 72.

68. In P. H. Boynton, *Literature and American Life* (Boston: Ginn & Co., 1936), p. 567.

69. *Autocrat of the Breakfast Table* (Boston: Houghton, Mifflin & Co., 1886), p. 89.

70. Boston: Houghton, Mifflin & Co., 1859, p. 402.

71. *Walden* (New York: Thomas Y. Crowell Co., 1899), p. 346.

72. *A Week on the Concord and Merrimac Rivers* (Boston: Houghton, Mifflin & Co., 1893), pp. 89 ff.

73. O. Shepard, "The English Bible and American Men of Letters," *Southern Workman,* LXIV (1935), 339 ff.

74. See N. Wright, "Biblical Allusion in Melville's Prose," *American Literature,* XII (1940), 185.

75. *Ibid.,* 185 f.

76. Lowell, "International Copyright," *Complete Writings,* XIII, 274.

77. "A She Precise Hypocrite," in R. Withington, *Essays and Characters: Montaigne to Goldsmith* (New York: The Macmillan Co., 1933), p. 186.

78. "The Everlasting Yea," *Sartor Resartus,* from *Sartor Resartus* and *On Heroes, Hero-Worship and the Heroic in History* (New York: E. P. Dutton & Co., 1908), pp. 148 f.

79. *Ibid.,* pp. 171 f., 198.

80. "Corn Law Rhymes," *Critical and Miscellaneous Essays* (Boston: Houghton, Mifflin & Co., n.d.), III, 222.

81. "The Hero as Prophet," *On Heroes, Hero-Worship and the Heroic in History,* from *Sartor Resartus,* etc., p. 282.

82. Prothero, *The Psalms in Human Life,* p. 325.

83. "The Hero as Prophet," from *Sartor Resartus,* etc., p. 284.

84. *Ibid.,* p. 168.

85. In W. Muir, *Our Grand Old Bible,* p. 191.

86. R. D. Mallary, "Macaulay's Use of Scripture in His Essays," *Old Testament Student,* VII (1888), 212.

87. In A. Cruse, *The Englishman and His Books in the Early Nineteenth Century* (New York: T. Y. Crowell Co., 1930), p. 253.

88. In "Leigh Hunt," *Critical, Historical and Miscellaneous Essays* (Chicago: Belford Clark, n.d.), II, 513.

89. "A Conversation Between Mr. Abraham Cowley and Mr. John Milton . . . ," *ibid.,* I, 101.

90. "Mill on Government," *ibid.,* I, 415.

91. "Southey's Colloquies on Society," *ibid,* I, 504.

92. J. H. Newman, in *Fine Gold of Newman,* ed. J. J. Reilly (New York: The Macmillan Co., 1931), p. 125.

93. *Ibid.,* p. 128.

94. *Ibid.,* p. 156.

95. *Ibid.,* p. 240.

96. W. G. Collingwood, "Ruskin's Bibles," *Living Age,* CCXXXVI (1903), 445.

97. "Praeterita," *Works* (Boston: Dana, Estes & Co., n.d.), p. 14.

98. "Our Fathers Have Told Us," *ibid.*, pp. 354 f., 360.

99. *Modern Painters, ibid.*, V, 438 f.

100. D. McCaslin, *Reaching Other Minds* (New York: Alfred A. Knopf, 1928), p. 265.

THE BIBLE ENCOUNTERS CERTAIN DRAGONS

1. "The 'Kultured' Evolutionist," in W. H. Brown, *Poems of Pep and Power for Public Speakers* (Cincinnati: Standard Publishing Co., 1918), p. 284.

2. "Speech at Oxford Diocesan Conference, Nov. 24, 1864," in *Hoyt's New Cyclopedia of Practical Quotations* (New York: Funk & Wagnalls Co., 1927), p. 26.

3. In Walsh, *Handy-Book of Literary Curiosities*, p. 62.

4. "Essays on Science and Education," p. 397, quoted in Lawson, *Greatest Thoughts About the Bible*, p. 133.

5. *Autobiography* (Boston: Houghton, Mifflin & Co., 1909), p. 3.

6. *Ibid.*, p. 11.

7. M. G. Machen, *The Bible in Browning* (New York: The Macmillan Co., 1903), p. 16.

8. *Works* (New York: The Macmillan Co., 1921), pp. 256, 241.

9. *The Poetry of Tennyson* (New York: Charles Scribner's Sons, 1900), pp. 391-437.

10. Robinson, *Tennyson's Use of the Bible*, p. 1.

11. In *Alfred Lord Tennyson: A Memoir by His Son* (New York: The Macmillan Co., 1897), II, 127.

12. *Ibid.*, 228.

13. *Ibid.*, II, 35; I, 495.

14. D. Muzzey, *Essays in Intellectual History* (New York: Harper Bros., 1929), pp. 76 f.

15. From "Dover Beach."

16. In J. I. Osborne, *Arthur Hugh Clough* (Boston: Houghton, Mifflin & Co., 1920), p. 20.

17. "The Latest Decalog," *Poems* (London: Macmillan & Co., 1920), p. 184.

18. Lowell, *op. cit.*, XVI, 73.

19. In Boynton, *Literature and American Life*, p. 561.

20. In Walsh, *Handy-Book of Literary Curiosities*, p. 62.

21. "The Ant," from *I'm a Stranger Here Myself* by Ogden Nash. Reprinted by permission of Little, Brown & Company.

22. J. S. Stevens, *Whittier's Use of the Bible* (Orono: Maine University Press, 1930), pp. 4 f, 96 f.

23. *Poems* (Boston: Houghton, Mifflin & Co., 1894), p. 442.

24. E. Markham, "Whittier." Reprinted by permission.

25. J. J. Chapman, *William Lloyd Garrison*, pp. 164 ff. Used by permission Little, Brown and Company and Atlantic Monthly Press.

26. In A. F. Gilmore, *The Bible, Beacon Light of History* (Boston: Associated Authors, 1935), p. 258.

27. In L. E. Richards and M. H. Eliott, *Julia Ward Howe* (Boston: Houghton, Mifflin & Co., 1915), I, 46.

28. From *Much Loved Books,* by James O'Donnell Bennett, p. 3. Published by Liveright Publishing Corporation.

29. A. S. Cook, "The 'Authorized' Version and Its Influence," *Cambridge History of English Literature* (New York: G. P. Putnam's Sons, 1910), IV, 57.

30. W. H. Crook, in C. S. Cooper, *The Bible and Modern Life* (New York: Funk & Wagnalls Co., 1911), p. 120.

31. A. Lincoln, in Tiplady, *The Influence of the Bible,* p. 116.

32. In W. R. Thayer, *Life of John Hay* (Boston: Houghton, Mifflin & Co., 1915), I, 206.

33. Authorship unknown.

34. *Shakespeare and His Forerunners* (New York: Doubleday, Page & Co., 1902), p. 7.

35. *Poems* (New York: Charles Scribner's Sons, 1918), p. 17.

36. In G. Taggard, *The Life and Mind of Emily Dickinson* (New York: Alfred A. Knopf, 1930), p. 69.

37. *Letters of Emily Dickinson,* edited by Mabel Loomis Todd (New York: Harper & Bros., 1931), p. 139.

38. See E. Dickinson, *Poems* (Boston: Little, Brown & Co., 1930), p. 296.

39. Dickinson, *Letters,* p. 164.

40. *Ibid.,* p. 148.

41. *Ibid.,* p. 218.

42. *Ibid.,* p. 93.

43. *Ibid.,* p. 37.

44. *An Autobiography* (New York: Harper & Bros., 1906), II, 936.

45. C. Van Doren, *The American Novel* (New York: The Macmillan Co., 1921), p. 123.

46. *Adventures of a Biologist* (New York: Harper & Bros., 1940), p. 202.

47. O. Nash, from "The Anatomy of Happiness," *I'm a Stranger Here Myself,* p. 147. Used by permission of Little, Brown & Co.

48. In McAfee, *The Greatest English Classic,* p. 182.

49. *Life and Letters of George Eliot* (New York: Thomas Y. Crowell Co., n.d.), pp. 721 f.

50. McAfee, *op. cit.,* pp. 172 f.

51. *Letters,* I, 237, in T. H. Darlow, *The Greatest Book in the World* (London: Hodder & Stoughton, 1927), p. 24.

52. "Bible Characters," in C. A. Dinsmore, *The English Bible as Literature* (Boston: Houghton, Mifflin & Co., 1931), p. 256.

53. In E. Wagenknecht, *The Man Charles Dickens* (Boston: Houghton, Mifflin & Co., 1929), pp. 250 f.

54. In J. G. Lawson, *op. cit.,* p. 112.

55. *Dombey and Son* (New York: P. F. Collier, n.d.), II, 931.

56. *Bleak House* (New York: P. F. Collier, n.d.), II, 720.

57. *A Tale of Two Cities* (New York: P. F. Collier, n.d.), p. 393.

58. J. R. Slater, *Recent Literature and Religion* (New York: Harper & Bros., 1938), p. 66.

59. Hardy, *Tess of the d'Urbevilles* (New York: A. L. Burt, 1921), p. 80.

60. *Ibid.,* p. 105.

61. G. C. Martin, "Thomas Hardy and the English Bible," *Bookman,* LXXIV (1928), 24-26. Used by permission of Hodder and Stoughton, London.

62. Hardy, *The Woodlanders* (New York: Harper & Bros., 1912), p. 444.

63. W. A. Neilson, in Crook and others, *The Bible and Its Literary Associations,* p. 374.

64. Quoted in Boyd, *Literary Blasphemies,* p. 244.

65. In Walsh, *Handy-Book of Literary Curiosities,* p. 972.

66. R. Buchanan, "The Fleshly School of Poetry," in Mordell, *Notorious Literary Attacks,* pp. 194, 201.

67. In A. C. Swinburne, *Complete Works* (New York: Wells, 1927), XIX, 109.

68. "Bill Jones on Prayer," in J. E. Meeker, *The Life and Poetry of James Thomson (B.V.)* (New Haven: Yale, University Press, 1917), p. 98.

69. E. Meynell, *The Life of Francis Thompson* (London: Burns, Oates & Washbourne, Ltd., 1913), p. 156.

70. R. Macaulay, *Some Religious Elements in English Literature,* p. 156.

71. F. Thompson, in Meynell, *op. cit.,* p. 173.

72. *"De Profundis," Complete Works* (New York: Bigelow, Brown, 1905), VIII, 116.

73. R. L. Stevenson, in J. Kelman, Jr., *The Faith of Robert Louis Stevenson* (New York: Fleming H. Revell Co., 1903), p. 84.

74. In *Essays on Literature, on Life* (New York: Charles Scribner's Sons, 1925), pp. 67 ff.

75. Stevenson, in F. W. Farrar, *The Bible, Its Meaning and Supremacy* (New York: Longman, Green & Co., 1897), p. 281.

76. *The Master of Ballantrae* (New York: Charles Scribner's Sons, 1895), p. 203.

77. *Letters* (New York: Charles Scribner's Sons, 1899), I, 236 f.

78. "Letter to W. D. O'Conner, July, 1885," in E. Bisland, *The Life and Letters of Lafcadio Hearn* (Boston: Houghton, Mifflin & Co., 1906), I, 350.

79. Hearn, *Books and Habits* (New York: Dodd, Mead & Co., 1921), p. 105.

80. In Work, *The Bible in Literature,* p. 213.

81. "The Bible on the Stage," *New Review,* VIII (1893), 187 ff.

82. *The Heart of Burroughs' Journals* (Boston: Houghton Mifflin & Co., 1928), pp. 111 ff.

83. W. F. Bade, *Life and Letters of John Muir* (Boston: Houghton Mifflin & Co., 1923), I, 27.

84. Muir, *Story of My Boyhood and Youth* (Boston: Houghton Mifflin & Co., 1913), pp. 244 f.

85. W. L. Stidger, *Edwin Markham* (New York: The Abingdon Press, 1933), pp. 143, 151.

86. *Wit and Wisdom* (New York: Longman, Green & Co., 1927), p. 1.

87. J. B. Reeves, *The Hymn as Literature* (New York: Century Co., 1924), p. 289.

88. B. McDaniel, "To Kiwanis," *Kiwanis Song Book* (Redlands, Calif., n.d.).

89. F. M. Whitcher, "Widow Bedott's Monologues," in Blair, *Native American Humor,* p. 274.

90. B. P. Shillaber, *ibid.*, p. 258.

91. Shillaber, in H. Gerwig, *Crowell's Handbook for Readers and Writers* (New York: T. Y. Crowell & Co., 1925), p. 495.

92. J. J. Hooper, in N. Wilt, *Some American Humorists* (New York: Thomas Nelson & Sons, 1929), p. 112.

93. W. T. Thompson, "Georgia Comedy," in Blair, *op. cit.*, p. 336.

94. H. T. Lewis, *ibid.*, pp. 388 f.

95. D. R. Locke, in Wilt, *op. cit.*, p. 223.

96. C. F. Browne, "Selections from Artemus Ward," in Wilt, *op. cit.*, p. 182.

97. C. F. Browne, *Selected Works of Artemus Ward* (New York: A. & C. Boni, 1924), p. 168.

98. Walsh, *Handy-Book of Literary Curiosities*, p. 513.

99. *Mark Twain's Notebook* (New York: Harper & Bros., 1935), p. 301 f.

100. *The Writings of Mark Twain*, Author's National Edition (New York: Harper & Bros., 1903), XXIV, 214.

101. Clemens, *Europe and Elsewhere* (New York: Harper & Bros., 1923), pp. 308 f.

102. *Carolyn Wells' Book of American Limericks*, comp. C. Wells (New York: G. P. Putnam's Sons, 1925), p. 51.

THE BIBLE WIDENS ITS BORDERS

1. "Old Joe Clark," in *Humor in American Song*, ed. A. Loesser (New York: Howell, Soskin, 1942), p. 53.

2. Anonymous bestiary, in Wells, *A Manual of the Writers in Middle English*, p. 183.

3. Anonymous, in J. O. Haliwell-Phillipps, *Popular Rhymes and Nursery Tales* (London: J. R. Smith, 1849), p. 153.

4. *Ibid.*, p. 164.

5. Sir J. Mandeville, *Travels* (London: Macmillan & Co., Ltd., 1923), pp. 46 f.

6. J. Skelton, "Phyllyp Sparowe," in J. Skelton and J. Donne, *Poetical Works* (Boston: Houghton, Mifflin & Co., 1855), I, 74 ff.

7. Anonymous, "Mirabile Dictu," in Adamson, *op. cit.*, p. 130.

8. J. Oldham, "Satires upon the Jesuits," in Disraeli, *op. cit.*, I, 282.

9. "Upon the Ass That Bore Our Saviour," *op. cit.*, p. 41.

10. From *The Poems of Emily Dickinson*, edited by Martha Dickinson Bianchi and Alfred Leete Hampson. Reprinted by permission of Little, Brown & Company.

11. "Daniel," *Collected Poems* (New York: The Macmillan Co., rev. ed., 1925), p. 159. Used by permission of the publishers.

12. New York: Harper & Bros., 1935, pp. 285 ff.

13. M. Kantor, *The Romance of Rosy Ridge* (New York: Coward-McCann, Inc., 1937), p. 26.

14. Anonymous, in V. Loggins, *I Hear America* (New York: T. Y. Crowell & Co., 1937), p. 283.

15. C. A. Smart, *R.F.D.* (New York: W. W. Norton, 1938), p. 280.

16. J. Steinbeck, "Saint Katy the Virgin," *The Long Valley* (New York: The Viking Press, 1938), p. 198.

17. W. J. Courthope, "The Song of Man," in H. J. Massingham, *Poems About Birds* (New York: E. P. Dutton & Co., 1922), p. 274.

18. *Wit and Wisdom of Sydney Smith* (London: Longmans, Green & Co., 1886), p. 330.

19. Anonymous, in Mencken, *The American Language,* p. 281.

20. See G. R. Owst, *Literature and Pulpit in Medieval England* (Cambridge, Eng.: The University Press, 1933), *passim.*

21. T. H. White, *England Have My Bones* (New York: The Macmillan Co., 1936), p. 8.

22. Anonymous, "Against the Friars," summarized in Wells, *A Manual of the Writings of Middle English* (New Haven: Yale University Press, 1926), p. 237. Used by permission of Connecticut Academy of Arts and Sciences.

23. Skelton, "Colyn Clout," in Skelton and Donne, *op. cit.,* I, 133.

24. Pope, *Poetical Works,* p. 187.

25. S. Smith, "Letter to Archdeacon Singleton," in *Wit and Wisdom of Sydney Smith,* p. 162.

26. G. W. Curtis, "Potiphar Papers," in *Half-Hours with Great Humorists* (Los Angeles: Sanderson Whittier, 1901), p. 24.

27. *Ibid.,* p. 27.

28. *Ibid.,* pp. 28 f.

29. In Blair, *Native American Humor,* p. 493.

30. *Degeneracy,* in A. Bates, *Talks on Writing English, Second Series* (Boston: Houghton, Mifflin Co., 1901), p. 9.

31. W. S. Miller, "The Champion of All Best Sellers," *English Journal,* XXXI (1942), 143.

32. C. D. Eldridge, *Christianity's Contribution to Civilization* (Nashville: The Cokesbury Press, 1928), p. 161.

33. In Walsh, *A Handy-Book of Literary Curiosities,* p. 319.

34. Perry, *North American Review,* CXCVIII (1913), 234.

35. "Impeachment of Warren Hastings," in M. W. Hazeldine, *Orations from Homer to McKinley* (New York: P. F. Collier, 1902), VI, 2, 237.

36. *Ibid,* p. 491.

37. "Speech on the British Slave Trade," in Hazeltine, *op. cit.,* VIII, 3, 453.

38. In T. H. Davies, *Spiritual Voices in Modern Literature* (New York: George H. Doran Co., 1919), p. 208.

39. A. W. Ward, "Historians Biographers and Political Orators," *Cambridge History of English Literature* (New York: G. P. Putnam's Sons, 1917), XIV, 146.

40. J. Bright, in W. Canton, *The Bible and the Anglo-Saxon People* (London: J. M. Dent & Sons., Ltd., 1914), p. 268.

41. "In Opposition to Writs of Assistance, in *The World's Famous Orations,* ed. W. J. Bryan. (New York: Funk & Wagnalls Co., 1906), VIII, 27.

42. *Ibid.,* pp. 63 ff.

43. Webster, in C. M. Fuess, *Daniel Webster* (Boston: Little, Brown & Co., 1930), I, 23.

44. Fuess, *ibid.,* I, 26.

45. In F. W. Farrar, *The Bible, Its Meaning and Supremacy* (New York: Longmans, Green & Co., 1897), p. 287.

46. *Speeches and Orations* (Boston: Little, Brown & Co., 1879), p. 603.

47. In *World Book Encyclopedia* (Chicago: W. F. Quarrie & Co., 1929), V, 2689.

48. In *The World's Best Orations from the Earliest Period to the Present Time,* ed. D. J. Brewer (St. Louis: F. P. Kaiser, 1899), X, 3951.

More genial and much neater was John Phillimore, of Glasgow: "Gentlemen, gentlemen! I have not yet ceased casting my pearls."

49. "The New South," in *Modern Eloquence* (New York: Modern Eloquence Corporation, 1921), II, 106.

50. "Oration at His Brother's Grave," in Hazeldine, *op. cit.,* XXII, 9585.

51. In M. R. Werner, *Bryan* (New York: Harcourt, Brace & Co., 1929), p. 16.

52. "The 'Cross of Gold,'" in Brewer, *op. cit.,* II, 694 ff.

53. C. G. Bowers, *Beveridge and the Progressive Era* (New York: Literary Guild, 1932), p. 425.

54. Beveridge, *ibid.,* p. 430.

55. "The First Banjo," in *Book of Humorous Verse, ed. C. Wells* (Garden City: Garden City Publishers, 1936), p. 672.

56. A. Manutius, in Brewer, *Dictionary of Phrase and Fable,* p. 333.

57. See Angoff, *A Literary History of the American People,* I, 238.

58. In Mordell, *Notorious Literary Attacks,* p. xxxiii.

59. "Journalism," in *Modern Eloquence* (New York: Modern Eloquence Corporation, 1921), VI, 106.

60. In W. W. Moore, *The Indispensable Book* (New York: Fleming H. Revell Co., 1910), p. 31.

61. In Tiplady, *The Influence of the Bible,* pp. 80 f.

62. In *Literary Digest,* LXXIX (1923), 34.

63. *Ibid.,* CIV (1930), 22.

64. In *Homiletic Review,* XC (1930), 52 f.

65. Hindus, *Green Worlds* (New York: Doubleday, Doran & Co., 1938), p. 348.

66. Simms, *The Bible in America,* p. 351.

67. J. A. Crone, "The Most Popular Book of the Day," *Independent,* CXII (1924), 7.

68. Simms, *op. cit.,* p. 213.

69. In *Literary Review,* III (1923), 503.

70. M. L. Guberlet, "The Classics and the Modern Magazine," *School and Society,* XXXIV (1931), 604.

71. T. R. Nunn and F. D. Curtis, "Biblical References, Quotations, and Allusions in Popular Magazines," *School Review,* LII (1944), 241.

72. H. C. Spillman, "Adjusting Ourselves to the New Era in Business," in *Modern Eloquence* (New York: Modern Eloquence Corporation, 1921 *et seq.*), VII, 367.

73. B. Barton, "Which Knew Not Joseph," in W. N. Brigance, *Classified Speech Models* (New York: F. S. Crofts & Co., 1928), pp. 26, 30.

74. W. Painter, "Give Moses a Chance," *Collier's,* LXXV (1925), 29.

THE BIBLE MEETS THE TWENTIETH CENTURY

1. In G. K. Chesterton, *Autobiography* (New York: Sheed & Ward, 1936), p. 157.

2. R. T. Oliver, "The Bible and Style," *Sewanee Review,* XLII (1934), 350.

3. F. Smith, "Fictionizing the Bible," *Homiletic Review,* XCVIII (1929), 188.

4. Loggins, *I Hear America,* p. 24.

5. S. Crane, in F. M. Ford, *Portraits from Life* (Boston: Houghton, Mifflin Co., 1912), p. 34.

6. *My Literary Passions* (New York: Harper & Bros., 1895), p. 174.

7. R. Page, *Thomas Nelson Page* (New York: Charles Scribner's Sons, 1923), p. 208.

8. In Oliver, *op. cit.,* p. 353.

9. *Loc. cit.*

10. B. S. Aldrich, *ibid.,* p. 354.

11. "Advice to Unborn Novelists," *Saturday Review of Literature,* XI (1935), 513-14.

12. In *I Believe: The Personal Philosophies of Certain Men and Women of Our Time,* ed. C. Fadiman (New York: Simon & Schuster, 1939), pp. 94 ff.

13. *Ibid.,* p. 335.

14. H. E. Luccock, *American Mirror: Social, Ethical and Religious Aspects of American Literature, 1930-1940* (New York: The Macmillan Co., 1940), p. 93.

15. *Jurgen* (New York: R. M. McBride & Co., 1919), p. 81.

16. See H. E. Luccock, *Contemporary American Literature and Religion* (Chicago: Willett, Clark & Co., 1934), p. 4.

17. Quoted in D. Karsner, *Sixteen Authors to One* (New York: Lewis Copeland Co., 1928), pp. 4 f.

18. Loggins, *op. cit.,* p. 129.

19. J. W. Thomason, Jr., "The Best Seller," *American Mercury,* XL (1937), 118.

20. New York: Harcourt, Brace & Co., 1920, p. 384.

21. New York: Harcourt, Brace & Co., 1925, p. 381.

22. *Ibid.,* p. 281.

23. *A Story-Teller's Story* (New York: B. W. Huebsch, Inc., 1922), p. 55.

24. *The Trouble with Tigers* (New York: Harcourt, Brace & Co., 1938), pp. 10 f.

25. M. Barish, "Hecht Pens Double-Edged Travesty of Modern Life," Los Angeles *Times,* June 25, 1939.

26. A. Bennett, *Journal* (New York: The Viking Press, 1933), p. 742.

27. In J. R. Slater, *Recent Literature and Religion* (New York: Harper & Bros., 1938), p. 71.

28. "Humanity Can Be Saved," *This Week,* Apr. 17, 1939.

29. In Luccock, *op. cit.,* p. 136.

30. R. Ogden, "The Literary Loss of the Bible," *Century,* LXV (1903), 629 ff.

31. T. S. Eliot, *Essays Ancient and Modern* (London: Faber & Faber, Ltd., 1936), p. 96.

32. H. S. Canby, "The Importance of Style," in Anonymous, *If I Could Preach Just Once* (New York: Harper & Bros., 1929), pp. 139, 145.

33. B. Rascoe, "The Biblical Style," *New Republic,* XXX (1922), 338.

34. B. Clegg, "Who Buys Religious Books?" *Publishers' Weekly,* CXXXI (1937), 936.

35. Utter and Needham, *Pamela's Daughters,* p. 740

36. New York: A. & C. Boni, 1911, *passim.*

37. In Boynton, *Literature and American Life,* p. 673.

38. *The Story of My Life* (New York: Grossett & Dunlap, 1905), p. 112.

39. *Joyous Gard* (New York: G. P. Putnam's Sons, 1913), pp. 135 ff.

40. *Jesus the Christ in the Light of Psychology* (Garden City: Doubleday, Page & Co., 1917), I, 152 f.

41. C. Hamilton, *Seen on the Stage* (New York: Henry Holt & Co., 1920), pp. 227 f.

42. *Reaching Other Minds* (New York: Alfred A. Knopf, 1928), pp. 267 f.

43. *Myself to Date* (New York: Review of Reviews, 1920), pp. 155, 157.

44. "In Memoriam, W. J. B.," *Prejudices, Fifth Series* (New York: Alfred A. Knopf, 1926), pp. 64 ff.

45. *The Gorgon's Head* (New York: The Macmillan Co., 1927), pp. 448 ff.

46. *Journal* (Boston: Houghton, Mifflin & Co., 1933), pp. 294 f., 431 f.

47. *Life and I* (Boston: Houghton, Mifflin & Co., 1928), pp. 155 ff.

48. Sir A. Quiller-Coüch, in Anonymous, *Reprinted from the Morning Post* (London: Griffiths, 1931), pp. 17 ff.

49. New York: The Vanguard Press, 1930, p. v.

50. *Autobiography* (New York: Harcourt, Brace & Co., 1931), II, 525 f.

51. "The Profits of Religion," in Luccock, *op. cit.,* pp. 216 f.

52. U. Sinclair, in Oliver, *op. cit.,* pp. 352 f.

53. *And Gladly Teach* (Boston: Houghton, Mifflin Co., 1935), p. 293.

54. *1066—And All That* (London: Metheun & Co., 1936), p. 32.

55. Kipling, *Something of Myself* (New York: Doubleday, Doran & Co., 1937), pp. 124, 135.

56. *Ends and Means* (New York: Harper & Bros., 1937), p. 1.

57. Copyright 1937 by Albert J. Nock. This and the following selections from Nock used by permission of Willam Morrow & Co.

58. *Ibid.,* pp. 264 f.

59. New York and Nashville: Abingdon-Cokesbury Press, 1937, p. 251.

60. Oct. 23, 1937, p. 1666.

61. *All Trivia* (New York: Harcourt, Brace & Co., 1938), p. 23.

62. Forster, In C. Fadiman, *op. cit.,* p. 79.

63. Van Loon, *ibid.,* pp. 303 ff.

64. "Gone With the Wind Trails Bible in Interest," Los Angeles *Times,* Jan. 22, 1939.

65. *American Mirror,* p. 52.

66. In E. V. Durling, "On the Side," Los Angeles *Times,* Mar. 11, 1938.

67. See Coleman, *The Bible in English Drama, passim.*

68. In Edwards, *New Dictionary of Thoughts,* p. 642.

69. Paull, *Literary Ethics,* p. 178.

70. W. A. Neilson, in Crook and others, *The Bible and Its Literary Associations,* p. 358. However, E. F. Hyde—*The Mystery Play: Medieval and Modern,* unpub. master's thesis (Columbia: University of Missouri, 1925), p. 142—says Given-Lally's *Jezebel* was licensed in 1912.

71. *Androcles and the Lion* (New York: Brentano, 1914), XIV.

72. "How to Print the Bible," *London Mercury and Bookman,* XXXVII (1938), 328.

73. In A. H. Quinn, *Representative American Plays* (New York: The Century Co., 1917), p. 207.

74. *The Print of My Remembrance* (New York: Charles Scribner's Sons, 1922), p. 455.

75. Luccock, *Contemporary American Literature and Religion,* p. 13.

76. *Three American Plays* (New York: Harcourt, Brace & Co., 1926).

77. W. L. Phelps, *The Twentieth Century Theatre* (New York: The Macmillan Co., 1918), pp. 87 f. Used by permission of the publishers.

78. M. E. McGinnis, *The Morality Play: Medieval and Modern,* unpub. master's thesis (Columbia, Mo.: University of Missouri, 1917), pp. 13 ff.

79. *The Miracle Play: Medieval and Modern,* unpub. master's thesis (Columbia, Mo.: University of Missouri, 1918), *passim.*

80. *The Mystery Play: Medieval and Modern,* unpub. master's thesis (Columbia, Mo.: University of Missouri, 1925), p. 313.

81. H. Hatcher, "The Literary Fourth Dimension," *English Journal,* XXVII (1938), 462.

82. Anonymous, "Religious Plays," Los Angeles *Times,* June 5, 1938.

83. C. A. Smart, *R. F. D.* (New York: W. W. Norton & Co., 1938), pp. 130 f.

84. From "The Strange Case of Mr. Ballantine's Valentine," *I'm a Stranger Here Myself* by Ogden Nash. Reprinted by permission of Little, Brown & Company.

85. "The Indian upon God," *The Collected Poems of W. B. Yeats* (New York: The Macmillan Co., 1934), p. 15.

86. In *Just So Stories* (New York: Doubleday, Doran & Co., 1907), p. 203.

87. Thomason, *American Mercury,* XL (1937), 117 f.

88. *Vanishing Roads* (New York: G. P. Putnam's Sons, 1915), conclusion.

89. In Anonymous, *The Literary Merit of the English Bible* (London: Griffiths, 1931), p. 50.

90. In Oliver, *Sewanee Review,* XLII (1934), 354 f.

91. In Stidger, *Edwin Markham* (New York: The Abingdon Press, 1933) pp. 97 f.

92. In E. L. Masters, *Vachel Lindsay* (New York: Charles Scribner's Sons, 1935), p. 75.

93. *Ibid.,* p. 115.

94. *Ibid.,* pp. 226 f.

95. In H. Monroe, *A Poet's Life* (New York: The Macmillan Co., 1938), p. 280.

96. Loggins, *op. cit.,* p. 108.

97. Robinson, *ibid.,* p. 56.

98. H. Hagedorn, *Edwin Arlington Robinson* (New York: The Macmillan Co., 1938), p. 72.
99. *Ibid.*, p. 362.
100. Frost, *ibid.*, p. 204.
101. In Oliver, *op. cit.*, p. 352.
102. L. C. Powell, *Introduction to Robinson Jeffers* (Dijon: Imprimerie Bernegand & Privat, 1932), pp. 14, 25, 52.
103. In introduction, *Christ in the Poetry of Today*, ed. M. F. Crow (New York: The Woman's Press, 1918). Used by permission of The Woman's Press.
104. L. E. Nelson, *Influence of the Christ on Modern American Poetry*, unpub. master's thesis (Lawrence: University of Kansas, 1921), p. 33.
105. M. P. Hert, *Influence of the Bible on Contemporary American Poetry*, unpub. master's thesis (Redlands: University of Redlands, 1939), *passim*.
106. Luccock, *Contemporary American Literature and Religion*, pp. 224 f.
107. In Los Angeles *Times*, Aug. 15, 1945.
108. *Publishers' Weekly*, July 24, 1943, p. 252.
109. *Ibid.*, Mar. 13, 1942, p. 1182.
110. "Popular Book," *Business Week*, Feb. 27, 1943, p. 48.
111. *Loc. cit.*
112. Los Angeles *Times*, Dec. 25, 1943.
113. *Publishers' Weekly*, Mar. 13, 1943, p. 1182.
114. *Newsweek*, XX (1942), 55 f.
115. *Pathfinder*, Jan. 10, 1944, p. 24.
116. P. Martin, "Bible Story," *Saturday Evening Post*, CCXI (1943), 23.
117. Lieutenant Colonel W. E. Dyess, *The Dyess Story* (New York: G. P. Putnam's Sons, 1944), p. 107.

INDEX